Air War Market Garden

Volume Three

The Shrinking Perimeter

Other volumes in this series

Air War Market Garden: The Shrinking Perimeter

Volume 1 The Build-Up To The Beginning
Volume 2 So Near And Yet So Far
Volume 4 A Bridge Too Far?

Air War Market Garden

Volume Three

The Shrinking Perimeter

Martin W Bowman

Pen & Sword
AVIATION

First Published in Great Britain in 2013
and reissued in this format in 2025 by
Pen & Sword Aviation
an imprint of
Pen & Sword Books Ltd
Yorkshire – Philadelphia

ISBN 978 1 39907 816 0

A CIP catalogue record for this book is
available from the British Library.

Typeset in 10/12pt Palatino
by GMS Enterprises
Printed and bound in England by
CPI Group (UK) Ltd, Croydon, CR0 4YY

MIX
Paper | Supporting
responsible forestry
FSC
www.fsc.org
FSC® C013604

The Publisher's authorised representative in the EU for product safety is Authorised Rep Compliance Ltd., Ground Floor, 71 Lower Baggot Street, Dublin D02 P593, Ireland. | www.arccompliance.com

For a complete list of Pen & Sword titles please contact
PEN & SWORD BOOKS **LIMITED**

47 Church Street, Barnsley, South Yorkshire, S70 2AS, England
E-mail: enquiries@pen-and-sword.co.uk
Website: www.pen-and-sword.co.uk
or
PEN AND SWORD BOOKS
1950 Lawrence Road, Havertown, PA 19083, USA
E-mail: uspen-and-sword@casematepublishers.com
Website: www.penandswordbooks.com

Contents

Acknowledgements

I am enormously grateful to the following people for their time and effort and kind loan of photos etc, not least to my fellow author, friend and colleague, Graham Simons, for getting the book to press-ready standard and for his detailed work on maps and photographs: My thanks and sincere appreciation to Nigel McTeer, whose uncle, a man by the name of Maloney, fought at Arnhem and killed two Germans, one with a pair of scissors and one by putting sand in his mouth. Thanks are due in no small measure to The Pegasus Archive website and the Maroon Beret's online news magazine for the wonderful collections of first-hand accounts faithfully compiled by the Association, its members and siblings of members. And to Deryk Wills, author of *Put On Your Boots and Parachutes!* My other favourite books on Arnhem and 'Market-Garden' include *The Longest Day* by Cornelius Ryan, *A Tour of the Arnhem Battlefields* by Major John Waddy, *Arnhem Lift* by Louis Hagen MM and of course *Arnhem 1944: The Airborne Battle* by Martin Middlebrook. My sincere thanks as always to Libby, Jenny and Lesley at the 2nd Air Division Memorial Library in Norwich. And also to Jim Borrett.

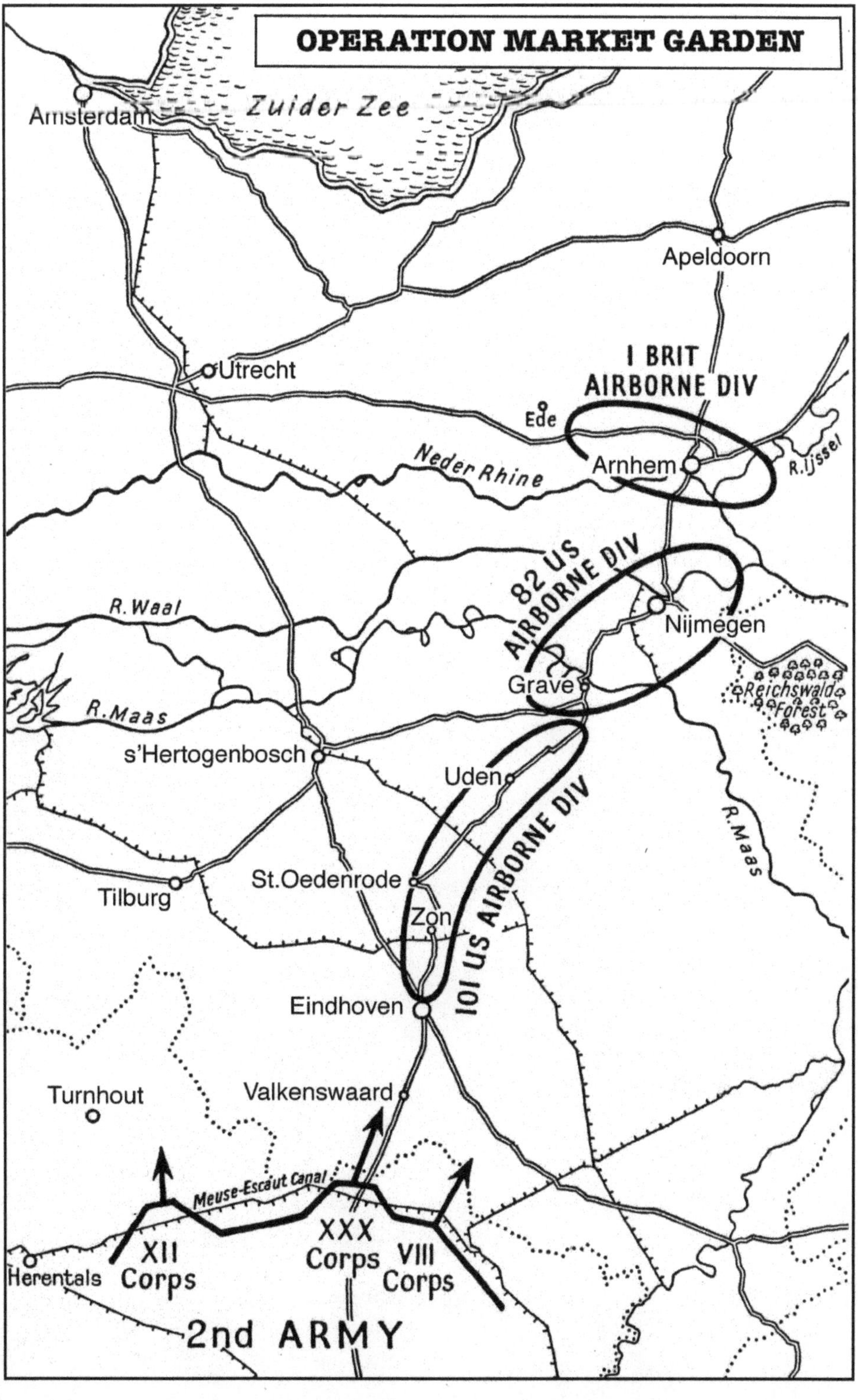
OPERATION MARKET GARDEN
Zuider Zee
Amsterdam
Apeldoorn
Utrecht
I BRIT AIRBORNE DIV
Ede
Neder Rhine
Arnhem
R. IJssel
82 US AIRBORNE DIV
R. Waal
Nijmegen
Grave
Reichswald Forest
R. Maas
s'Hertogenbosch
Uden
101 US AIRBORNE DIV
R. Maas
St.Oedenrode
Tilburg
Zon
Eindhoven
Turnhout
Valkenswaard
Meuse-Escaut Canal
XII Corps
XXX Corps
VIII Corps
Herentals
2nd ARMY

Chapter 1

'Hell's Highway'

'We saw this incredible armada go over us in an absolute unending stream. I don't think it occurred to us that anybody could possibly stop us. We might have delays such as roadblocks, but nothing serious.'
Major Peter Martin of the 2nd Cheshires.

The morning of 18th September had come too quickly for Sergeant Bill Tucker in the US 82nd Airborne Division and there was firing to the left. The Third Platoon was there, moving along the road towards the forest and on the right, the First Platoon was moving too. The mortar squads were to follow behind. They were told to expect bombers to come in towing the gliders carrying equipment so they had to hold the Landing Zone at all costs. By dawn on the 18th the 82nd were under simultaneous German attack not only at the bridge and in Nijmegen but to the east of Gavin's perimeter by the captured bridges and the ten-mile-long Grave-Nijmegen road and near the drop zones near Groesbeek Heights, where the rest of the division's artillery was to land at 10 o'clock that morning. A resupply drop of ammunition was also scheduled there. The local German command nearest the Groesbeek Heights had assembled a force under the operational control of the 406th Division, totalling around 2,300 men supported by five armoured cars and three half-tracks mounting 20mm flak guns. This force was grouped into four Kampfgruppen which were ordered to move against the south and east side of the Groesbeek Heights. Wyler was still under threat and the 508th PIR could not take and hold it. Fortunately, the German advance was extremely slow, because the bulk of the troops were very badly equipped and untrained in infantry work. One contingent consisted of over-age men recently called up for PoW guard duties.

Bill Tucker and Jim Downing scouted ahead for an observation point since the First and Second Platoons seemed to have made contact with the enemy up ahead. They knew that the Third Platoon had been firing and fighting all morning. Norell Blankenship was hit, others too. Finally Tucker ran into Tony Crineti who told him that Staff Sergeant Clarence Prager had been killed on the road out in front. It seems that Prager was leading the Third Platoon when they ran into a German patrol. He waved a flag to the Germans and hollered to them to surrender. They waved a flag in return and three stepped out on to the road. Prager went after them, but the Germans jumped into a ditch and opened up with machine-guns. Prager was badly hit, but he kept alive and fighting where he was. He was recommended for a Medal of Honor for his tremendous action in bringing the Third Platoon down the road and holding the flank. Staff Sergeant Clarence Prager was posthumously awarded the Distinguished Service Cross. His death was a great loss because he was a soldier without equal. He was a tough guy and everyone was concerned at losing a top man.[1]

Downing and Tucker were still scouting around for an observation post and came across a deserted farmhouse. By this time they had passed through a big iron gate which separated Germany from Holland. They were in Germany - maybe the first Americans to cross the German border - they'll never know. In the farmhouse they found the table set with a roast duck, hot potatoes and vegetables. Evidently they were the first to go into this area since they had strayed away from the First and Second Platoons. The two made themselves comfortable and polished off as much of the duck as they could, carrying the rest of it away. The firing got heavier. Suddenly about six Me 109s appeared and began to strafe. If the Germans had airplanes in this area it was going to be rough. The 505 were in Germany so they were in for it anyway. The Mortar Squad moved towards the firing, setting up the guns at every opportunity. Bass, Logan, Lester and Intrieri were doing real well for the new men and Wingfield was Wingfield. He and Tucker decided to go up with the First Platoon to see what was going on. They saw that the Second Platoon was stuck over on the right and it seemed to be having a fight in a little town. Leo Lopez was the only one who had been hit with a shot through his helmet. It had a hole in it but that was all. There was a dead man in the middle of the road as they passed by the Second Platoon. It turned out to be young Everett Gilliland who had just married a girl in England who he hardly knew. Gilliland was either shot by a sniper or during a strafing. The Germans were about 300 yards away. Finally Tucker and Downing got to the front of the combat line and it happened to be Tommy Thompson's Squad. Louis Russo had a machine-gun in action and there seemed to be Germans in a cluster of houses about two hundred and fifty yards away. They all opened fire. Gliders were coming in and many were burning, tipping over and crashing. The Second Platoon was still in the town on the right. Tucker got into a deep hole with the Executive Officer, Tommy and a few guys and they all took it easy for a while.

Further south, a fierce battle was in progress at Eindhoven. The 101st Airborne's 506th PIR led off the assault from Bokt into the city. After wiping out German infantry pockets in the fields on the outskirts, the troopers entered the north edge of town along Vlokhoven Street and began clearing German troops one house at a time. Two flak guns held up their progress and 88mm flak rounds killed and wounded some troopers before the they were flanked by troopers who used a mortar, rifle grenades and M1s to destroy the German crews and capture both guns. Colonel Robert Sink soon established his regimental command post in a school beside the Vlokhoven church, it was here that a British Recon car entered Eindhoven after circling the perimeter and made first contact between XXX Corps and 506th troopers. XXX Corps had been delayed, but had now made up much of the time lost at Son and covered more ground in two hours on the morning of 19 September (D+2) than they had on the two previous days. Horrocks had planned to be at the Neder Rijn

1 Later it was found that Prager's body had been buried in a shallow grave by the Dutch and remained there between the lines until March 1945. His action prevented Groesbeek from being overrun by the attacking Germans.

bridgehead on D+2: the Grenadiers Group of the Guards Armoured Division, the unit spearheading the XXX Corps advance, were now in Nijmegen, just eight miles from Arnhem and still had six hours in hand to get to Arnhem.[2] As the fighting continued deeper into Eindhoven it became necessary to move the HQ nearer the centre of the city. The Philips office buildings were cleared by the 506th. Thousands of Dutch civilians poured into the streets offering apples, ice cream, sandwiches and beer to the paratroopers. Kissing, dancing, singing and celebrating liberation day with orange bunting displayed everywhere; the populace was in a joyful frenzy. The Dutch now carried out reprisals, cutting off the hair of women collaborators and shot many male Dutch Nazi sympathisers. The various reprisals and celebrations would seriously delay the flow of northbound British traffic. Even without the crowds, the proposed route up Hell's Highway involved many twists and turns just to get through Eindhoven. Some troopers boarded the Sherman tanks of the 15/19 Armoured Regiment and patrolled to the northwest of Eindhoven, while others probed toward a Panzer staging area at Helmond via Nuenen and some were sent to secure the airfield west of the city.

Unsure of what division he was facing in Nijmegen, General James M. Gavin, commanding the 82nd Airborne headed his jeep for Colonel Roy E. Lindquist's headquarters. The bridge, now surrounded by German armoured forces, no longer seemed so important and anyway, Gavin did not have enough troops to capture the bridge until reinforcements arrived in the next air lift but the 325th Glider Infantry Regiment was not due to arrive until D+2. At about 1200 hours the 505th received orders to attack Nijmegen.

'We hiked for three or four miles' recalls James Coyle 'and as we came to the outskirts of the city we met a column of British tanks from the Guards Division. I was relieved to see that the British XXX Corps had reached Nijmegen. Looking back towards the south, the road was full of tanks and Bren gun carriers as far as the eye could see. This was a reassuring sight. I was surprised that the tanks were American Shermans, but the guns had been replaced by British 17 pounders, a long cannon with muzzle brakes that I had never seen before. We came into the city like a Victory Parade. The Dutch people lined the roads in crowds that cheered us on our way. Captain James J. Smith, the Company Commander, informed us that 'E' Company was to be the lead Company in the attack on the Nijmegen Bridge across the Waal River and the First Platoon would lead the assault. As we moved through the city towards the bridge, a Dutchman came up to me and asked me, in English, for a cigarette. I gave him a few and asked if he was familiar with the area at the bridge approach and he said he was. I asked him if there were many German soldiers there and he replied that there were a great many in Hunner Park in front of the bridge.[3]

2 *The Battle for the Rhine 1944: Arnhem and the Ardennes; the Campaign in Europe* by Robin Neillands (Weidenfield & Nicolson 2005).

3 Before the war the Dutch had fortified the Hunner Park which stretches both east and west of the Arnhemseweg and in 1940 had held it for three days. Looking north, the more extensive west side of the park is dominated by a lookout point, the Belvedere and further to the west, by the Valkhof, the ruin of a palace of Charlemagne. The Germans in turn had strengthened the defences of the park, especially those of an old medieval fort and a large wooded knoll, the Valkhof.

However, when I asked him if there were anti-tank guns in the German defence position, he said there were none. I felt that with all the British Armour, we could handle the enemy infantry. He was correct about the large number of enemy forces in the area, but not about the absence of anti-tank guns.

'On approaching the last houses before the open area in front of the bridge, the lead tank began firing its cannon. The roar was deafening and I am sure they were not firing at any particular target but to pin the enemy down. I was moving up alongside the third tank in the column. When I cleared the last house and could see the bridge, I got quite a shock. I didn't expect it to be so large. (I learnt after the war that it was the largest single-span bridge in Europe). As I moved up the street to the park the two tanks right in front of me exploded and caught fire. The third tank next to me went into reverse and backed up about fifty feet to the houses we had just left. I still could not see any enemy anti-tank guns or troops, but I and a few of my men were left out in the open with no support. I went storming back to the third tank shouting at the commander to get back with us. He said he was hit - I told him he was not hit as I could not see a mark on the tank. A British sergeant jumped out of the tank and said, 'What's that then, mate?' pointing to a large hole on the other side of the turret which I had not seen. I felt about two feet tall. I don't know how the tank took that hit without suffering any wounded or catching fire. I could see that the tanks were not going to make a move at that point and I was trying to figure a way to get into a position where I could observe the situation without being spotted. Just then an elderly man and woman came out of the back door of one of the houses on my left which faced the park and ran as fast as they could back the way we had come. I realised that if I could get the men in the second floor front rooms of the row of attached houses, we would be able to observe and fire on the enemy.

'I moved the platoon quickly into two of the buildings cautioning them not to open fire before I gave the command. I knew that as soon as we opened fire we would receive heavy fire in return. I hoped that we would be able to spot the anti-tank guns and knock them out so the tanks and the rest of the Battalion could advance on the bridge. The men kept back from the windows so they would not be seen by the enemy and set up their machine guns on tables near the front windows of two of the adjacent buildings. I could see German soldiers streaming across the bridge from the other side on foot and on bicycles. It was difficult to keep the men from opening fire because I wanted to get as many men in a firing position as possible before we gave our location away. The Germans had no idea we were there. I knew this for certain when a crew man-handled a 57mm anti-tank gun out of the park and proceeded to set it up in the street not thirty feet in front of us, pointing it up the street to our right where the tanks had been knocked out.

'Lieutenant Colonel Benjamin Vandervoort and Captain Bill Harris, the S-3 (Plans and Training), came into the room where I was setting up our position. I explained my plan to him and he approved. He saw the Germans coming over the bridge and the anti-tank gun right in front of us. I told him I knew we could knock out the gun as soon as we opened fire. I told the Colonel I would hold our fire for five minutes. He agreed and would try and move the British tanks forward when we opened up. Then he left to contact the British Commander. Just before the five minutes were up, someone opened fire from the building next door (I later learned that a British soldier had walked into the room where our men were waiting and seeing the Germans in the street in front of us, opened fire on his own). I immediately had the men in our house open fire with the machine-gun and Browning Automatic Rifle and Pfc John Keller knocked out the anti-tank gun with a rifle grenade. We had only been firing for a minute when there was a terrific explosion in the room and it filled with plaster dust, blinding everyone. When it cleared I could see that an anti-tank shell had come through the wall from the room in the house next door on our left and continued through the wall to the house on our right. By some miracle, the only man hit was Private Carl Beck, but he was seriously wounded in the left side on his head and face. We pulled him to the back of the house and some men got him out to the backyard where the Medics could pick him up.'

Private Carl Beck in Company 'E' and his buddy, Pfc Earl 'Pete' Hable, were working their way down to the Nijmegen Bridge. 'We went into the houses from the front and out the back, over the fence and into another house. Then out the front door, go across the street and into the front of another house. We did that all the way down to the bridge. In a second floor window we set up our light machine-gun on a table and waited for the order to open fire. The Jerries were down in the street. Before the order came a British sniper opened up so we began shooting into a large group of Jerries. This is when I got hit. A shell came through the wall and a piece of shrapnel went into my mouth and came out of the left side of my head, taking everything with it. I woke up in the 119th General Hospital in England, nineteen days later. I didn't know where I was or what the hell had happened to me. I know now that it was my Lieutenant, James Coyle, who saved my life by his prompt first aid.' [4]

James Coyle continues:

'Pfc Clyde Rickert and I then manned the machine-gun and reopened fire but we could not see exactly where the anti-tank gun firing from our left was located. Just as I realised that tracer rounds included in the ammunition were pin-pointing our position for the enemy, another shell burst into the room from the left, hit the wall on our right and fell to the floor in the room. We could not continue firing and we moved back out of the front room. I went to the front room next door where the other squad of my men were to check them out. No Company 'E' men were hit, but a British observer with a radio who had moved into our position without my knowledge, had been killed by concussion when the shell had gone through that room. He did not have a mark on him.'

Company 'D' had also moved into Nijmegen until they hit stiff German resistance as Pfc Frank Bilich recalls. 'We occupied a row of houses on the Oude Wertz, the second or third one down and took over the upstairs rooms. Captain Taylor Smith told us to stay there, nobody was pulling out. 'We are going to hold this position,' were his last words. All of a sudden the Germans were all over the nearby railroad track and we were cut off. What we didn't know was,

4 His great buddy, Pfc Earl 'Pete' Hable was later killed in action in the Ardennes.

the Company had all pulled back leaving us to our fate. There were three of us, myself, Bill McMandon and another guy. With us were three members of a Dutch family, the mother who spoke English and her two young daughters. That Dutch family's name was Palmen. The girls were Trudie (or Judie) and Theresa. Around my neck I had my dog-tags and a rosary my mother had given me. The Dutch lady asked if I was Catholic.'

'The Germans were getting very close so we went down into the basement from the kitchen. Those houses were built so there was another door and stairs from the basement that came up under the back porch, into a fenced back yard. All three of us were hiding under the stairs as a German officer brought his Platoon into the building. Twice he came halfway down the stairs from the kitchen to give orders to the Dutch lady to fix coffee or something. By then the shooting had died down and it was all quiet. Every time he came down we thought about shooting him, but the rest would have got us. Her daughters were against a wall - she had only one small light on and we had not been spotted in the darkness. By about 2.30 in the morning all was quiet. We knew there was a guard on the back porch. If we stayed until daylight they would soon find us. The three of us had a whispered council of war. It was decided that we would make a run for it just before dawn. We talked about who was going first, second and last. The way out would be up the stairs and out under the porch. Again the officer came half way down the stairs from the kitchen and asked for coffee. After he went back we decided that this was our chance, we came up to the backyard and saw a wooden fence with a gate blocking our path. McMandon took off, hit the gate with such a force that it burst open and went through, I followed. There was a call to halt in German and somebody fired some shots. We were all through the gate and running down the backs of those houses, running until our lungs were ready to explode. We ran across a road and right over a Company 'E' machine-gun position and fell into a ditch. All the Company 'E' boys could say was, 'Where the hell have you come from?' We didn't care, we had made it.

'Later that day, 19th September, First Lieutenant Waverly W. Wray yelled at Pfc's 'Barney' Silanskis, Joe Rajca and John Rasumich and Private Jacob Herman to follow him to the railroad track leading to the rail bridge. As Wray raised his head over the track he was killed by a sniper's bullet in the head, fired from a signal tower. Herman was also killed. Silanskis had a bullet ricochet into his mouth off a tank car. He said later that he had his mouth open shouting orders. Luckily its force was almost spent and it bounced off a tooth, turned up into his cheek bone and lodged under his eye, leaving him with a permanent crooked smile to this day. The next day Charlie Miller rescued three crew members from a British tank that was on fire outside their house. Three times he went into that burning tank and the Germans were shooting at him all the time. He took the wounded men into the Palmen's house. Charlie should have had a medal for that. They said they would write him up for one, but he never heard any more about it.' [5]

5 After the battle for the bridge was over we drove out of Nijmegen in trucks, down the main road and I saw the two Palmen girls on the sidewalk. They recognised me and hollered at me - 'Thank you, Thank you.' Since the war I made several attempts to find them, without success.'

[Staff Sergeant Paul Nunan in D company was to be wounded himself a few hours after Lieutenant Wray was shot and killed.] 'As I was moving towards the railyard with my Platoon and Lieutenant O. B Carr, our Platoon Leader; Pfc Frank Silanskis approached me holding a hand over his mouth. Blood was seeping between his fingers. He informed me that Wray had been killed. Frank had a large lump on his left cheekbone, but the skin was unbroken. I examined his mouth and saw that the blood was coming from between his lip and the gum. Frank later told me the lump in his cheek was a bullet. The Medics made an incision from the outside over the bullet. Apparently the bullet had ricocheted, striking him between the front teeth and the inside of his lip, coming to rest over his cheekbone. I was hit later in the day when I tangled with an anti-aircraft gun and its crew. Using a British made Gammon grenade and a Thompson sub-machine-gun, the issue was decided in my favour at the cost of a fair sized hole in my left leg. I was subsequently evacuated by ambulance, truck and hospital train all the way back to Normandy, near where I had landed on D-Day just over three months before. I had what we Yanks called a 'million dollar wound'. Bad enough to keep you out of combat for a while, without being permanently disabling.'[6]

In Groesbeek Pfc Gordon Walberg in the 80th Airborne Anti-Tank Battalion received word that they could expect the German tanks to come down from Nijmegen to try to cut them off. 'We set up our anti-tank gun along the highway and had to cut down several trees to give ourselves a better field of fire. In the warm sun of a beautiful day we rested by the gun until I was rudely awakened by a grenade that came sailing through the air. As I stood up to see who had thrown it, an explosion in a tree above me knocked me on my back. I hollered out for everybody to get the culprit but another grenade exploded and knocked me down again. By this time I was getting smart and stopped looking for the enemy and I vaulted over a fence with my rifle. Pfc Malcolm Neel was with me at that time. The last grenade explosion set fire to our supplies, ammunition and camouflage net. For a while we were pinned down by the exploding of our own shells. Some of the 505 Parachute Infantry boys came along and helped by smothering the exploding ammunition with sand. Our tactics now consisted of going to wherever we were needed to stop the Germans from mounting their counter-attacks.

'We knew that we had to hold on to Berg en Dal, the highest ground in the area. As we approached the Hotel Hamer we felt we were being observed and I mentioned this to Herbert Moline, a boy from Chicago. Mortar fire began to fall on us and we jumped into a foxhole that was already dug in the parking lot. The two of us looked very odd in this place but the mortar fire was very accurate and we had no choice. A few paratroopers searched the Hotel Groat de Bergendal and found and killed an enemy observer in the tower. He could see where we were and was able to call for artillery and mortar fire when needed.'

At Lindquist's HQ Gavin was told that more men were needed to hold off the attacking German troops and Gavin gave orders for Lindquist to retrieve

6 *Put On Your Boots and Parachutes!: The United States 82nd Airborne Division* written and edited by Deryk Wills (self published, March 1992).

the battalion from Nijmegen to bolster the defences around Wyler even though it was exhausted from a night of fighting in Nijmegen. Gavin was then driven to Ekman's 505th. As he arrived, the Germans were preparing to attack Groesbeek and Colonel William Ekman, the 505th CO too was short of troopers, which held a tenuous 7-mile line. The 505th managed to keep the main German attack from taking Groesbeek but other German troops attacking from the Reichswald reached the landing areas. Gavin needed men to clear the LZs and as the situation worsened in the late morning he reinforced Colonel Benjamin Vandervoort's divisional reserve with two companies of engineers from the 504th and dispatched them on an eight-mile forced march to help clear the landing zones. It was perhaps fortuitous therefore that bad weather in England delayed the lift and the first gliders did not arrive at the LZ until 1400. The second lift consisted of 36 75mm Pack Howitzers and 1,866 men of the 456th Parachute Field Artillery Battalion and the 319th and 320th Glider Field Artillery Battalions, a battery of eight 57mm anti-tank guns and some engineer and medical units. Benjamin Vandevoort's 2nd Battalion launched a bayonet charge in a last ditch effort to clear at least part of the LZ as the first gliders began to land. Many of the German troops were low calibre and they began to break and run. American casualties were high and included Captain Anthony Stefanish who had been the heavyweight boxing champion of the division and was known for his humour, toughness and devotion to his men. Just before he died of wounds, he whispered 'We've come a long ways together. Tell the boys to do a good job.'

1st Sergeant Leonard A. Funk marched at the head of the force, shooting his way across 800 yards of open ground. Spotting four 20mm guns, Funk, with two others, then attacked and destroyed each gun and crew. Then he turned on three anti-aircraft guns close at hand and, leading a small group, he put them out of action, killing fifteen of the enemy. Vandervoort's men killed fifty soldiers and captured a further 150. Gavin wrote later of the action:

'A highly creditable performance and one that I never would have thought possible as I watched them approach the landing zone.' Of the 444 Waco gliders that left England, 385 reached the release point and 250 landed on, or close to, the designated LZ. The remainder were scattered around the surrounding area and 25 gliders of the 319th Field Artillery Battalion continued over the zone, beyond the Reichswald and landed about five miles inside Germany. About half the men got back to the division within a few days. The glider pilots explained that they had failed to get a green light signal from the tugs and thought they should not release. Other gliders that landed near the Reichswald came under intense and damaging fire. Flak hit glider pilot Flight Officer Lawrence W. Kubale in the right side of his head. He blacked out momentarily. Coming to, he found the sergeant, a gliderman who was by no means a pilot, at the other controls doing his best to fly the glider-and so far succeeding. Blood streaming from his right temple into his eyes, shrapnel in each of his arms, in severe pain, Kubale nevertheless took over again. He skilfully managed to land right on target when released. The landing was complete by 1430. Thirty of the 75mm Pack Howitzers were recovered, along with 78 of the 106 jeeps and all the 57mm anti-tank guns.

It was getting towards sunset. The firing died down and there was a chance for Bill Tucker and his squad to eat. He realised that it got dark a lot earlier in Holland than it did in Normandy. Just as the sun was going down about a hundred B-24s came over with equipment bundles. They were released at about six hundred feet over the Drop Zone. The German 88s on the right were firing at the bombers but not one was hit. Their speed was terrific, over 200 mph and many of the chutes did not open. It was a beautiful sight with the sunset behind the Liberators as they went over. The 82nd were getting their supplies and the troopers could feel their strength.

The supply-carrying B-24 Liberators of the 8th Air Force 2nd Bomb Division arrived over LZ 'N' Knapheide-Klein Amerika (Little America) near Groesbeek having been briefed at their bases in Norfolk and Suffolk the day before for a practice mission 'with a real twist' as Robert E. Oberschmid, a pilot in the 93rd Bomb Group at Hardwick recalled: 'A number of 93rd Group aircraft (18?) together with approximately 102 B-24s from other 2nd Division Groups would assemble and fly a loose bomber stream to an area north of London, descend to treetop level and return to our home base on the deck, individually hedge-hopping all the way. What a fascinating opportunity that turned out to be. About as much fun as I ever had flying a B-24 and I'm sure there are bovine descendants that still cringe when a plane passes overhead.'

That night, motor trucks brought supplies to the bases in the region and men loaded each Liberator with about 6,000lb of perishables and fuel supplies for the armies in Holland. Because of an administrative error, aircrews from the 20th Wing did not receive their pictures of the dropping zones until shortly before take-off. Individual crew briefings, addressed to the 20th Wing, had gone to the 14th Wing and vice versa, leaving crews to familiarize themselves with the correct details en route. The 20th Wing Liberators, each carrying twelve supply packs stowed in the bomb bays and with trained personnel from the special 9th Troop Carrier Command to supervise the drop, took off early that afternoon. Ball turrets and turret fairings had been removed to allow the bundles to be released through metal chutes. The Liberators took off from their airfields in Norfolk and Suffolk and almost immediately things began to go wrong. Just out of Orfordness, leading elements of the 20th Wing were forced to make a 360 degree turn to port to avoid veering into a C-47 unit. This confused the Groups following and the 448th lost sight of the force completely in the sea haze and continued alone while five 93rd Bomb Group Liberators returned to Hardwick.

Carroll A. Berner, a pilot in the 93rd recalled: 'This was our third mission. The group proceeded toward the mainland while descending in altitude and was at approximately 75 feet above terrain crossing the coast. Flying that low, formation became virtually impossible so we continued essentially as individualism, feeling comfortable if we could see one or two other B-24s - three was a bonus. Needless to say, we flew lower and lower - often at 25 feet and rarely above 50 feet. Church steeples, power lines and tall trees did present a very real concern. The Dutch citizens, mostly women and girls, came out in the yards and streets in their brightly coloured clothing, waving kerchiefs or bare hands as we passed over. At that altitude it was easy to distinguish the beautiful from the good looking and the young from the old. I thought they all looked great because they were obviously cheering us on. At one point my supply man called on the intercom and in an emotional voice said, 'A little round hole just opened up behind my knees and another about face high in front of me.' I asked if he was hurt and when he said 'no'. I said 'good.' End of conversation. I heard later from another crew that one man was busy waving at the girls when he saw a lone man in the street and decided to also wave at him. He then realized that the man was wearing a uniform and had a machine gun on his shoulder - pointing up! We did receive one more bullet hole but it did not pass between any knees.

'I will never understand how our navigators did it, but we reached the drop zone almost dead centre. It was a rather open field one-half to one-quarter of a mile in diameter. I pulled up to the designated drop altitude of 500 feet and while the crew in back was pushing out the cartons I gazed at a picture that war bomber pilots rarely see. There before me was the biggest collection of wrecked military hardware I had ever seen: unnumbered airplanes, German and Allied, dozens of gliders, several C-47s and C-46s, Me 109s and, I believe, Stukas; an unbelievable number of tanks German and Allied; also trucks and jeeps. The one that really impressed me was a P-47 in a 3-point position 'nose and main gear' but, other than the unusual position, it appeared to be undamaged. As soon as the supply man said, 'last chute is out,' we dropped down as low as we dared and still being able to turn. Since it was a right turn, I told the co-pilot to take it and keep his eye on the right wing tip and that I would look ahead for problems. We proceeded back toward England without incident, still waving at the populace. [7]

Robert Oberschmid found himself flying 20 feet above the ground, 'engines howling in protest of a power setting far above normal and the engine instruments in the 'red' or close to it'. Oberschmid continues: 'We had an indicated air speed of 205-210 with the wind whistling through more holes than anyone would ever count, still taking hits from small arms fire and no effective means of fighting back. I didn't even have my trusty 45. Where and when, you say? OK, follow me where angels fear to tread but where 'all those fine young men' would go so many, many times.

'It was a 'no mission credit' kind of trip. No flak vests or steel helmets but they added a load master for some obscure reason. It wasn't going to be as much fun as the practice mission either, because the trip would be at 500 feet instead of on the deck and we would have fifteen P-51s to intercede for us. They wouldn't be necessary of course, but just in case. I was decked out in a pair of oxfords, pink pants, green shirt, A2 jacket and 30 mission crush hat. Piece of cake. We were doing our pre-flight when jeeps began running all over the place, picking up our navigators to re-brief. Somebody somewhere had decided we were going to the wrong place. Seems we were not going to Arnhem after all - now it was Oosterbeek. Talk about confusion - if ever the alarm bells in my head had gone off this would have been the time, but no matter, away we went, we were

7 *Monty's Folly: Operation 'Market-Garden'* by Major Frederick D. 'Dusty' Worthen USAFR (Retd) and others; Edited by Lieutenant Colonel Carroll A. Berner USAFR (Retd) California Aero Press 1999).

invulnerable, we were good and this was gonna be fun, at least someone said that. 'At its best, the North Sea is an ugly, incredibly cold, foreboding body of water. This day it was fairly calm, but the debris of war was scattered from England to Holland. At the top of the list were several Horsa gliders awash in the sea and one of them had at least three British troops sitting on the wing. We reported their plight to 'Colgate' (air sea rescue) but the troops were a long way from shore and had already been in the sea at least 24 hours. Poor odds, I'd say.

'Landfall was on time, uneventful, on course and at 500 feet, very beautiful. Holland in the fall is truly a poet's inspiration. It was a clear day with the Dutch countryside before us when all hell broke loose. It started with a loud bang from the front of the plane and our nose gunner, Nick Flureas, said he had been hit and the turret was knocked out. Now anyone who flew 25 or 30 missions with the Mighty 8th knows how such an event can focus one's attention. Our bombardier, Al Faulhaber, gave him first aid and said the injury wasn't very bad, but we had lost the turret we would so desperately need. On to Oosterbeek - but now we were really on the deck in a very loose gaggle rather than a formation. A number of the planes had been hit and the radio was alive with the concerns of the various crews, to wit; what the hell's going on and didn't they say this was going to be a fun 'no mission credit' trip and where are our little friends and hey, a guy could get hurt doing stuff like this. I was flying 10 to 15 feet above the ground and was actually pulling up to cross dykes and roads. I could see some large electrical transmission towers ahead and I made the decision to fly under the wires rather than pull up again. Now just sit back and reflect on that manoeuvre for a few minutes and you can't help but wonder where you and I and all the rest of us got the courage to make a decision like that. And the courage of my crew was equal to or greater than mine - they knew what I was going to do and no one uttered a peep. Our top turret gunner Glenn Thompson says he still has a tendency to duck his head driving under a high line.

'From here on things just got worse. We came to a guard tower at the corner of a large fenced area, which turned out to be a PoW camp. I lifted the left wing over the first guard tower and flew the length of the fence, waving at the prisoners who were really animated at the thought that deliverance was at hand - little did they know. At the end of the fence I lifted the wing again to clear a second guard tower and there, not more than 30 feet from my face and eyeball to eyeball were two German soldiers with a machine gun in full automatic. They stitched our plane from end to end but didn't hit anything vital; however, my navigator Jerry Baughman developed a blister on the back of his neck from a round that passed a bit too close.

'From then on things just got worse than worse. We were flying about 30 feet above a canal that ran along one side of a small town. My left wing was over the street and the right wing over green fields. Soldiers of all nations gravitate toward towns and this idyllic village was no exception; it had German soldiers every place I looked. One guy on a bike going our direction looked over his shoulder when he heard us coming and somersaulted but came up on his feet with a pistol in his hand and put a few more holes in us. There were soldiers walking, riding in trucks, half tracks and tanks and they were all shooting at us. We passed a church and a priest was in the belfry waving down at us - at least he wasn't shooting. Approaching

Oosterbeek we pulled up to 500 feet, formed up, opened the bomb bays and made the drop on target. Two of our bundles did not release and our engineer, Fred Johnson, did his usual circus trick of going into the bomb bay without a parachute to release them. As we made a left turn away from the drop zone I could see that the trees across the river from our drop point were sprinkled with the parachutes of our paratroopers and many of those men were still hanging there.'

Theodore J. Gourley, a pilot in the 93rd Bomb Group, said, 'One could not forget the excitement demonstrated by the Dutch people. They were waving bright coloured cloths, which we assumed to be parachutes from previous cargo drops. Each colour would identify the contents of the material contained within the package or containers. The farm animals were in panic. Cows and horses were jumping through fences. The chickens were going wild.' 'We made landfall over Schouwen Island' recalled 'Dusty' Worthen, a bombardier 'then let down to about 50 feet to 100 feet. The view along the route to the drop zone was incredible. Crashed C-47 planes, burned outlines of crashed glider, gliders nosed up or on their back - a general mess. Our flight was mostly over farming areas. We could nearly see the flying feathers of the fluttering chickens; the cows were in a full gallop - right through fences and bushes. The Dutch farmers were waving happily. It was certainly a different sight than we would see at our usual 22,000 foot altitude. As we neared the target, the small arms fire became intense. We were hit several times. One slug stopped in the backpack parachute of our tail gunner, Chuck. Our waist gunner, Sid, had a bullet graze his leg.'

Another pilot, Arthur W. Cable, saw Dutch civilians running out into the streets 'from the small pubs in the small towns frantically waving their beer mugs in salute' the next instant he was over farmland 'with a German soldier trying to spray us with a 9 mm machine pistol.' Gene Hoffman saw a German in a slit trench swinging his machine gun and firing as they went by. 'One of his bullets hit about a foot under my seat and went straight through the plane; in one side and out the other. Going down the main runway of a German airfield, flak towers were actually firing down on us while our gunners answered with their 50s.' Alan Barber, a navigator, recalled: 'They told us not to fire at the ground to avoid killing any of our Dutch allies'. Charles R. Bastian, a co pilot, recalled that they 'rumbled inland right over a big town;' which he thought was Rotterdam. 'We lifted up to clear the taller buildings and then dropped down again to the open areas. The town had a lot of brown/red brick buildings and I can remember looking level right into the third storey window of one of them and seeing a German rifleman aiming back at me. On top of this building was a tripod mounted machine gun with two more German gunners shooting down at a plane ahead of us. A gunner in our flight knocked some bricks off the building and the Germans ducked out of sight. It appeared that the whole civilian population was out on the streets totally ignoring any danger and many of them were waving orange flags, the royal colours of Holland. We thought that the civilians would be cowed by the presence of the Germans but here they were - out in the open and waving flags like on a Fourth of July parade! Their support really gave us a morale boost and, despite the obvious danger, this was actually a fun mission.'

The Liberators flew so low that crewmen could see the expressions on the faces of the Dutch civilians, Sherman F. Furey could see people below shooting from the streets and others waving at them. A black kitten that he took along slept on his shoulder all the way to the drop zone. 'Our flight was through a lot of small arms, .50 calibre and 20mm fire. Both of my wingmen received hits.' David P. Glick, a navigator, quickly learned how difficult it was to navigate at such a low altitude, since features flashed by so swiftly. On the way to the drop zone he clearly recalled seeing 'countless gliders grounded at various angles and positions.' Oddly he recalled one fleeting glimpse of a Dutch housewife 'doing her laundry spread over hedges and bushes outside her house'.

James M. Davis, another pilot, saw the last of the gliders releasing and headed toward the ground. 'The fields seemed covered with gliders and as we approached I wondered how they could find a place to land because of the multitude of gliders scattered over the area, as well as the fences and many other obstacles on the ground. We passed just over some gliders that were attempting to land with no clearing. I saw one in particular, which did get on the ground only to collide with another glider and I can still recall seeing bodies of soldiers as they were flung through the air. At that instant, I was glad to be in a B-24 at 50 feet rather than in that glider.' As they entered the flooded countryside of Holland looking up at flak towers, Donald B. Day, a co-pilot, spotted a man walking across a footbridge - dead ahead and 'perpendicular to our 'water-skimming path. 'Will he see us in time? Yes, finally and over the side-rail he went, head first. I can still see the hobnails on the soles of his boots.'

Lloyd D. Hubbard, a waist gunner was releasing jerry cans when he saw one big roll of wire go through its harness and skim barely over a house, disappearing in the garden 'in a huge spray of dirt'. 'what tickled me most was a lady who was milking a cow and as we roared over the cow took off and the woman sat there with the milk pail between her knees and I swear I could almost read her lips as she flared up at us. I saw a field of PoWs and a girl pedalling a bicycle right through the battle zone after the drop we went right down on the deck. I remember seeing our wingman on one side of a big haystack and us on the other...' Bill A. Rosser piloting a B-24 saw 'every bush and hedgerow come alive' as men came out to retrieve the supply bundles. 'At least one plane had dropped some bundles near a village and the locals were out opening packages very quickly! Hope they got K-rations and not mortars.' One Liberator overshot the LZ and must have flown over German territory because 'a farmer, with his wife standing beside him, fired a shotgun at them'. After the supplies were kicked out of James W. Berry's B-24 he put the Liberator into a steep bank to turn away when a German bullet shattered the side window putting two holes in his flak helmet and peeling away the right side of his head before passing out through the cockpit roof. 'I thought something had blown up; he said. 'I could see my helmet between the rudder pedals and that there was blood all over. My right eye was full of Plexiglas. That son-of-a-gun who shot me was either the luckiest shot in the German Army or he was a pretty good duck hunter.' [8]

One bullet, well spent by the time it reached the B-24, hit Ted Parker, waist

8 Berry was awarded the DFC for his handling of the bomber after he was shot and spent more than a year in hospital. *Monty's Folly: Operation 'Market-Garden'* by Major Frederick D. 'Dusty' Worthen USAFR (Retd) and others; Edited by Lieutenant Colonel Carroll A. Berner USAFR (Retd) California Aero Press 1999).

gunner in a nine-man crew in the 491st, in the cheek. Parker's B-24 carried a dropmaster. At one point the drop was in jeopardy, as Ted Parker wrote: 'The moment we took off the Quartermaster froze with fright and I got no help from him. I placed him on the forward deck and covered him up to keep him warm. He was shaking like a leaf. At the target I opened the hatch in the floor and had to work quickly because we would be passing the dropping zone fast and at low altitude. In my haste my leg became entangled in the parachute straps attached to the ammunition track and I was pulled out of the hole when the last bundle went out. I just managed to cling to the track but my legs were dangling out of the hatch. The Quartermaster ignored my calls for help. Finally the tail gunner heard me and came to my assistance.'

Their B-24 flew on the left wing of the lead ship *I'll Be Seeing You,* which was flown by Captain Jim Hunter and carried Captain Anthony Mitchell, the Air Commander. Hunter's ship was hit after the formation had dropped its bundles of supplies. Ted Parker watched the Liberator take one bounce, strike a haystack and explode in a large orange flame. Frank DiPalma, one of the gunners, was the only survivor; he was badly burned but survived after treatment by some Dutch doctors in the vicinity and was then hidden by some Franciscan monks in Udenhout until liberated.

As Robert Oberschmid headed home he thought it was obvious 'that a disaster of major proportions had been brought down on our heads.' We never did see our little friends but were told later that they had been devastated on the way in and the trip out was just an extension of that mess. We were on the deck indicating about 210 when a terrific explosion occurred in the cockpit. A fire broke out in the fuse panel on my left and the cockpit area was full of smoke and debris. It took me a few seconds to realize I was still alive, if somewhat rattled. When I turned to Fred, who always flew standing between our co-pilot Art Antonio and me; I saw a picture of total amazement. Fred had been wearing a baseball cap and the visor was gone. The only remnants were a few threads hanging down his forehead. Anyone who believes 'close only counts in horseshoes' has never been shot at and missed. Over the North Sea headed home we watched one of our Group go in the water. Technically it was a perfect ditching, but there were no survivors. Not even a cushion floated after the second impact which also broke the plane in two. We also saw another B-24 and a C-47 go down in the water. Approaching Hardwick I requested an ambulance for my nose gunner but it proved unnecessary as his injuries were quite minor. So minor that my recommendation for his Purple Heart wasn't even acknowledged. We were greeted by a number of staff and medical personnel whose curiosity immediately shifted to questions such as, 'Where is everybody?' When we informed them that 'everybody' was scattered and splattered from Hardwick to Arnhem, Nijmegen, Oosterbeek and back, the mood became sombre indeed.' [9]

Two Groups of escorting Thunderbolts Jailed to nullify the almost constant small-arms fire and 16 Liberators were shot down while seventy were damaged and 21 fighters were shot down. The 446th and 448th each lost three Liberators and had many more damaged. These included twenty-five out of the thirty-six

9 *Operation 'Market-Garden'* by Lieutenant Colonel Robert E. Oberschmid, writing in the 2nd AD Journal.

dispatched from Bungay. But despite some 453rd crews having to make three runs over the dropping zone and the 448th releasing the supplies some five miles short, the 1st Allied Airborne Army recovered 80 per cent of all supplies dropped by the 20th Wing at Groesbeek. The 14th Wing, meanwhile, with the 491st Bomb Group at its head, was en route for its dropping zone at Best. First Lieutenant Pete Henry flew as deputy lead of the third squadron in the 44th formation in a brand-new ship, later named *Henry* after the King Features cartoon character. When the 44th released its supplies, it reverted to flying on the deck (having gone in at about 500 feet over the dropping zone). Many B-24s received hits, including Pete Henry's. His leading edge on the left wing was holed by a 0.30 calibre shell which cut the line supplying manifold pressure. It also holed the fuel tank and petrol began leaking into the bomb bays. Pete Henry got his aircraft home but one Liberator from the 44th was forced to ditch in the North Sea. Only three crewmen were seen scrambling from the stricken bomber.

Shortly after the drop Bill Tucker and his squad moved over to the left about 500 yards to set up their own position. The Second Platoon manned a roadblock and the First and Third Platoons were sent to the left and right of the line respectively. However, under Captain McPheeters's plan, which was a good idea, the Mortar Squads were set up right next to the Command Post. Paul Hill and Mike Terella were there and they all dug in. The CP had a lot of runners now. This is where they remained for a while so Jim Downing and Tucker went out again in search of an observation post. About fifty yards in front of the Third Platoon's lines they found a house which had good cover and good visibility in every direction. The Wyler family's cellar was full of potatoes. They only intended to stay temporarily since it was out in front of the combat lines, but it was such a good observation post they stayed for the entire day. The Third Platoon and Hallahan with his machine-gun were behind them for safety. They ate a lot of potatoes. The farmer, his wife and six small children were living in a deep hole in the front yard. They too were hoping to stay with their house and land. Tucker felt sorry for them and sympathised with their plight. The farmer was a sturdy character. [10]

The Germans attacked, but not in too much strength. The observation post was the most vulnerable position in the whole line. During the day while some German planes were coming over, Hallahan took the opportunity to cut down a fat cow with his machine-gun. The cow belonged to a rich farmer who lived next door to the Wyler family. The cow's owner did not like it but it was cut up and they gave some of it to the Wylers. It did the guys good to see him get some meat for his kids. He didn't have a cow of his own and as Tucker was eating his potatoes, it was a fair swap.

When night came, Tucker and Downing crawled back to the CP, as it would have been crazy to stay out there all night. However, Sergeant Melvin told them that since it was a good observation post they had better stay there. Tucker was frustrated but they had to go back. Moe Green came with them and they dug in under the hay and hid. So for the rest of the night the three took turns sleeping under the hayloft, but there was no attack. It was learned that the

10 The Wyler family, husband and wife are deceased as of 1985. They had a total of fourteen children. Tucker visited the family several times after the war, in 1970 accompanied by his wife and two children.

Germans had issued an order that the 82nd must surrender or be annihilated. The order was ignored. Still no heavy attack, although the Second Platoon received some pressure. The mortar squad was ordered to move over to the right and support them. The CP stayed where it was but Tucker moved out and wound up in an apple orchard which had a greenhouse - a glass greenhouse - in it. Everybody did a lot of digging in and found a lot of food again. Just behind the Second Platoon there was a windmill. This was to be a windmill of destiny and Tucker took it over as an observation post. One of them would have to be up at the narrow window at all times, but the first night they were too interested in setting up the guns. So they were not there when the Company Commander tried to reach them on the telephone. Ed Morrissey was on the road block under attack and calling for support. Tucker finally reached the window and fired the guns. Somehow he got lined up on the wrong target and nearly hit Leonard's position with the mortars. Morrissey was really sore at this and the Captain gave Tucker hell. With the Second Platoon so close the following day Tucker got the chance to go and talk to them. There was no food, no supplies and everything was scarce. While Tucker was talking to Matash, Matash was chasing a skinny old chicken. During the chase, Lieutenant Colonel Krause came up and told them they would have to forage for food off the land.[11]

Wallace was now with the Platoon again and they stayed there for another day and did quite a bit of firing. By that time they were well acquainted with the terrain and picked many targets to use. Just about the time when they were reaching the end of the rope at the windmill, the 325th Glider Infantry Regiment came in to relieve them. Tucker didn't know where they were supposed to go but the news came through that they were going to Nijmegen to help in attacking the bridges. The Battalion stopped for a rest in a very beautiful pine forest. As it was said, this was a playground for the Dutch people and it was very beautiful. They made several stops up in the forest and the first time they contacted the Second Platoon they noticed there was something wrong. The previous night the Platoon had sent out a patrol and as it was coming in one of the men had been killed by one of the others, who was immediately transferred out to another Company.

After a long march through the woods they boarded British lorries to go north to Nijmegen. There was no firing on the way - just beautiful country. On the approach to Groesbeek they noticed that the rear elements of their outfit had themselves pretty well set up there. There seemed to be plenty of dairy products and everybody had some butter and cheese. The country from Groesbeek to Nijmegen was not as flat as they thought Holland was. This was more like Germany than Holland. The houses were beautiful, with some of the corners completely covered by glass windows. Most of these windows were broken now but these houses compared very well with the best of houses in the US. By the time they reached Nijmegen they found that both the big bridges had been taken by the 504. The way they took them will go down in history.

11 Edward Krause was promoted to Lieutenant Colonel in August 1944 and made the Regimental Executive Officer..

D+1 Resupply by Bomber Timeline

The bomber resupply mission to the 82nd and 101st Divisions was to arrive 20 minutes after the troop carriers, drop time being set for **1557**. It was to be flown by 252 B-24 Liberators of the 2nd Bombardment Division from bases in Norfolk and Suffolk. Supplies were trucked in on the night of the 17th. The ball turrets were removed and each plane was loaded in bomb racks, waist and bomb bay with about two tons of supplies packed in 20 containers. A trained dropmaster of the 2nd Quartermaster Battalion was assigned to each B-24 to direct the pushing of bundles through the turret well and the rear hatch. The bomber staff, new to this sort of mission, had been in great doubt as to tactics and particularly as to what would be the best altitudes for the bombers to maintain. Finally it decided to imitate the troop carriers by having them fly at 1,500 feet to the IP, descend to about 300 feet for the drop and make a climbing turn to 1,500 feet or higher for the trip back. Formations would be nine-ship V's in trail at 30-second intervals. The speed would be 165 mph along the route and 150 miles when dropping. Except for leaving England at Orfordness, a headland two miles south of the troop carrier departure point, the Liberators would follow the northern troop carrier route out and back in order to benefit from the marker boat, anti-flak operations and ASR facilities provided for their predecessors. At the IP the 20th Wing with 131 B-24s would proceed to DZ 'N' with supplies for the 82nd Division and behind it 121 Liberators of the 14th Wing would turn southward to drop on DZ 'A' and DZ 'W' for the 101st. The same visual aids set out on the zones for the troop carriers were to be provided for the bombers, but since the B-24s were not equipped with 'Eureka', the pathfinders were to provide radio 'buncher' beacons to guide them. Each flight was to drop its loads when its leader dropped and he was to do so directly over the T.

The bombers were given fully as much support as the transports. The ADGB fighters covering the troop carrier missions were in a position to protect the Liberators over most of their way to the IP and four of the P-51 groups flying area cover around Eindhoven and Nijmegen remained throughout the supply drop. Two groups of P-38s and P-51s flew 104 sorties as close escort from landfall to drop zone and two groups of P-47s bombed and strafed flak positions between IP and drop zones five minutes before the bombers were due to arrive. No hostile aircraft were sighted, but the flak-busters had a hard time. Clouds were rolling in below 1,000 feet; the haze was thickening as the afternoon wore on; and the German gunners were perfecting their hit-and-hide tactics. In 88 sorties the P-47 group lost 21 fighters and had many damaged, while destroying only 6 gun positions and damaging about 15.

Over the middle of the Channel the 20th Wing make a 3600 turn to the left and the 14th, anxious to keep its assigned position, turn with it. The turn, which was made to avoid running into a belated serial of the 442nd Troop Carrier Group, causes delay and confusion, particularly since the haze makes it easy for a group which lags a little to lose sight of the one ahead. In the 20th Wing the 448th Group becomes separated from the others and proceeds independently and five pilots in the 93rd Group lose their way and have to abort. Thanks to good navigation, greatly aided by 'Gee', all but those five appear to have reached the IP. The 20th Wing has some trouble locating DZ 'N'. The radio beacon is not on and most formations see neither panels nor smoke. Part of the 489th Group miss the zone on its first run, circle, turn away on its second run to avoid other formations and drop on the third try. The 448th Group probably misled by evidences of paratroop operations on DZ 'O' drop five miles short near that zone at 1630 hours. Some incoming flights have to swerve to avoid those returning. Many appear to have used glider concentrations as drop points and since the gliders are spread up to 3,000 yards north, west and south of DZ 'N', the drop is similarly dispersed. The prescribed altitude is well maintained, almost all drops being made from heights between 250 and 400 feet. Most of the bundles land within the lines of the 82nd Division and about 80 percent of the 258 tons dropped are recovered. Estimates vary as to the percentage collected, but the value of the ammunition and other items delivered is unquestionably great. General Gavin considers them 'vital to our continued combat existence.'

The 446th Bomb Group experienced an easy approach over several miles of friendly territory dotted with waving paratroops and Dutch civilians and it returned almost unscathed. The others reported small arms and light flak, which in places was intense and accurate. The wing lost four B-24s, had about 38 damaged and had at least 16 men wounded. The flights of the 14th Wing had overrun each other in the haze and reached the IP in great disorder at altitudes ranging from 500 to 1,500 feet. They received little or no assistance from the pathfinders, who apparently got their equipment into operation too late to be of use. However, with one exception, all the 121 pilots found their way to the general vicinity of DZ's 'A' and 'W' and dropped their loads. Most dropped from about 300 feet as prescribed, but some flights came in on the deck as low as 50 feet, too low for accuracy. For the others the gliders on DZ 'W' were the most obvious landmarks. The results were not good. Even the wing commander admitted that the bundles were badly scattered. Some 238 tons were dropped. On DZ 'W', where 108 of the Liberators were to drop, only about 20 percent of the supplies were recovered. This is less damning than it appears, since the gliders used as checkpoints were at the west end of the zone and a deviation of less than a mile to the west of them would suffice to put the bundles in the hands of the Germans in the Best sector. The failure, however understandable, caused the 101st Division serious shortages of food and other essentials. The 501st PIR had been given a drop on DZ 'A' by 13 B-24s. Although the supplies they brought were rather scattered, they were centred 1,000 yards west of the zone. A small-scale German attack in this area had been routed about an hour earlier and the 501st had both time and men to spare for collection details; under these relatively favourable conditions it was able to retrieve slightly over 50 percent of its bundles. The 14th Wing had had very little trouble with ground fire on the way in and some flights which stayed low and skimmed out on the deck came back untouched. However, most pilots who had dropped on DZ 'W' made a climbing turn to the right, as planned. This tactic posed them like clay pigeons directly over the guns of the Germans at Best. For a minute or two the Germans gave the wing what even the bomber men regarded as a very rough time. Three of their planes were shot down, one crash-landed at Brussels and four crash-landed in England fit for nothing but salvage. At least 32 others received some damage. Next day the returned pilots agreed unanimously that the climbing turn was a mistake.

US Airborne Divisions' Timeline 18th September D+1

Eindhoven Sector

In the 101st Division's area of responsibility the 506th Parachute Infantry Regiment marched south at dawn, reached Eindhoven at 0900 and took the town before noon over the resistance of about a battalion of Germans. The bridges there were unharmed. Two British armoured cars on reconnaissance got through to the 506th about 1230, but the rest of the British armour was still five miles to the south, bumping along from road-block to roadblock. Not until 1830 did the Guards reach Eindhoven and they halted for the night outside Son on the south side of the Wilhelmina Canal while their engineers laid a Bailey bridge over the centre trestle of the damaged highway bridge there.

The 501st PIR have a relatively easy day. It repulses four or five feeble attacks made by improvised German forces gathered west of it at Schijndel and 's Hertogenbosch. Much more serious is the situation of the 502d PIR. Its 3rd Battalion begin the day in battle with superior forces at the Best highway bridge. The rest of the regiment, excepting the 15t Battalion, which remains at Sint Oedenrode, moves to assist it and is also engaged and pinned down. Early in the afternoon the Germans attack with artillery and tank support against the paratroops, still without artillery. 'Enemy closing in, situation getting desperate,' reads the entry in a battalion journal. Bombing and strafing by five P-47s, which arrive in the nick of time, enables the troops to repel that attack, but bitter and indecisive fighting continues throughout the day in the Best sector, within 1,000 yards west and southwest of LZ 'W'. This situation presents an unexpected hazard to the glider missions landing on W that afternoon.

Nijmegen Sector

The 82nd Division is faced with a threat which for a time is serious indeed. At first everything seems promising. The 508th PIR has extended its lines westward to make contact with the 504th at the site of Bridge 9, thus giving the division a neat sausage-shaped perimeter with its north side on high ground and its south protected by the Maas. Except for Nijmegen the enemy has shown little strength and the 508th is deploying for a stronger thrust at the Nijmegen Bridge. Then between **0800** and **1000** the Germans surge down the road from Wyler, push back the one company of the 508th which has been left to guard LZ 'T' and seize an ammunition dump. About the same time, other forces attack out of the Reichswald Forest and overrun DZ 'N'.

The 82nd seems close to disaster. If the Germans hold the zones when the gliders landed there would be a slaughter which would make that on LZ 'W' in Normandy seem insignificant. If the attackers break through the perimeter into the woods around Groesbeek, it would scarcely be possible to drive them out and with enemy troops at its centre; the division's carefully chosen ring of defensive positions would become precarious. Fortunately the German troops involved are a hastily gathered assortment, no match for the paratroops in either quality or quantity and the postponement of the glider missions to **1400** gives sufficient time to counterattack and clear the landing zones. News of the change in schedule has reached the division at **0840** about the same time as the first reports of the German attacks.

General Gavin throws his only ready reserve, two companies of the 307th Engineers, into the gap between the 505th Regiment and the 508th and orders the two regiments to hold their lines along the ridge at all costs and to retake their landing zones ('T' and 'N') in time for the glider missions. The 508th pulls back its companies in the Nijmegen area, redeploys on the ridge and at **1310** launches an attack on LZ 'T'; by **1400** it has regained that area and captures 149 prisoners and 16 guns. The 1st Battalion of the 505th is directed to attack eastward at **1240** and clear LZ 'N'. Already engaged in stiff fighting at Riethorst and Mook, the battalion can spare only Company 'C' to do the job. However, with help from Company 'I' they are able by **1350** to push off the zone the relatively weak enemy force. At **1415** the Germans again attack out of the Reichswald with three companies supported by eleven armoured vehicles. The 3rd Battalion of the 505th repells this thrust with the help of artillery support, which knocks out five of the vehicles. The landing zones have been saved, but they are far from safe. The Germans have dug in near enough to LZs' 'T' and 'N' to rake them with small a fire and bombard them with mortars.

While carrying on a defensive battle around zones, the 82nd captures another bridge over the Maas-Waal Canal, valuable insurance in case anything happens to the one at Heumen. During the morning a patrol of the 508th PIR pushes north to Honinghutie, the point where the main road crosses the canal. Checked by stubborn resistance on the approaches to the east end of the bridge, it calls for assistance from the 504th which sends a platoon to assist it. About noon this unit moves stealthily onto the west end of bridge, takes the Germans by surprise and slaughters them. However, the Germans damage the structure making it unsafe for heavy vehicles.

US Airborne Divisions' Timeline 18th September D+1

Eindhoven Sector

In the 101st Division's area of responsibility the 506th Parachute Infantry Regiment marched south at dawn, reached Eindhoven at **0900** and took the town before noon over the resistance of about a battalion of Germans. The bridges there were unharmed. Two British armoured cars on reconnaissance got through to the 506th about **1230,** but the rest of the British armour was still five miles to the south, bumping along from road-block to roadblock. Not until **1830** did the Guards reach Eindhoven and they halted for the night outside Son on the south side of the Wilhelmina Canal while their engineers laid a Bailey bridge over the centre trestle of the damaged highway bridge there.

The 501st PIR have a relatively easy day. It repulses four or five feeble attacks made by improvised German forces gathered west of it at Schijndel and 's Hertogenbosch. Much more serious is the situation of the 502d PIR. Its 3rd Battalion begin the day in battle with superior forces at the Best highway bridge. The rest of the regiment, excepting the 15t Battalion, which remains at Sint Oedenrode, moves to assist it and is also engaged and pinned down. Early in the afternoon the Germans attack with artillery and tank support against the paratroops, still without artillery. 'Enemy closing in, situation getting desperate,' reads the entry in a battalion journal. Bombing and strafing by five P-47s, which arrive in the nick of time, enables the troops to repel that attack, but bitter and indecisive fighting continues throughout the day in the Best sector, within 1,000 yards west and southwest of LZ 'W'. This situation presents an unexpected hazard to the glider missions landing on W that afternoon.

Nijmegen Sector

The 82nd Division is faced with a threat which for a time is serious indeed. At first everything seems promising. The 508th PIR has extended its lines westward to make contact with the 504th at the site of Bridge 9, thus giving the division a neat sausage-shaped perimeter with its north side on high ground and its south protected by the Maas. Except for Nijmegen the enemy has shown little strength and the 508th is deploying for a stronger thrust at the Nijmegen Bridge. Then between **0800** and **1000** the Germans surge down the road from Wyler, push back the one company of the 508th which has been left to guard LZ 'T' and seize an ammunition dump. About the same time, other forces attack out of the Reichswald Forest and overrun DZ 'N'.

The 82nd seems close to disaster. If the Germans hold the zones when the gliders landed there would be a slaughter which would make that on LZ 'W' in Normandy seem insignificant. If the attackers break through the perimeter into the woods around Groesbeek, it would scarcely be possible to drive them out and with enemy troops at its centre; the division's carefully chosen ring of defensive positions would become precarious. Fortunately the German troops involved are a hastily gathered assortment, no match for the paratroops in either quality or quantity and the postponement of the glider missions to **1400** gives sufficient time to counterattack and clear the landing zones. News of the change in schedule has reached the division at **0840** about the same time as the first reports of the German attacks.

General Gavin throws his only ready reserve, two companies of the 307th Engineers, into the gap between the 505th Regiment and the 508th and orders the two regiments to hold their lines along the ridge at all costs and to retake their landing zones ('T' and 'N') in time for the glider missions. The 508th pulls back its companies in the Nijmegen area, redeploys on the ridge and at **1310** launches an attack on LZ 'T'; by **1400** it has regained that area and captures 149 prisoners and 16 guns. The 1st Battalion of the 505th is directed to attack eastward at **1240** and clear LZ 'N'. Already engaged in stiff fighting at Riethorst and Mook, the battalion can spare only Company 'C' to do the job. However, with help from Company 'I' they are able by **1350** to push off the zone the relatively weak enemy force. At 1415 the Germans again attack out of the Reichswald with three companies supported by eleven armoured vehicles. The 3rd Battalion of the 505th repells this thrust with the help of artillery support, which knocks out five of the vehicles. The landing zones have been saved, but they are far from safe. The Germans have dug in near enough to LZs' 'T' and 'N' to rake them with small a fire and bombard them with mortars.

While carrying on a defensive battle around zones, the 82nd captures another bridge over the Maas-Waal Canal, valuable insurance in case anything happens to the one at Heumen. During the morning a patrol of the 508th PIR pushes north to Honinghutie, the point where the main road crosses the canal. Checked by stubborn resistance on the approaches to the east end of the bridge, it calls for assistance from the 504th which sends a platoon to assist it. About noon this unit moves stealthily onto the west end of bridge, takes the Germans by surprise and slaughters them. However, the Germans damage the structure making it unsafe for heavy vehicles.

US Airborne Divisions' and XXX Corps' Timeline

19 September (D+2)

Weather and tactical developments produce several changes in the plans for D+2. On the evening of the 18th General Brereton decrees that all airborne missions next day would take the southern route and that the drops and landings would begin at **1500** hours instead of **1000.** His preference for flight over friendly territory dictates selection of the southern route. Predictions of extensive fog in northern areas and almost unbroken low clouds further south on the morning of the 19th account for the postponement. By afternoon, the fog would be gone and the clouds were expected to lift a little. The 101st Division has decided it wants artillery in the third lift, so the five serials originally detailed to drop supplies to it are transformed into glider serials to bring in guns and gunners. Instead of 191 Wacos the division would receive 382 and to this are added three more carrying the loads of gliders which had aborted earlier. In addition, the low attrition rate in the previous missions makes it possible to increase the number of gliders going to the 82nd Division from 209 to 219, the resupply aircraft for that division from 142 to 167 and the planes carrying Polish paratroops to Arnhem from 108 to 114. The RAF would send to Arnhem a parachute resupply mission of 163 planes and a glider mission of 52 aircraft, including seven added to bring in replacements for gliders which have aborted on previous missions.

0645 Bailey bridge completed across the Wilhelmina Canal at Son by sappers of the Royal Engineers bridge-building teams [12] and the XXX Corps advance resumes at dawn. The second lift of the 101st Airborne leaves England, 428 gliders setting out with two battalions of the 327th Glider Infantry Regiment and parts of division support units. Eighty-two gliders

12 Plans had been made for the situation where the enemy might demolish one or more of the vital bridges along the axis. This possibility alone meant including in the column no fewer than 9,000 sappers with 5,000 vehicles full of bridging equipment.' *The Guards Armoured History.*

break their tow combinations over England, 17 land in the Channel and 16 in Germany, 31 in friendly territory and 26 remain unaccounted for. Between 209 and 213, or only half the force make it to the landing zone, which nevertheless brings in 146 jeeps and 109 trailers and a bulldozer, in addition to sorely needed infantry. The lift costs the Division 29 killed and 41 injured in crashes and a total of 225 men remained unaccounted for. The next task of the 101st Airborne, now supported by British tanks, artillery and infantry from the two other British Corps of Second Army, the VIII and XII, is to keep the main road open in the face of strong counter-attacks from German forces to the east and west and, if possible, widen the Allied thrust.

0730 Guards Armoured Division arrives in Veghel and by 0820 the Household Cavalry has covered another 14 miles of road to the north and makes contact with the 82nd Airborne at Grave, where Browning and Gavin are waiting for Horrocks. The Grenadiers arrive two hours later. The journey of 53 miles from Joe's Bridge to Nijmegen has taken the Guards Armoured 42 hours and 130 casualties. The advance by VIII and XII Corps on the flanks of XXX Corps has made little progress. Horrocks and Browning, concerned at the plight of 1st Airborne Division at Arnhem, instruct Gavin to plan urgently an attack to capture the Nijmegen bridges. German reinforcements have been building up on both sides of the narrow Allied salient, first to contain it and then to destroy it. Model has forbidden the bridges at Arnhem and Nijmegen to be blown so that they could be used for a counter-offensive. **1000** Tanks of the Household Cavalry and Grenadier Guards Group start to cross the Maas to the outskirts of Nijmegen, 42 hours after crossing their start line. As the leading tanks of the Grenadier Guards Group pass over the bridge at Heumen and enter the outskirts of Nijmegen to link up with 82nd Division it is learned that the road and rail bridge over the Waal which were to be taken by the 1st Battalion, 508th PIR, commanded by Lieutenant Colonel Shields Warren, are still in German hands and fighting is raging in the town.

German pressure from Best continues. 101st Division mounts a three-battalion attack with British tank and artillery support and finally takes Best, killing 300 and capturing 1,000 German soldiers, mainly of the 59th Infantry Division. Enemy probing attacks come in against Veghel and Sint-Oedenrode. Tanks of 107 Panzer Brigade shell Son bridge from the east, halting traffic on the axis for 24 hours. The Grenadiers and 2nd Battalion, 505th Regiment are ordered to rush the Nijmegen bridges. The Guards advance is delayed by the detour via Heumen Bridge. The combined attacks start mid-afternoon, but these are held by stubborn defence by the SS troops, 300 yards from the railway bridge and 500 yards from the road bridge. The Coldstream Guards Group is placed in support of 82nd Division. It is not until **1830** that Warren is able to send a force - albeit small - into Nijmegen. Dutch reports were that there were only 19 Germans at the bridge but the platoon radio fails and no word is received that night.

The 508th PIR is harassed by increased German infiltration from the Reichswald near Berg-en-Dahl, including seven battalions of German II Parachute Corps.

Weather conditions prove to be much worse than had been predicted. Throughout the day haze and stratus blankets the Grantham area and great masses of low cloud persist over the Channel and the Low Countries. Along most of the troop carrier route haze limits visibility to about half a mile. The only area on the route with even relatively good weather is that around Arnhem. Lowering clouds over the bases of the 50th and 52nd Wings force the postponement of the 82nd Division's third lift consisting of 428 gliders carrying mainly two battalions of 325th Glider Infantry at 1000. A few aircraft and gliders get off the ground but are recalled almost immediately. The others remain grounded all day. Gavin is forced to organize 450 of his glider pilots into an improvised battalion and is supported by 8th Armoured Brigade and the Guards Armoured.

The resupply mission of 167 C-47s, which was to drop 265 tons of supplies to the 82nd, did somewhat better, because it staged from the bases of the 53rd Wing in southern England and two serials had been sent to those bases on the day before. One serial of 25 aircraft flown by the 439th Group ran into heavy cloud off the Belgian coast and broke up. One of its planes followed the gliders going to LZ 'W' and dropped its bundles near there. Another gets far enough to be damaged by anti-aircraft fire. (One of the crew bails out in the mistaken belief the aircraft is about to blow up). The rest apparently turn back before reaching the Continent. The other serial, 35 aircraft of the 61st Group, begin taking off from Aldermaston at **1250.** They fly across the Channel through dense haze under a 200-foot ceiling. Over Holland the weather improves greatly, but flak is heavy and no friendly fighters are sighted north of Gheel, Two aircraft are shot down, one west of Veghel and another shortly after making its drop. Fifteen are damaged and five men are missing, including a quartermaster bundle-dropper who fell out the door of his aircraft.

As a result of its struggle for LZ's 'N' and 'T' on the previous day, the 82nd Division has decided to use DZ 'O' as both drop and landing zone for the time being, so its pathfinders set out their aids on that zone. Although one squadron claimed it got no response, the 'Eureka' was probably functioning effectively. The panels and smoke on the zone were clearly visible. One pilot dropped his bundles prematurely near Hertogenbosch and another straggled off and followed a RAF formation to Arnhem. However, 32 planes reached the vicinity of DZ 'O' at **1530.**

Remembering their stinging reception on the previous day, the troop carriers made a fast, high drop. Authorized to go in at 1,000 feet, they let go their bundles at speeds up to 135 mph from as high as 2,500 feet. The results are decidedly unsatisfactory. The airborne calls the amount recovered 'negligible' and official estimates put it at only 20 percent of the quantity dropped. The failure of this mission is a real blow to the 82nd Division, since it is becoming critically short of both food and ammunition.

Escort and cover duties between England and the southern IP near Gheel have been assigned to 15 Spitfire squadrons of ADGB but because of the widespread bad weather only one of the Spitfire squadrons carries out its mission as planned and only 68 of the Spitfires make sorties. The rest have to turn back. All responsibility for protection of the troop carriers from air action between 's Hertogenbosch and Arnhem, originally delegated to the 9th Air Force, is given to 8th Air Force. Of seven groups of P-51s which the 8th Air Force is to furnish for perimeter patrols and area cover, five groups are able to reach the battle area and make a total of about 180 sorties. (Two P-47 groups and the rocket squadron for anti-flak work south of 's Hertogenbosch are unable to make any sorties). Flak neutralization beyond 's Hertogenbosch for missions to Nijmegen and Arnhem is a responsibility of 9th Air Force units based in northern France. These dispatch 171 fighters, but few reach the front and none go into action. The principal reason for this failure is the impossibility of attacking ground positions through low clouds and thick haze. Thus weather prevents any effective operations against AA positions.

Two of the P-51 groups have to battle German fighters which are seeking to penetrate the perimeter. At **1445** near Wesel the 364th Group sights and engages more than 30 enemy aircraft. It reports the destruction of five of them and the loss of one of its own. The 357th Fighter Group, which has 54 planes on patrol in the Arnhem area, has four such clashes. It encounters 25 Bf 109s at **1610** hours, about 30 FW 190s at **1620,** between 20 and 30 assorted fighters at **1705** and 15 Bf 109s at **1720.** The group claims to have shot down 18 of the enemy and lose five of its aircraft. Except for the fight near Wesel these air battles are fought after the troop carrier serials have left the combat area, but they undoubtedly save the airborne troops some punishment. If the Luftwaffe had struck earlier, their chances of getting at the troop carriers would have been better, since because of the weather two P-51 groups on area patrol are late in getting into position.

Glider missions by 80 American and 10 RAF aircraft to land the 878th (US) Aviation Engineer Battalion on LZ's 'X' and 'L' are postponed. The gliders stand ready; the weather at their bases is favourable; but the land on which to build an airstrip outside Arnhem has not been won and, indeed, never was won; so the engineers wait and their aircraft stand idle.

The glider mission to the Eindhoven area flown by the 53rd Wing and 442nd Group for the 101st Division takes off between about **1130** and **1320** in ten serials containing 385 plane-glider combinations. The weather over the assembly area around Greenham Common is barely passable with visibility poor and clouds closing in at about 1,200 feet. Beyond Hatfield conditions deteriorate rapidly and before reaching the coast the serials ran into deep, dense clouds in which visibility is zero. Glider pilots unable to see their tugs have to guide their craft by the tilt of the tow rope and by telephone conversation with the plane crew. At most points over the Channel it is possible to get under the clouds by going down to about 200 feet, but even then visibility is generally half a mile or less.

Many gliders break loose, cut loose (when an aircraft banked in the overcast its glider was apt to turn on its back and go out of control. necessitating release) or are brought back; the whole last serial is called back after it is well out over the Channel. Of these gliders, 80 land more or less smoothly in England and two in the last serial collide over their base, killing their pilots and six troops. Another 17 gliders have to be ditched in the Channel, but are located by rescue launches in time to save all personnel. During the flight over friendly Belgium 31 more gliders break loose or are released, all presumably as a result of the weather. Three of them crash, killing five men, injuring four and putting two jeeps out of action. The rest land well and all the troops and materiel aboard them reach the 101st within a week. Contrary to expectations, the route instead of passing over the new salient runs just west of it and with visibility so low, the airmen probably blundered over some strongpoints they would normally have avoided. In spite of clouds and mist German gunners sent up intense and accurate light flak from Rethy, Moll and Best. Small-arms fire, probably aided by the fact that the mission had to fly low (the ceiling in the release area is about 600 feet and visibility less than a mile), also took its toll. The troops on LZ 'W' could see the formations approaching over the battlefield between Best and the zone and could certainly have saved some losses by recommending a detour if a ground-air radio had been provided. As it is 17 aircraft, 7 percent of those making sorties, are destroyed (another 17 land at Brussels, partly because of damage and partly because of the weather. Five others have to be salvaged after landing at friendly bases. Almost all received the fatal damage before reaching the LZ. Among the crews 31 men are dead or missing. Approximately 170 of the returning planes have been damaged, but this ratio, 70 percent of those exposed, is offset by the fact that in most cases the damage is slight.

About half of the pilots whose aircraft are shot down manage to release their gliders on or close to LZ 'W'. Among the bravest and the luckiest were 1st Lieutenant Jesse M. Harrison of the 435th Group and his co-pilot. Although their aircraft was already on fire, they brought their glider over the zone for a good release, then jumped through the flames and lived. Many gliders are shot loose, break loose or are prematurely released as a result of enemy action. One squadron in the next-to-last serial releases 15 gliders by mistake nearly 10 miles west of the zone. In all, 16 gliders land safely in enemy territory, their occupants and most of their cargoes eventually reaching the 101st Division. Another 26 Wacos are unaccounted for, almost certainly because they have come down in hostile territory and all aboard them were killed or captured.

Of 213 gliders reaching the drop zone one is shot down, two or three crash and 209 made good landings with very little damage, a remarkable performance under the circumstances even if some allowance be made for the smooth and spacious character of the landing zone. Landings begin at **1437** and end about **1600.**

The mission has carried 2,310 troops, of whom 1,341 safely reach their destination, 11 are dead, 11 are injured and 157 are missing. The remainder have been returned to England or landed safely somewhere short of the zone. Out of 136 jeeps loaded into the gliders 79 arrive at the zone in good condition, as do 49 out of 77 trailers and 40 out of 68 guns. By far the most depleted unit is the 907th Field Artillery Battalion, which had been carried by the last two serials and one flight of the serial preceding. Of its 89 gliders

57 have been returned to England, 4 have ditched and about 17 are missing or down in enemy territory. Only 24 men of the battalion and none of its twelve 105mm howitzers are landed in the vicinity of LZ 'W'. (In order to give the airborne more firepower the 105mm howitzer had been redesigned so it could enter a C-47 or a Waco without being disassembled. Its dimensions had been cut from 238 x 82 x 60 inches to 157 x 67 x 55 inches and through the use of light alloys its weight had been reduced from 4,235lbs to 2,500lbs. The 907th has been chosen to give the new weapon its first combat test in 'Market', so the ill-fortune of the serials carrying it is particularly regrettable). The other units carried are the 81st Airborne Antitank Battalion, the 321st Glider Field Artillery Battalion and portions of the 327th Glider Infantry Regiment, the 377th Parachute Field Artillery Battalion and divisional artillery headquarters. These come in at between 55 and 95 percent of strength. The antitank battalion has on hand only 14 of the 24 guns with which it had started, but the 377th Field Artillery has all 12 of its 75mm howitzers in position and ready to fire by **1710,** an hour and forty minutes after it landed.

The guns which do arrive prove their worth almost immediately. About **1700** a German force with tanks and self-propelled guns strike at Son from the east and get to within a few hundred yards of the Son Bridge, which the 502nd PIR has left lightly defended while it concentrates on winning its battle at Best and guarding its landing zone. Since by that time the landings are over and victory has been won at Best, the 502nd has ample resources to counter the threat. Antitank guns of the 81st Battalion knock out two German tanks and the rest retreat. Had this thrust come a couple of hours earlier, it might have achieved the destruction of the bridge, a most serious possibility.

20 September (D+3)

As revised on the evening of the 19th, plans for troop carrier operations call for all missions to take the southern route and for four of them to arrive simultaneously at their zones at **1500** hours. Again the timing is dictated by predictions of extensive fog throughout the forenoon. The original southern route is modified to permit the missions to fly up the British salient and pass close to Eindhoven with missions to the Arnhem and Nijmegen sectors using Schijndel as their IP. At the last minute Eindhoven is made IP for all airborne missions this day, Schijndel being regarded as too 'hot a spot'. In an effort to make up for lost time 1,047 aircraft and 405 gliders are to be dispatched, with all the gliders and 317 resupply aircraft flying along the centre lane to DZ/LZ 'O' for the 82nd Division. A 51-plane paratroop and resupply mission for the 101st would follow the right lane to DZ and 114 aircraft of the postponed Polish paratroop mission to Arnhem would use the left lane. Overhead would fly 160 RAF aircraft with supplies for 1st Airborne Division.

Escort as far as Schijndel was to be furnished by ADGB. The 8th Force is to fly its usual perimeter patrols between Maastricht, Wesel, Apeldoorn and Zwolle, supply area cover beyond the IP and attack positions between the IP and Nijmegen. The 9th Air Force is to neutralize flak batteries between the IP and Arnhem, but it did not seem to receive a clear statement of its assignment until **1430.** Once again unfavourable weather grievously curtails the troop carrier operations. During the morning the weathermen decide the overcast will lift later than they had thought so arrival time for the missions is put back from **1500** to **1700** hours. Then in view of the urgent need of the British at Arnhem it is decided to split the RAF resupply mission and send 67 of its aircraft to drop at **1345.** Arrival time for the other missions is moved to **1720.**

Morning Elements of the 504th, supported by Guards Armoured Shermans set out to begin clearing the south bank of the Waal close to the road bridge but the first units of the German II Parachute Corps - (seven under-strength infantry battalions - 2,000 men in all) supported by 88s, mortars and multi-barrelled Nebelwerfers put in a strong attack on the Allied line around Mook and Riethorst. The enemy attack makes some progress until the early afternoon, when it is halted and driven back by the Coldstream Guards Group.

HQ Airborne Corps at last makes radio contact with HQ 1st Airborne Division and receives the first direct report of their serious situation. At Son Major Freiherr von Maltzahn leads the remaining tanks of the 107th Panzer Brigade in an attack at first light. Again the German tanks sweep the bridge with fire and race forward. As success seems within range of the 107th Panzer Brigade, a group of British tanks belatedly answering Taylor's call for reinforcements blast the attack to a halt. With four tanks knocked out in succession, Maltzahn again orders his unit to withdraw. The bridge at Son remains firmly in Allied hands. German attacks on Veghel are also repulsed by aggressive counter-action by 101st Division, supported by British tanks. German parachutists in strength make two attacks against the Groesbeek area and take Beek, Wyler and Mook, the latter only 1 mile from Heumen bridge axis. Gavin deploys his five remaining parachute battalions and the Coldstream Guards and in a series of actions regains the ground lost. The 505th PIR and the Grenadier Guards, in three columns, renew attacks against Nijmegen road bridge. **1500** After hard fighting all day Hunner Park and the Valkhof (a medieval observation tower called the Belvedere, at the southern end of the bridge) which dominate the bridge are captured. The 504th PIR and Irish Guards clear the west suburbs of Nijmegen downstream of the railway bridge and by noon are on the river bank, awaiting the delayed arrival of the boats for the planned assault crossing at **1400.**

Twenty minutes before H-Hour that afternoon 26 assault boats arrive and at about **1500,** supported by artillery, mortars, tanks of the Irish Guards and by RAF Typhoons, the 3rd Battalion, 504th PIR, commanded by Major Julian Cook, row across 400 yards of the fast-flowing Waal river by members of C/307th Engineering Battalion, make a gallant assault, supported by fire from two squadrons of British tanks, part of another 504th battalion and about 100 American and British guns. A shortage of paddles requires some troopers to paddle the craft with rifle butts. Under fire all the way, the water lashed with machine-gun fire and mortar bombs, about half of the first wave get across. Those who land scramble up the bank and dash for the shelter of a bank some distance away while the sappers who had crossed with the US paratroopers paddle the boats back for the next lift. In all, the 11 boats that survive the first two crossings make six crossings of the river, taking across the 3rd and 1st battalions of the 504th PIR in the face of enemy fire. Once on the north bank the 504th proceed to attack the enemy positions defending the road and rail bridges. The paratroopers are accompanied by British sappers of the 615 Field Squadron and 11th Field Company, Royal Engineers, who make five river crossings in all, taking heavy equipment and ammunition across before a small bridgehead is established on the north bank. C/307th cross the Waal five times while ferrying across two battalions of the 504th. The surviving paratroopers then assault across 218 yards of open ground on the far bank and seize the north end of the bridge. The costly attack is nicknamed 'Little Omaha' in reference to Omaha Beach. German forces withdraw from both ends of the bridge which is then rushed by tanks of the Grenadier Guards Group and the 2nd Battalion, 505th PIR, securing the bridge at **1830,** D+4. The American paratroopers push on to the railway bridge at lent and patrols reach the road bridge at **1915.** Colonel Vandervoort's battalion of the 505th PIR, supported by Grenadier Guards' tanks and infantry, wear down the resistance in Nijmegen.

By **1700** British tanks and American infantry have driven the Germans back to the bridge. It is discovered that 34 machine guns, an 88mm gun and two 20mm cannon are mounted on the bridge, with snipers and machine-gunners deployed on the girders. As the enemy are pushed out of Nijmegen, they are able to cross the bridge and reinforce the SS troops fighting with the 504th paratroopers on the north bank but a troop of Guards' tanks, led by Sergeant Peter Robinson of the Grenadier Guards, cross the Nijmegen bridge from the south end under heavy fire, arriving at the far end just as three troopers of the 504th PIR run to meet them. The Guards reach the north end at **1830** and push on to link up with the Americans in Lent. A squadron of Grenadiers and two companies of Irish Guards cross during the night, but make no further advance. There are at that time, on the road to Arnhem, only detached pickets of 9th SS Panzer Reconnaissance battalion at Elst and south of Arnhem. Despite the capture of Nijmegen Bridge and the clearing of the town on the previous evening, the five tanks of Guards Armoured Division which are across the river do not advance. The Division resumes its advance about 18 hours later, at noon. Lieutenant General Brian Horrocks claims he needs this delay to sort out the confusion among his troops that had resulted from the battle in Nijmegen. The Coldstream Guards Group are repulsing an attack on the Groesbeek position, the Irish Guards Group has returned to Eindhoven to meet another attack, the Grenadiers have just captured the approaches to the bridge with the US paratroops and got five tanks over it to support the Airborne bridgehead and the Welsh Guards are in 82nd Airborne reserve. The Guards Armoured Division is scattered over 25 square miles of the south bank of the Waal.

By nightfall The Germans have set up a rudimentary blocking position north of Lent. The 43rd (Wessex) Division have crossed the Meuse-Escaut Canal and, after some delay due to the detour round Eindhoven, the leading 130th Infantry Brigade reached Grave bridge in the afternoon, where it stops for the night. The Irish Guards do not receive orders to advance north to

Arnhem until **1100.** The advance starts at **1230** but they soon lose a number of tanks on the high-banked road by accurate anti-tank fire and are stopped by tanks two miles short of Elst. The Welsh Guards try a left flank move but are also held. 130 Infantry Brigade spends all day defending the bridges north of Grave and in unnecessarily clearing the rest of Nijmegen. One battalion crosses Nijmegen Bridge late in the day. 214 Brigade comes up to the Grave area and is ordered to cross the Waal and attack round the left flank of the Guards Division, but is later delayed in Nijmegen. During the morning 64 Medium Regiment, Royal Artillery, makes radio contact with HQ Royal Artillery 1st Airborne Division. Firing at extreme range from Nijmegen, the medium guns give invaluable support to the airborne troops defending the Oosterbeek perimeter. At **1700** the Polish Parachute Brigade are to drop just east of Driel, but due to weather en route 42 aircraft are ordered to return to base, with one and a half of the Polish parachute battalions. The Germans, thinking that the Poles will attack and recapture Arnhem Bridge, withdraw troops and tanks from Oosterbeek to reinforce their positions between Arnhem and Elst.

The big glider mission marshalled for the 82nd Division is also grounded by the fog in the Grantham area. Fortunately the resupply mission to that division had been delegated to the 53rd Wing and its bases in the south are comparatively clear. Beginning about **1430** the wing put 310 aircraft in the air with the 434th, 435th and 438th Groups contributing one serial each and the 436th and 437th Groups two apiece. (One additional aircraft towed a Waco, which had been on call with a ton and half of supplies, making the total dispatched 311). They carry a cargo of 441 tons, of which the greater part is ammunition. One aircraft has to turn back with pararack trouble. The others fly over the southern route, close to Eindhoven, past Best, then up the road to DZ 'O'. Fighter cover is good and in spite of the lack of anti-flak activity, ground fire is conspicuous by its absence. Some serials could report that not a shot was fired at them. Not an aircraft is lost and only six are damaged. This experience, so different from that of the British mission that day, can be attributed to the fact that the Americans were over friendly territory almost all the way to their drop zone.

The lead serial reaches DZ 'O' at **1648** and the others follow at extremely irregular intervals, some arriving almost simultaneously, others as much as 20 minutes apart, with the last one turning up at **1749.** In addition, most of the serials are loose or broken, probably because of bad weather en route. However, since the pilots and navigators of the 53rd Wing have become fairly familiar with the southern route as far as Best and the way from there up the road to the Grave Bridge is unmistakable, none of the stragglers lose their way. As might be expected, the drop is disorganized and spasmodic with each serial or separate element using its own tactics. Some release their bundles as low as 400 feet, others as high as 1,800 feet. Although there is the usual difficulty getting bundles out the door in time and 14 parapacks stuck, over 99 percent of the cargo is delivered but the bundles land in a pattern about two miles wide and six miles long centred considerably northwest of the zone. The 82nd Division reports recovering 60 percent of these supplies with Dutch assistance and according to some estimates 80 percent is ultimately recovered, but the hunt is long and difficult. It is sheer good luck that most of the supplies land in friendly territory. The value of the mission is very great nevertheless. The supply dumps of the 82nd are running low and it has not yet received any supplies by road. Indeed, the first truck convoys for the division have just reached the Meuse-Escaut Canal; some of those first trucks had been loaded with shells of the wrong calibre; and others by some strange oversight were empty. The 101st Division, being in firm contact with the Allied ground forces, has much less need of supply by air. However, 35 aircraft of the 442nd and 439th Groups take off from Greenham Common with 17 tons of supplies for that division. They fly unharmed over the new southern route to DZ 'W' and drop their loads at **1748.** Again the drop is inaccurate and only about 30 percent of the bundles are reported as recovered. (This figure represents an average for several categories of supplies, a few items in one category being counted as equal to tons in another. It is further distorted by the fact that hardly any of the rations which are dropped are reported as collected).

A paratroop mission is also flown to DZ 'W' by 12 C-47s of the 442nd Group carrying Battery 'B' of the 377th Parachute Field Artillery. The troop carriers have to fly to Ramsbury to take on their load, 125 artillerymen and six 75mm howitzers. Somewhat late in arriving, the planes are not loaded until about **1500** and in the turmoil the pilots are not informed of the changes made in the southern route. They therefore take the D-Day route west of the salient and run into intense light flak and small-arms fire which damages five of the C-47s, one severely. The mission does not reach the zone until **1831** by which time the sun is setting and the haze is growing thick. In the face of these difficulties the pilots make an accurate and very compact drop from perfect formation. An hour after its jump the battery has assembled 119 men and almost all its equipment, including five howitzers, ready for action. The other howitzer is ready by morning.

21 September (D+4)

A German attack made against Beek is repulsed. The 101st Division extends the depth of their protection on either side of the axis. North of the Waal the Germans counter-attack with infantry and tanks from the east, which check the Allied advance. Knaust's Kampfgruppe with SP guns and Panther tanks cross Arnhem Bridge during the morning and establish a blocking position around Elst at noon.

1330 While some Guards' Armoured tanks from Nijmegen have to be sent south to deal with German units attacking and sometimes cutting the road in the 10lst Airborne sector, between Eindhoven and Nijmegen, XXX Corps resumes its thrust for Arnhem. This, after the ground ahead (known as 'The Island' - flat low-lying land, drained by innumerable ditches and waterways, which separate its fields instead of hedges) has been reconnoitred by armoured cars of The Household Cavalry. The cavalry encounter enemy tanks at Elst, south of the Arnhem Bridge, which is now in German hands. The Guards' advance along the main road to Arnhem which runs between deep, wide ditches, within which the advancing tanks were firmly enclosed, is quickly opposed by elements of 9 and 10 SS Panzer with Panther tanks and 88mm guns. Five tanks of the leading Irish Guards are destroyed and they block the road. The Guards have very few infantry and little artillery and it is decided therefore that the Guards Armoured should be replaced as the XXX Corps spearhead by the 43rd Infantry Division, commanded by Major-General Ivo 'Butcher' Thomas. This decision cause delay, as the 43rd Division must battle its way through Nijmegen and along a road jammed with tanks, troops and vehicles and under attack to the south by the German 15th Army.

Appalling weather in the Grantham area makes it impossible to dispatch the gliders marshalled for the 82nd Division. Although conditions at the bases of the 53rd Wing in southern England are better, they are bad enough to ground the gliders intended for the 101st Division also, particularly since the 101st is in no great need of reinforcement. The parachute resupply mission set up for the 101st is sent, but it is reduced to two small serials. Another serial with emergency supplies is arranged for the 82nd Division. The 438th and 437th Groups dispatch 15 aircraft apiece carrying about 16 tons of rations to LZ 'W' for the 101st. During the early part of their flight they have to contend with haze, which limits visibility to as little as half a mile and with 7/10 cloud between the altitudes of 500 and about 6,000 feet. Three pilots straggle, lose their way and return because of the weather and three others turn back because of mechanical difficulties. The remainder, 12 in each serial, fly unopposed over the southern route and drop their loads over DZ 'W' at **1631** and **1640.** Although as a result of the weather the drop is not well concentrated, it is fairly accurate and about 31 percent of the rations were recovered. All aircraft return undamaged, having probably been over friendly territory all the way.

Another 33 planes with about 15 tons of rations are dispatched by the 438th Group to DZ 'O' for the 82nd Division. Two of them abort on account of the weather. The rest reach the drop zone at **1700** after a difficult but uneventful trip and make a somewhat scattered drop from a height of 1,500 feet.

Chapter 2

'Death Of A Dutch Town'

The worst mistake of the Arnhem plan was the failure to give priority to capturing the Nijmegen Bridge. The capture would have been a walkover on D-Day, yet the 82nd Division could spare only one battalion as they must at all costs secure the Groesbeek Heights where the Corps HQ was to be sited.'

Major-General John Frost, who as a Lieutenant Colonel commanded the 2nd Parachute Battalion at the Arnhem Bridge.

These rainy days, the 82nd Airborne Division is sweating it out in Holland' said Martha Gellhorn in her *Collier's Magazine* article, *'Rough and Tumble,'* radioed from Holland during the campaign. 'This rain is the heartbreak rain that washes away men's hope of peace and home and it is the rain which warns you of the ugly winter ahead - another ugly winter of, war. In this rain, in the flat, dreary country of southern Holland, the paratroopers live and now fight a deadly little nibbling campaign which is not their style and they do not complain, since they are tough boys and not given to complaint. Besides, they are volunteers and a volunteer is a man who says to himself that he damn well got into this and there is no use beefing and where do we go from here?

'The troops of the 82nd Airborne Division look like tough boys and they are. They are good at their trade, too and they know it and they walk as if they knew it. This trade is war: most of them are too young to have learned any other profession. The general, who is himself thirty-seven, received many official communications about the soldiers' voting act and how soldiers were not to be influenced and how ballots were to be made available and all of this was evidently most important, though in the middle of the campaign in Holland it was perhaps hard to attend to these matters. Anyhow, quite worked up and conscious of his duty, he went around to the battalions to see that all was in order and discovered that in one company only two men were old enough to vote and that this odd state of affairs was the usual form in his outfit. Finally, after a careful check-up, it was learned that the average age of the 82nd Airborne Division paratroopers is twenty-two and if you subtract two or three years for Army life you will see that these young men have not had much time to study any subject except the technique, mechanic and principles of killing other men. They walk as if they know how good they are and they walk like individual men. All combat troops have a special pride and style. All combat troops despise garrison life and garrison soldiers and all combat troops look like something very rare and would shock anyone with stern ideas about uniforms and compartment. But these airbornes seem to me even more remarkable than most and, seeing them now, you notice every face, for every 'face is that of an entire man and you notice that each man wears his soiled and baggy clothing as if it had been designed for him alone and was not Army issue at all.'

In Nijmegen, Martha Gellhorn caught up again with 'Ted' Bachenheimer 'who had moved into the headquarters of one of the branches of the Dutch underground and at their request he took over command. He was very busy sending out patrols to mop up Germans in the town of Nijmegen and other patrols to get information on German dispositions in the town and around the bridges, so that he could keep his regiment informed. He also opened bakeries and organized civilian billets and nightly he visited the cellars where the citizens of Nijmegen were living in justifiable fear of the shelling. That job of maintaining civilian morale is what he is proudest of now. He says he didn't feel any too sure of anything himself, but he made the people believe everything was fine and dandy. I can only say that I think this was a terrific piece of work, because Nijmegen is not fine and dandy now and it must have been pretty appalling during Bachenheimer's early days there. His headquarters is a very small crowded room in a former Nijmegen schoolhouse. Bill One and Bill Two work with him in this room. They eat here and they have a neat, small arsenal hanging on the walls. They collect their souvenirs in one corner and they have the most fantastic list of callers every day. I listened to Bachenheimer interrogating an Alsatian prisoner and never saw a prettier or more thorough job; next he received a German informer from whom he wanted to get some information about German defense constructions in the region; then, two sergeants from other regiments who were also engaged in collecting information came and had a brisk argument about a patrol which they wanted Bachenheimer to send out and which he deemed unsound. English officers, also, arrived from time to time and Dutch undergrounders and Dutch civilians who wanted to get collaborators arrested or wanted to get people released from jail on the grounds that a mistake had been made. Nothing seemed to worry Bachenheimer, who is an extremely competent and serious boy and nothing seemed to shake his modesty. His previous training for this work consisted of one job in America - he had briefly been press agent for a show that failed. He was not in his office when I went to say goodbye; he had crossed over behind the enemy lines.

'You are always happy with fine combat troops, because in a way no people are as intensely alive as they are. You do not notice the rain too much, or the ugly soaked flat land, or the sadness of the yellowing trees that are rotting limply from summer into the nakedness of winter. You do not think much about what war costs, because you are too busy being alive for the day - too busy laughing and listening and looking. And, you forget about the crude wooden crosses that mark where just such boys lie in Sicily and Italy and France and now Holland. You forget about the hospital in Nijmegen where devoted, weary men work in operating rooms that never cease to be appalling, no matter how many such operating rooms you have seen. You forget, too, that the boys who last it out intact and whole have nevertheless given up these years which were intended to be young and happy.

'There were seven German counterattacks on Nijmegen. At one time, the

82nd Division had 2,200 prisoners who were being guarded by American glider pilots, the only men who could not be spared; they had hundreds of their own paratroopers wounded; they were at half strength and being attacked by the Germans in regimental strength from the north and the south while they held the tiny island of Nijmegen, about as practical a place to hold as a sand-bar with the tide coming in.

'The mission of the 82nd Airborne Division in Holland, which takes only one sentence to write and only a minute to say aloud, was completed in three fierce and sleepless days. It was entirely and successfully completed with a total of five bridges and a piece of essential ground taken. Then, it became necessary to hold and they are holding still-sweating it out in the long rain that means another ugly winter of war.'

Martha Gellhorn's story did not go into detail on the long gruelling battles fought on the German border or at Kiekberg, Mook, Wyler and the brilliant use of Anglo-American Artillery in the two months that the 82nd held the Nijmegen salient into Holland and across the German border, but 'Rough and Tumble' expressed, better than anything written thus far, the esprit de corps, individual bravery and cocky self-reliance which motivated the men of the 82nd. Shortly after Miss Gellhorn's story was written, Bachenheimer was killed while laying a telephone wire to the underground in German occupied northern Holland. He had just received a field commission as a 2nd Lieutenant when his death occurred. Theodore Bachenheimer is buried in Holland along with approximately 800 other 82nd troopers.

'Death of a Dutch Town' was the title of another Martha Gellhorn story in which she reported on the dangers and hardships to the Dutch civilians in Eindhoven who coped with the daily allotment of broken glass, always sweeping it up 'in a despairingly tidy way.' She also explained why one never saw any Jews in Nijmegen. They had been deported to Poland, she told her readers in *Collier's* and she described in considerable detail the tiled 'baths' that were in reality gas chambers. Hard on her heels on the 18th came Marjorie 'Dot' Avery of the *Detroit Free Press* and Catherine Coyne of the *Boston Herald* who drove to Nijmegen with Flem Hall of the *Fort Worth Star-Telegram* and Ervin Lewis, broadcaster for Station WLS, Chicago. The trip was unsettling.

'The battles had been recent ones,' Dot noted 'and I got a fresh view of the aftermath: bricks and debris tumbling into the streets of clean little Dutch towns. Dead bloated cows with stiff legs outstretched in a sort of dumb protest. Freshly dug graves. A few still unburied Germans lying like heaps of rags. The smell of decay.'

As they walked in the cool autumn sunshine in the grounds of a hotel that Wehrmacht officers had only just abandoned some admiring paratroopers took their pictures, while solemn-faced blond children trotted behind them, nodding when they spoke, but saying nothing themselves. A major from Baltimore in the 82nd Airborne invited Catherine Coyne to accompany him to the command post of a parachute regiment. They arrived in time for supper and were just having coffee when a thunderous roar was heard. 'You're lucky,' the colonel in command told her, 'you'll get a good show.' Officers ushered her to a top-floor dormer window, which provided an excellent view of enemy aircraft dropping flares over the command post. The great road bridge, their target, was silhouetted cleanly against the moonlight, while flares on the opposite shore started fires that turned the velvety sky a pale pink. Catherine was particularly impressed by the pattern of orange tracer bullets that merged to form a great wall of fire in the sky: 'There was about it constant beauty, constant movement, a kind of grace... Certainly nothing could get through that steadily moving wall of fiery bullets! Then the planes roared in. The flares, the moon and the tracer bullets made it as light as day. I leaned out the window to get a look at the planes silhouetted against the sky. The ack-ack batteries went into action. Great puffs of black exploded high in the air. You could feel the concussion in the very air you breathed. Then I was aware there was no air in front of me to breathe. Just a hot sensation of emptiness that passed quickly. The building vibrated. When it happened I don't believe I was aware of sound. Then I knew, even without recognizing sound, the planes had dropped their bombs.

'They didn't get the bridge. The ack-ack stopped. The tracer bullets disappeared into nothingness. The flares burned low... Most of the bombs on that run landed in the river. One was close enough to damage one of our supply sheds and killed a soldier. All the glass in the windows on the two lower floors of our building was blown out ... Major Ireland suggested we take advantage of the lull to get back across the river. We got into his jeep, drove carefully through the moonlight dusk to the bridge, then dashed madly over it to the other side. It was a cold starlit night. I tried not to think of the boy who had been killed. The major sang phrases from popular songs - he did not seem to know a whole song - probably to keep up that daredevil attitude that characterizes the paratrooper. 'Doesn't this remind you of football weather back home?' he asked...

'As we rode through the quiet streets of Nijmegen, we heard the faint rumble of planes. They were returning. The cold starlit sky was changed again into a pattern of dazzling orange and golden light. The air was rent with the explosions of flak and of bombs. Now it did not seem so beautiful, for we could smell the burning homes. We could smell charred and burning wood, first the hot smell, then the acrid odour of water having been poured on the fire; then we could smell the bombs and the tracer bullets - they smell just like old-fashioned fireworks. In the faint light we could see silent Dutch families standing close to their dignified and substantial homes looking skyward, silent.'

James Coyle, still fighting in Nijmegen had received word that the American attack had been held up and that they were to hold their position. 'Enemy fire had stopped and I placed men in three of the houses on the ground floor to prevent enemy infiltrators from getting into the position. I was in the upper front room shortly after dark observing the enemy area in front of us as best I could. Suddenly a British tank opened fire across my front from the right and a German tank replied from my left. I don't know how they could see each other in the dark, but a terrific cross-fire of heavy calibre tracers continued for almost five minutes. When the firing ceased, I saw that the tracer fire had set a public building in the park on fire and I could now observe the area to my front by its light. I saw the German tank, an old French model, knocked out near the traffic circle to the left of our position. The Company runner came and gave me a message to report to the Company 'E' Command Post located about two blocks behind the First Platoon's position. When I got there, the CO asked me to plot my platoon's position on the Company overlay. I had just completed the map when my Platoon runner came in with the information that a patrol was moving in front of our area. The men guessed the patrol was British and had not fired on it, but others thought it was an enemy patrol.

'I returned to the Platoon and went to the front of the house where Sergeant Ben Popilsky was observing from the doorway. He reported that two men had walked past on the sidewalk earlier but he thought they were British tankers. Just then the two returned and I could see in the light of the burning building that they wore the helmets and smocks of German paratroopers. Popilsky and I opened fire with our Thompson sub-machine-guns. One of the Germans went down but the other ran to our left and got behind a tree. He yelled at us in German and Ben who understood German said he was asking if he could come back and help his comrade. I told Ben to tell him that we would take care of his comrade who was groaning on the sidewalk. When Popilsky yelled back, I realised that Ben was speaking Yiddish to the German. The German then called us *'Verdamt Americanishe Schweinhunts'* and we called him a *'Kraut Bastard'*. I wanted the wounded German as a prisoner and I was not about to let the other man come back and pick us off in the doorway now that he knew exactly where we were. He finally ran away, but when we crawled out to get the wounded German we discovered that he had died. Later that night another German came right up to the window of a building where Pfc George Wood was on guard and Wood shot him in the head with a pistol as he started to climb in.'

Sergeant Don McKeage in Company 'F' in the 505th PIR recalls:

'On 19th September the Second Battalion headed into Nijmegen and the next day took part in the battle for the Nijmegen Road Bridge. It was a very hot fight, but like all the battles we came out on top, although with a terrible loss of life. As the men of Company 'F' were heading into Nijmegen, working our way to the park and main highway bridge, we came under heavy enemy artillery fire. Word was passed that Private Arnold Palmer had been killed in the last artillery volley. Captain Robert H. Rosen my Company Commander halted the company in front of a Dutch residence. The lady of the house came out, telling Captain Rosen that she had a British flier hiding in the house for many months and that he would like to speak with one of the Americans. The Captain motioned for me to check the house, while this lady wrote down Rosen's name, rank etc. I entered this Dutch residence, the dining room table was moved, the carpet rolled up and a floor access panel removed. There hiding in a crawling space was the British flier being only allowed to come out of hiding at night. I assured him that we were in town to stay and within hours we would have the German troops routed. He was very happy and at last he would be returned to freedom. I rejoined the Company and we once again resumed our forward progress. Captain Rosen was killed the next afternoon at the park before the bridge.'

'Captain Robert 'Doc' Franco was in his jeep moving north up one of those lovely tree-lined roads, now totally jammed with Bren gun carriers and personnel carriers of, I believe, the British Grenadier Guards. In front of one of the houses a group of old 'gaffers' gathered with their brass horns, trumpets, cornets, trombones and a tuba and started to play with the greatest imaginable discord. A young Guards officer in the vehicle in front of mine caught my eye and smiled. 'A bit grim, what?' he said. It was a British understatement. A couple of hours later my driver and I were in the city about 150 metres away from the guns on the roundabout on the bridge approach. The tracers from the 88mm guns went down the street just above the bumper to bumper line of tanks. The din was, as usual, terrific. My young driver yelled at me to look. Three British tank men were sitting in the middle of the road around a can of gasoline soaked sand, that had been lit and they were brewing their tea. This mode of combustion was apparently popular in the desert.'

Earlier, during the morning Pfc Gordon Walberg and his fellow troopers were still holding on to Berg-en-Dahl when they heard of another probe by the German tanks in the Beek area. 'We chose the high ground overlooking the town, facing the German border. As we moved into position we came across a wounded Glider Pilot who had been shot by a machine-gun. I counted at least five wounds in him. The pilot, his voice was very weak, asked if we could help him. I told the jeep driver, I believe it was C. Perry, to unhook the gun and we carefully lifted the wounded man onto the jeep and Perry went in search of an Aid Station. We hoped the pilot made it but I was doubtful with so many wounds. We met some local Dutch people by the name of Schretlen and they gave us food and drink.

'It was decided that if an attack came it would be from the flatlands in front of Beek, so we relocated our gun. Our new location was in front of the Bad Hotel across the street from the Hotel Rusthof. In preparing for an attack we tore the bricks out of the pavement and used the sand to fill one hundred and fifty sandbags. A British tank came up behind us and the Tank Commander asked us to show him where we thought the Germans were located. He then proceeded to shoot up everything he could and the Germans returned the fire. They had better observation than we did. Their first shot hit a 508th Parachute Infantry Regiment's heavy mortar pit, knocking out the mortar, killing two and wounding another. The next hit was on a British M-4 tank and some of the crew were killed. One round hit the lounge of the Bad Hotel where we had been eating a short time before and blew out part of the heavy glass window. Corporal Ernie Seddan jumped up and finished knocking out the rest of the plate glass window because he did not want more glass raining down on our foxholes. Then our jeep was hit - which we had tried to hide - and the tyres caught fire.

'The town of Beek was now in ruins, ringing with the screams of wounded civilians and military. Private Charles E. Kidd, one of our crew, said he would move out to the left and see if he could protect our flank. Ernie Seddan and I were wondering how long we could hold out. Ernie, a Normandy veteran, suggested we place two grenades in the front edge of the foxholes along with extra clips of M-I ammunition. We took our trench knives and stuck then in the ground to our front. About this time a 508 trooper with an asbestos glove on his hand holding a still hot 30 calibre machine-gun came by and told us there was nothing on our left except Germans. I took the firing pin from the 57mm and started up the hill towards Berg-en-Dahl. On the way we located one of the wounded 508th mortar crew. Robert Hayden had picked up an abandoned 45 pistol and as the wounded man was unarmed, Hayden gave him the 45. We knew that we would get our 'ears chewed off' for losing the 57mm gun - and we did. Lieutenant Colonel Louis Mendez, the 508's Third Battalion Commander, gave us hell, but backed off a little when we explained that there were only two of us left and without a jeep were unable to move 2,600lbs of equipment by ourselves. He said Company 'H', 508, would retake the town of Beek and we were to stand by. At 0230 we were sent with a jeep and driver and told to go back into Beek and recover our 57mm gun and anything else we could locate. At the time I told Ernie Seddan that I doubted if the Germans would still be in Beek and that turned out to be the fact. We pulled our gun out and were then assigned to protect the two Nijmegen bridges across the Waal River from German river craft.' [13]

By now Gavin had established contact with XXX Corps and was aware of the situation at the Son Bridge and at Best. XXX Corps had got through Eindhoven, but they would be held up until their engineers got a bridge across the river. So, while the arrival of the additional artillery gave Gavin far greater firepower, he still lacked the troops to meet the growing enemy strength. Air cover remained grounded and artillery support remained concentrated on keeping the corridor open. While Gavin anticipated the arrival of the 325th Glider Infantry Regiment he would simply have to hold with what he had.

It was on D+2 that XXX Corps' Grenadier Guards Brigade Group reached the Grave Bridge and Lieutenant General 'Boy' Browning and Gavin greeted them there in person during the late morning. The arrival of the Grenadier Guards gave Gavin British armour and infantry support he desperately needed and so he decided to make another try for the bridge at Nijmegen without waiting for the 325th Glider Infantry, which was fortuitous because the third lift, scheduled for that afternoon, was postponed due to bad weather in England.

The Reverend Leslie Skinner of the Sherwood Rangers Yeomanry in 8th Armoured Brigade following The Guards Armoured spearhead wrote: 'Moved off at 0600 into Holland and over canal - not so big as the Albert Canal at Gheel. Action and movement all day pushing steadily up the one road ... only road possible in this country of dykes and canals as we move further into Holland. Devil of a long convoy - Sherwood Rangers plus Squadron of Royals with Armoured Cars; plus Ack-Ack plus Battery of Essex Yeomanry; Company of King's Royal Rifle Corps; our Regimental Echelons and Recovery Unit, parts 552 Company RASC and Field Ambulance and our Medical Aid sections - all making a column stretching along nearly seven miles of road. Squadron of

13 'On the night of 28 September, or early on the 29th, German frogmen swam down the river and were able to place charges and blow a span out of the railroad bridge into the river. We now know a few names of those German frogmen. They were, Heinz Bretscheider, Jager, Gert Olle, Wolchendorf and Hauptman Hellmer. Out of the original twelve, only two landed safely near Aachen. The other ten were either killed or captured.' Because of the casualties, Gordon Walberg took charge of a Squad after the first week in Holland. His Commanding Officer, Captain Arthur G. Kroos, previously Ridgway's Aide in Normandy, had been shot down in his glider and taken prisoner. *Put On Your Boots and Parachutes!:The United States 82nd Airborne Division* written and edited by Deryk Wills (self published, March 1992).

tanks with some armoured cars and infantry up front and at rear, with other 'fighting elements' scattered throughout the column. All making a hell of a target. Shot up once or twice. Lost one or two vehicles but no men. Leagured up as were on road about 0200hrs to snatch some sleep. Air raid again. Again lucky.' [14]

Jack Pritchard, No 4 Company 1st Battalion Grenadier Guards reached Marienboom on the outskirts of Nijmegen at about mid-day on 19 September, where the formation of his convoy was changed. 'The slogan for the Company; came from the letters that were stenciled onto every one of our vehicles; 'S.O.B'; The 'Shit or Bust Company of the 'Fighting First'! We moved off and entered the suburbs of Nijmegen to find it almost deserted. The only Americans I saw that afternoon were a group of five or six, who walked towards us and then as they turned, they fired small mortars which were attached to the heels of their boots in the direction they had just left. Cautiously we approached the center of the town, but had to abandon the protection of our half-track as we got nearer to the bridge. Taking cover we rested for a time, while a plan was hurriedly devised for the capture of the bridge. We had received some information from the Americans that the Germans had installed a mechanism for blowing the bridge, in the post Office on the south side of the river. It became obvious that the Americans had not penetrated so far into a town, when a patrol, sent out by the Grenadiers, found the post office undefended and consequently this was chosen as a suitable site for our Company Headquarters. No demolition equipment was found at the post office.

'The following morning, 20th September, we were told of the desperate situation the Airborne troops at Arnhem were in and that it was essential for this attack to succeed. Further incentive was provided by the announcement that anyone wounded in the engagement would be immediately flown back to England. Number 4 Company would take the left hand side of the street approaching Hunner Park and the Kings Company would take the right hand side. The information supplied said that three 88mm guns protected the approaches to the bridge, that they were well dug in and had to be eliminated before the tanks of the Second Battalion moved into the attack. Moreover, German infantry were entrenched in Hunner Park and had either to be captured or killed with bayonet charge if necessary. This daunting task was programmed to begin at 4 pm that afternoon. Strong points had been established by the Germans along the streets leading to the bridge and the centre of the town had been set on fire to prevent infiltration by the enemy. A unit of the 10th SS Panzer Division, under command of SS general Euling together with a company of Engineers, had been allowed to take up defensive positions on the southern end of the bridge, while Hauptsturmführer Reinhard's Battalion of SS troops were well dug in on the northern end.

'The attack was spearheaded by Lieutenant Prescott's tank, which immediately drew heavy enemy fire, as it positioned itself in the centre of the street. I took the Section into the only cover that was available, which was behind the tank. All went well for about 30 yards, when the Sherman came to

14 Quoted in *The Words of War* by Marcus Cowper (Mainstream 2009).

a halt, still firing all of its weapons. We dived for cover into the terraced houses on the left side of the street. Firing at anything that moved, we rapidly made our way from house to house along the street, but the nearer we got to our objective the more resolute became the opposition. After a particularly heavy burst of machine-un fire and anticipating that there would be a brief lull, my section ran for the cover of the next house. It was there that my luck run out. I was suddenly headlong through an open doorway and found myself lying on the floor, with my Tommy gun at the other side of the room. How long I laid there I don't know. No-one was near me and the sound of gunfire had receded. I tried to stand, but my left foot gave way and my right arm hung limply at my side. Struggling to my right foot, I opened the door. The street was deserted, except for the tank which remained about twenty yards away, where I had last seen it. Not a thing moved and I slowly made my way back to the shelter of the building we had stayed in overnight. Stretcher-bearers appeared and after being injected by morphine, I was stretched onto a 30 cwt covered truck and driven through a deeply wooded area to a First Aid post.

'What had happened to the six men of the section I had led into the attack on Hunner Park and the German gun positions guarding the approach to the Nijmegen Road Bridge ?I didn't know any of the men I led that day, for they were all replacements for men previously wounded or killed in action. There could not be so many of us left, for there were not so many of us to begin with. Infantry of the Kings Company and Number 4 Company of the First Battalion Grenadier Guards, supported by a troop of four tanks commanded by Sergeant Peter Robinson were given daunting task of capturing this bridge intact.

'It wasn't until days later that I found out what had happened to the men I had left behind at Nijmegen. Both Number 4 Company and the Kings Company had gained their objectives on the approaches to the road bridge, clearing Hunner Park and the Valkhof of German troops and capturing their heavier weapons. The way was now clear for the tanks of the Second Battalion to storm the bridge. Major John Trotter, commanding number 1 Squadron of the 2nd Battalion Grenadier Guards, ordered Sergeant Robinson to make the first attempt, but his Sherman was hit twice by anti-tank gun fire and he was forced to pull back for minor repairs. It wasn't until dusk was falling that a second attempt was made. This time sergeant Robinson's troop of four tanks were used. Sergeant Pacey led the attack, with Sergeant Robinson's tank following and Sergeant Knight together with the 4th Sherman of the troop in the rear. The two rearmost tanks were hit and had to be abandoned, but realizing that his vehicle had not caught fire, Sergeant Knight ordered his crew to remount. They then followed the two leaders who were nearing the northern end of the bridge, which was guarded by an anti-tank gun. Sergeant Robinson's gunner knocked out this formidable weapon with his second shot and fearing that the bridge would be blown at any time, the tanks smashed through all other obstacles until they halted a mile away. Their objective had been achieved and they established a bridgehead and stayed isolated overnight. Here they were joined by a party of Americans, who had crossed the river four hours earlier at a point near to the railway bridge, which was about three-quarters of a mile upstream'.

Between 16-21 September the Guards Armoured Division lost 130 men all ranks, with the battle for Nijmegen Bridge accounting for the majority of those killed.

'Market-Garden' was seriously behind schedule and the British 1st Airborne Division had been fighting alone in Arnhem for three days. Montgomery had dispatched two of his liaison officers from TAC HQ to report on the progress of the advance. One of them was Major Carol Mather, who recalled: 'The road was no wider than an average room, but there were side roads coming in and when the Germans counter-attacked there was a major melee on the road. There were polders on either side and the land fell away to marshy fields. It was a scene of the utmost confusion, but everything was at such close quarters that no one really was able to use their weapons very much. I remember we were almost in touching range of Tiger tanks and I found myself to the north of this bottleneck, cut off from home. That was the only occasion when I failed to deliver my message to Monty at six o'clock in the evening. We spent the night sleeping in a kind of tavern of some sort, but the next day we managed to get through this blockage and report to Monty. And this did give him an absolute bird's-eye view of the situation and the difficulties. And he was obviously quite worried by this.' [15]

Conditions along the road leading through Grave and Nijmegen to the outskirts of Arnhem can be gauged by what happened to Flight Lieutenant Turner DFC, the pilot of a Stirling employed in dropping supplies to the airborne troops. On 21 September he was shot down near Nijmegen and presently arrived there on foot with his crew. Here they were given food, a three-ton lorry and an order to make for Eindhoven. Five miles from that town they were told that two German tanks - Panthers, it was thought - and a body of SS troops were moving against the road from the north-east and would arrive at any moment. 'We had two revolvers and a Sten gun between the nine of us,' said Turner. Judging this armament insufficient with which to attack tanks, the party drove to Veghel, a small village close by, where they presently fell in with 'an Army Lieutenant and three Bofors guns.' All at once returned to the main road, determined to fight their way through. The opportunity to do so soon arrived, for the German tanks made straight for them. The first was knocked out by the Bofors firing at a range of 400 yards, but in the ensuing battle with the second and the SS infantry accompanying it, the Army Lieutenant became a casualty, two of the three Bofors were destroyed and the available ammunition for the third fell to fourteen rounds. So the crew of the Stirling moved off the road once more and joined thirty British infantry who were without officers but had machine-guns. Though lacking all experience in ground warfare, Turner at once took command. Tiger tanks, suddenly appearing, drove the party back to Veghel, where the lorry, into which they had all clambered, was ambushed and destroyed. Undismayed, the survivors lined a ditch by the roadside, held off the enemy for ten hours with small-arms fire till darkness fell and then retired with their wounded to a neighbouring house, whose owner gave them all the food he had - one slice of bread and butter and one apple to each man. By then

15 Quoted in *'D-Day To Berlin'* by Andrew Williams (Hodder & Stoughton, 2004).

there was almost no ammunition left and they therefore lay quiet listening to the Germans fifty yards away, who, badly mauled, made no further attack. Late in the next afternoon the advanced guards of the leading British armoured division arrived and Turner was able to hand over his command, abandon fighting on land and return eventually to the air, a more familiar element. [16]

Browning's Advanced Corps HQ meanwhile, had received a brief situation report from the GHQ Liaison Regiment, or 'Phantom' team attached to 1st Airborne Division indicating all was not well at Arnhem, a verdict reinforced by occasional, brief reports from the Dutch resistance coming through the local civilian telephone network. Browning urged Gavin therefore to get across the Waal by the following day at the absolute latest. This was now easier said than done. On the north bank were sited 72 artillery pieces, some of which had been commandeered from an abandoned train in Arras during the retreat from Normandy; and 29 88mm guns that Allied intelligence estimated for the defence of Nijmegen and more 20mm anti aircraft guns.

Gavin decided to use the Grenadiers' tanks and the 2nd Battalion, 505th Parachute Infantry but the attack was delayed until the late afternoon, partly because the Grenadiers had to take the roundabout route over the Maas-Waal Canal via the Molenhoek Bridge because the Honinghutje road and rail bridge, the most direct route to Nijmegen, was blown up by Germans. The railway bridge was destroyed and the blast badly damaged the road bridge. The Grenadiers also had to pick up Vandervoort's battalion at the LZ and this caused a further delay. Vandervoort's troopers rode into battle on the backs of more than forty British tanks and reached the centre of Nijmegen near the bridge approaches at the south end without much difficulty and then the 505th PIR split, half for the road bridge and the other half for a railway bridge that ran near it. One joint force, paratroopers mounted on tanks, went off to the post office to relieve the US troops and Dutch civilians trapped there since D-Day. When the attack did go in at 1530, high-velocity 88s, self-propelled guns and well-placed machine guns blasted the tanks back and the troopers raced for cover. Company 'D' of the 505th, commanded by First Lieutenant Oliver Banks, climbed onto five British tanks and some other vehicles and set off for the rail bridge: they were halted by an 88mm gun at the road junction and heavy machine-gun and rifle fire about 1,000 yards from the railroad. The Guards and the Airborne spent the rest of the day battering at this position but could make no progress. The German defenders, mainly the 10th SS Panzer, stopped both attacks 400 yards from the bridges, destroying at least five tanks. The Grenadier Guards and the 2nd Battalion, 505th PIR fell back and the SS set fire to buildings to illuminate the approaches to their positions.

'We had about half the infantry we needed' said Gavin. 'Our survival depended to a large measure on the help we got from the Dutch - and we got that in abundance. Six hundred Dutchmen joined me. All they asked from me were rifles and pistols and weapons of the dead and wounded - expressing a fully worthy commitment to join us in battle on the grounds of knowing the dangers of what would happen if they were caught - and they would have been

16 Flight Lieutenant Turner was awarded a Military Cross.

assassinated of course for they were only wearing civilian clothes with their armbands. They proved to be among the bravest and most patriotic people we had liberated. That made a big difference.[17]

'I met in front of the Malden schoolhouse, right on the sidewalk [in a roadside cafe close to the Grenadiers' Group HQ in the monastery at Marienboom] General Horrocks, General Allan Adair and 'Boy' Browning, Commander of the British Airborne Division.[18] General Horrocks said to me, 'Jim, we've got to get on the other side (of the Waal) and get to Arnhem right away!' And I said, 'But we have no way to get there really, but we might find a way.' I asked Browning, 'How bad is the situation in Arnhem?'

'Well, I don't know, it is pretty bad. We know they are in real trouble and we have got to get there within 24 hours,' replied Browning. That meant right away as far as I was concerned.'

'I turned to Horrocks and asked him if he had an Engineer Battalion that would have boats. He turned to his Staff who were gathered in a circle around us and they said 'Yes.' They thought that XXX Corps had boats down the road, perhaps just fifty miles away on this side of Eindhoven. And I asked him when he could let me have them and he said, 'I will get them up during the night.'

The boats were part of the standard equipment for the Bailey bridge teams of the Royal Engineers. Originally, the plan had called for a night assault, but now Gavin and Lieutenant Reuben 'Rube' Tucker figured that the British in Arnhem could not hold until dark. The attack had to go as soon as the boats arrived.

'Well, if you can get them up' Gavin said 'I will cross the river during darkness. Crossing this fast moving river against some entrenched Germans on his side of the river was in any case very difficult, but at night we had no problem. We were very adept in handling German Infantry having a lot of experience especially in Africa. Colonel Warren Williams came to my Headquarters near Malden and got his orders from me at 11 o'clock at night to make the crossing. We got prepared to go and get the job off around 7

17 First Sergeant John Rabig, Company 'D', 505th PIR, recalls: 'One of those 600 Dutchmen who fought with the 82nd during those critical days was Agurdus Leegsma, a young man who was living in Nijmegen. He volunteered to join Company 'G' of the 508th Parachute Infantry Regiment as a rifleman and was immediately taken under their wing. Nobody could pronounce his name so the troopers called him 'Gas'. On 23 September 'Gas' was wounded during the Company's attack on Thorensche Nolen and was taken to a field hospital for treatment. He soon returned to take his place in the line with Company 'G' north of the river. Agurdus Leegsma made such an impression with the troopers that President Roosevelt awarded him the Medal of Freedom together with a Purple Heart. Queen Wilhelmina presented him with a Bronze Cross on behalf of the Dutch Government. This was not to be the end of his military service, for in April 1945 the Dutch Army sent him for officer's training to the Military Academy at Sandhurst, England. Before retiring in 1962 he had reached the rank of Captain in the Dutch Army. *Put On Your Boots and Parachutes!: The United States 82nd Airborne Division* written and edited by Deryk Wills (self published, March 1992).

18 Also present were Norman Gwatkin of the Fifth Guards Brigade, Lieutenant Colonel Reuben Tucker of the 504th PIR; Colonel George Chatterton, the commander of the Glider Pilot Regiment, Lieutenant Colonel Edward Goulburn, Major A. H. M. Gregory-Hood and Captain the Duke of Rutland Charles John Robert Manners of the Grenadiers.

o'clock while it was still dark. But at 7 o'clock the boats were not to be seen. So about 10 o'clock I went down to the crossing site at the power plant to take a look. About a half a mile from the river I ran into a platoon of German Infantry coming towards me like 'gute soldaten' about four hundred yards away. Sergeant Walker E. Wood, my bodyguard, who was with me and who had a lot of combat experience - that was why he was with me - jumped beside the building and gave his covering fire as fast as he could and they were all on the ground in a few minutes. (Also there, but not mentioned was Hugo Olsen, an officer and trusted confidant of Gavin throughout the war). Then I started to get back to Colonel Warren Williams in his Headquarters to tell Colonel 'Rube' Tucker, his Regimental Commander, 'We do not even have a site where we can launch the boats yet.' He said, 'I will get there as fast as I can.' Tucker was a very tough capable combat commander. He had just come from Anzio with his Regiment where they had some hard fighting. He had jumped into Sicily and he fought the Hermann Goering Division and defeated them. We were ready to go if we could get up there and get the boats in the water. He told me to get the boats up at 1.30 pm at the power plant.'

The planned German counterattack was launched on Wednesday, 20 September (D+3). An artillery barrage hit the landing zones near Gavin's headquarters and two German combat teams struck out of the Reichswald Forest toward the thinly held 505th and 508th areas. The Guards Armoured Division arrived in Nijmegen and the battle was on. Captain (later Lord) Carrington, second-in-command of 1 Tank Squadron, 2nd Battalion, Grenadier Guards, the first British officer across the bridge, recalls: 'There was no significant opposition that morning until we got to Nijmegen. There may have been the odd skirmish on the way but nothing slowed us down until we got to Nijmegen and found ourselves in the middle of a battle. That brought the column to a halt and I remember meeting Chester Wilmot, the war correspondent, who helped drink my last bottle of liberated champagne.

Wilmot noticed a sign put up by what he called' some over-conscientious sapper', who believed that the other stretches of the road would be as dangerous: 'DON'T LET THIS HAPPEN TO YOU. KEEP ON THE ROAD. VERGES NOT CLEARED OF MINES.' Wilmot was certainly one of the first Australians to land in France on D-Day, his reporting from the battlefield thrilled his radio audience in Britain and further afield. His recording of the chiming of the church bells of the first village liberated in France was heard around the world. [19]

Vandervoort's battalion and British armour and infantry crept forward house by house against the German positions, but when afternoon came, they still had not broken through to the bridge. Colonel Ben Vandervoort would later write: 'The troopers fought over roof tops, in the attics, up alleys, out of bedroom windows, through a maze of backyards and buildings. The tanks were the firebase providing covering fire and blasting

19 Chester Wilmot died in the crash of a Comet airliner in 1954.

strong points. Where feasible, tanks served as bulldozers, smashing through garden walls, etc. A tank cannon thrust through a kitchen door really stimulates exodus... In the labyrinth of houses and brick-walled gardens, the fighting deteriorated into confusing face-to-face, kill or be killed show downs between small momentarily isolated groups and individuals.'

James Coyle took five men through the back yards of the buildings on their left and worked their way to the end of the block where he hoped to be able to spot the anti-tank gun which had fired on them.

'When we got up into the attic of the corner building, I could see the gun with its crew in the street at the corner. We opened fire with M-ls from the attic window. The crew could not spot our firing position and when one of their men was hit they abandoned the gun and withdrew to a nearby trench to join with other enemy troops. We continued to fire down on them and hit some. The rest retreated into the park. While waiting to see if they would reactivate the gun, I sent Private Gill back to the Company Command Post to tell the CO where I was and what we were doing. When he didn't return as I had instructed, I sent another man. This man returned immediately and reported that Gill was lying wounded in the backyard next door. Gill told me that as he started back he had been shot from the back door of the adjacent house. We pulled him to cover. We threw grenades into the windows of the house but the Germans kept firing out of the door. Corporal Thomas Burke tried to rush the door but was hit with machine pistol fire and killed instantly. While we were firing into the building I saw our Medic, Ralph Hopkins, signal me over the brick wall of the next house. He had heard us firing and had come up by himself from our Platoon CP to see if anyone was wounded. He shouted to me that Sergeant Ben Popilsky was lying dead on the other side of the wall. Popilsky had apparently heard the firing from the attack, came to see if he could help and had been killed by the Germans in the house as he climbed over the wall. These had later wounded Gill. A grenade flew out of a window and badly wounded Corporal Richard Crouse. He later died. Realising we had no cover we had to get out of the yard and despite all our fire the Germans were in a position where we could not hit them but they could hit us. I pulled the men out of the yard and blew in the back of the house with a bazooka round. Then I took the men back to our original position down the block. We had knocked out the anti-tank gun. The Germans abandoned it and did no more firing, but we lost three men killed and one wounded.'

Tom Horne and other members of Company 'H', 508th PIR were digging foxholes near a church in Nijmegen when a priest and a tall young boy of about 15 in a Boy Scout uniform approached. Horne recalled: 'The priest motioned for me to get out of the hole and give my entrenching tool to the young man. I did so and the boy dug a big, wide, deep hole for me. As I went to get into the hole, the priest motioned for me to wait and he sent the boy off on an errand. A few minutes later the boy came back with a small mattress which he put in the hole for me. By this time it was very late in the evening. After I was in the hole for a while, the priest came back pushing a wheelbarrow with a large pot in it. He came around to each trooper's hole and served hot beef stew. These people were showing their gratitude by serving us with hot food.'

Bill Downs, CBS War Correspondent called Nijmegen: 'A single isolated battle that ranks in magnificence and courage with Guam, Tarawa and Omaha Beach. A story that should be told to the blowing of bugles and the beating of drums for the men whose bravery made the capture of this crossing over the Waal possible.'

The rest of the corridor was attacked and the 82nd Airborne were forced to abandon the Reichswald Forest drop zone. Gavin went to Mook where the 505th PIR was reported to be holding but he found Mook had been overrun. Gavin wrote, 'As I arrived... a tremendous amount of small-arms fire passed overhead. About 25 yards from the railroad overpass a paratrooper was in a foxhole with a bazooka. He seemed a bit shaken and he was all alone... By then the town was overrun and the Germans were upon us.' Gavin immediately sent a runner for reinforcements from the Coldstream Guards. He turned to the rail embankment and saw a cow walking up the side. When it reached the crest, impacting bullets shook its body and it flopped back down. Gavin moved to the top of the embankment and began engaging Germans pouring from the town ahead, firing his M-1. The troopers rallied and the German battle groups wavered and then fell back. Soon Colonel William Ekman launched a counterattack and retook Mook. Gavin then rushed to the 508th at Beek where the German infantry was supported by armoured vehicles and half-tracks with 20mm anti-aircraft guns, but the troopers held. Gavin ordered Lindquist to hold and then he moved among the troops to give as much encouragement as he could.

The only troops available to plug that gap that would be left by withdrawing a battalion of men from the line to cross the Waal in boats to attack the north end of the bridge as the British rush the south were the glider pilots of the 50th Troop Carrier Wing under Major Hugh Nevins. The pilots, bivouacked west of Groesbeek, armed with nothing heavier than .45-calibre automatics or M-1 carbines were ill-equipped to do the job but at 2200 Nevin spoke to them and explained the situation, asking for 295 volunteers. It was pitch-dark. Nevins said, 'I don't know how many stepped forward, but with tears in my eyes, I selected the first 295 men in the line, touching and counting each man. I was very proud of them.'

The change took place around midnight of 19 September - two Glider Pilots into each foxhole, replacing two troopers. The glider pilots would not sleep for another 36 hours. The pilots, though they were spared a frontal attack, were under steady fire from small arms, machine guns and hourly attacks by mortars, 88s and the 'screaming mimis' (Nebelwerfers). However, according to Nevins, 'The single most devastating ordeal was lack of sleep which was really worse than the enemy fire.'

In daylight on 21 September Nevins was checking positions overlooking Mook when he spotted eight of the formidable Tiger tanks moving in on his lines from the Reichswald. The tanks, 'looking like enormous crawling prehistoric monsters, were creaking up the railroad around our right flank. If they got behind us, they would slaughter us piecemeal. Over the field phone, I alerted battalion and division command posts, asking for anti-tank support as quickly as possible. I'm sure my voice was shaking.' Within minutes, two bazooka teams appeared and began to stalk the tanks. When they had crept up within less than fifty yards of the lead tanks, they cut loose and 'literally detonated the first three tanks.' The others withdrew back into the woods. When the GPs were relieved at noon on 21 September they had suffered 12 casualties, including two killed. [20]

General Gavin wrote '...One thing in most urgent need of correction, is the method of handling our glider pilots. I do not believe there is anyone in the combat area more eager and anxious to do the correct thing and yet so completely, individually and collectively, incapable of doing it than our glider pilots. Despite their individual willingness to help, I feel that they were definitely a liability to me. Many of them arrived without blankets, some without rations and water and a few improperly armed and equipped. They lacked organization of their own because of, they stated, frequent transfer from one Troop Carrier Command unit to another. Despite the instructions that were issued to them to move via command channels to Division Headquarters, they frequently became involved in small unit actions to the extent that satisfied their passing curiosity, or simply left to visit nearby towns. In an airborne operation where, if properly planned, the first few hours are the quietest, this can be very harmful, since all units tend to lose control because of the many people wandering about aimlessly, improperly equipped, out of uniform and without individual or unit responsibilities. When then enemy reaction builds up and his attack increases in violence and intensity, the necessity for every man to be on the job at the right place, doing his assigned task, is imperative. At this time glider pilots without unit assignment and improperly trained, aimlessly wandering about cause confusion and generally get in the way and have to be taken care of. In this division, glider pilots were used to control traffic, to recover supplies from the LZs, guard prisoners and finally were assigned

20 Over 90 percent of the glider pilots did their best in a difficult situation and served faithfully on guard and supply details and even as infantry. At midnight on the 20th, when the Germans were pressing the 82nd Division very hard, 300 glider pilots then in their bivouac, a barracks about a mile north of Mook, were called out, organized into companies and used as infantry at the front or in reserve. Most of them did not see much action, but about 100 men of the 313th and 61st Groups under able leadership from Captain Elgin D. Andross, Group Glider Officer of the 313th, who had previously served in the infantry, took over a section of the front near Mook for the 505th PIR and held it until relieved late on the 23rd by other glider pilots, who in turn were relieved next day by the 325th Glider Infantry. Living in fox-holes, under frequent shelling and mortaring, soaked by repeated rains, almost without food except for raw carrots and turnips grubbed from the fields around them Andross and his men did their best for three, days and nights in the unfamiliar role of combat infantry. The glider pilots were put on 26 empty trucks headed for Belgium and evacuated on 24 September. In the 101st's sector, just south of Veghel the convoy was ambushed by Oberst Freiherr von der Heydte's 6th Parachute Regiment. Captain Andross, at considerable risk to his own life, organized his troops, who eventually fought their way out of the ambush, killing over 100 German paratroopers. Thirteen glider pilots had been casualties and three others were captured.

a defensive role with one of the regiments at a time when they were badly needed.

'I feel very keenly that the glider pilot problem at the moment is one of our greatest unsolved problems. I believe now that they should be assigned to airborne units, take training with the units and have a certain number of hours allocated periodically for flight training.'

Meanwhile, on the 20th, one mile downstream from Nijmegen, to the northwest, Major Julian Aaron Cook, a 27-year old West Pointer, the commander of the 3rd Battalion of the 504th PIR, waited for the British boats to arrive. [21] He was the man Gavin and Tucker had charged with the assault river crossing of the Waal west of the railway bridge with two battalions of the 504th PIR when the 33 canvas assault boats arrived. Prior to going overseas, Captain Adam Komosa was the S-3 (Plans and Training Officer) of the Third Battalion. Lieutenant Colonel Leslie Freeman was the Battalion Commander, with Captain Julian Cook as the Executive Officer. Komosa planned and the Third Battalion executed a simulated river crossing at Coolie Conch Lake at Fort Bragg. When given the river crossing mission at Nijmegen, Colonel Tucker remembered this. This was not really the place for a Battalion Commander, but in the true paratrooper's tradition Cook chose to lead his men across the Waal in one of the boats on this dangerous mission. 'I' and 'H' Companies would be the first to cross, along with 'C' Company of the 307th Engineers. When Major Edward G. Tyler of the Irish Guards, whose tanks were to give fire support, asked Tucker if his men had had any small-boat training, calmly chewing a cigar, the 'Little Colonel', responded, 'No, they're just getting on-the-job-training.'

That morning Cook had gone to the top of a tower at a nearby power station to survey the opposite hank of the Waal. A young captain with Cook wrote in a letter home: 'When we reached the top of this tower and had a glimpse of this scene, which is indelibly imprinted on my mind forever. I felt rather funny inside. I think everyone else did too although no one said a word - we just looked... What greeted our eyes was a broad flat plain void of all cover or concealment. The first terrain feature which would offer us assistance was a built-up highway approximately 300 yards from the shore against the bank of which we would get our first opportunity to get some protection and be able to reorganize... We could see all along the Kraut side of the river strong defensive positions, a formidable line both in length as well as in depth-pillboxes, machine gun emplacements and, what was really wicked looking, one or two old Dutch forts between the place where we were landing and the two bridges.'

'At 1.30' continues Gavin 'I was at the power plant ready to help get the thing launched and order support. We were supposed to have air support to strafe the slope, but with the bad weather - like today - they didn't fly. So then the Irish Guards were going to give us artillery support, but the

21 The 2nd Platoon, Company 'B', 307th Airborne Engineer Battalion commanded by Lieutenant Adrian J. Finlayson was ordered to collect any boats he could find on the Maas-Waal Canal. The platoon gathered 27 rowboats of all kinds, but they were not used during the Waal River crossing. Jan Bos.

wind was so bad and the smoke blew away. It was broad daylight - What are we going to do? There were two and a half thousand of the British left out of their great combat division of ten thousand. Two and a half thousand left to be killed and sacrificed and we could not cross the river. We had checked, of course, all along the forest side and under the town. We could not expect the people to swim the river. So finally about 2 o'clock we both went out and we were ready to go. Well, would you believe it? we were out to watch the river crossing and at that very moment I had a phone call on the radio from my Chief of Staff up near Groesbeek. He told me we were going to lose the whole area of the Division to the Germans if we did not get back and make some decisions. Molenhoek had just been overrun. This was very important because the only bridge which we had to get tanks across was here at Nijmegen. Furthermore, Beek had just been overrun, so we were being pinched out on two sides, while we were deciding to cross the river here. What could we do?' There was only one thing to do and that was to call the infantry to make a supreme effort as they could. This was a tough good infantry. We decided to go ahead. At about that time I went back to Molenhoek it was overrun. In fact the troopers were in the cellars. Anyway they took to the cellars and I sent for the Coldstream Guards to come running from three miles away to save our situation in Molenhoek. And we drove the Germans out of Mook without the Guards being involved - we didn't need them.

'I captured some German prisoners and talked to them, they were making a counter attack. They were part of a combat team that had a mission of driving through Mook, Molenhoek and joining up with an attack through Beek. 'So having settled that issue we had to get Molenhoek back and hurry up to beat them off. To get across a ridge I got on my stomach to cross the macadam road and got up there to talk to the troops in the foxholes. There was a very steep hill there and there is a serpentine road going to the bottom. The German armour had got stuck half way up. They could not get up and they could not get down. So all we had to do was deal with the German infantry. That was all right, we liked that. So we dug in and I talked to the troopers as they were digging the holes. And at that time I made a decision to attack, probably during the night. We got Molenhoek back and we attacked out of Beek towards the flatlands during darkness at about 3 o'clock in the morning. By daylight we were way up by Erlecom. The 82nd Airborne Division's left flank was at Erlecom and the right flank at Molenhoek.'

In the meantime, Julian Cook and his troopers prepared to cross the Waal, which was about four hundred yards wide at this point with an 8-knot current. 'The Waal' was, according to Martha Gellhorn 'a very un-European river, being wide, swift and deep and the road bridge across it is the longest span bridge in Europe and looks like an American job, the Eads bridge across the Mississippi, for example. The Grave and Nijmegen bridges are huge steel-girdered structure's spanning the Maas and the Waal. The roads are either raised up on dykes, or they are narrow flat strips passing through bare country which gives no cover. The two rivers are broad, between high banks and at Nijmegen the Germans had a most convenient fort which commanded the approaches to the railroad bridge and the road bridge. There was, likewise, the enemy in force and determined and well equipped; there was, for a change, German aviation. You must now imagine a very American-looking bridge - no quaint little arched stone job, but a double-lane roadway which, I believe, some proud Dutchman told me was the second longest bridge in Holland.'

The two Companies from the Third Battalion would swing right and attack the road and the rail bridges. Company 'H' would take the rail bridge and Company 'I' would carry on further to the road bridge. The First Battalion would follow across and capture the fortifications at Lent. The assault had now been postponed several times and having been set for 1pm, was postponed two hours again because the boats had still not arrived. Finally, at 1430, RAF Typhoons bombed the Germans across the river and the bank seemed to disappear behind a screen of dust and smoke. Twenty minutes before jump-off time, the trucks with the boats pulled up. There were twenty-six of them, 19 feet long, with a plywood floor and canvas sides and room for sixteen men - thirteen paratroopers and three engineers in each boat. They were once equipped with paddles, but most of those were missing, so the troopers prepared to flail along with rifle stocks. There were not enough boats for the whole battalion so two waves were improvised. The engineers manning the boats would have to return for the rest of the battalion. H and I Companies and forward obsever teams from the 376th Parachute Field Artillery Battalion, whose guns were positioned on the west bank of the Maas-Waal Canal made up the first wave. Due to their heavy equipment, several 376th observers had to stand up, esxposed, in the boats.

They jumped off on time, at 1457, but the Germans quickly sighted the boats and opened up with every gun they had. A trooper in one of the boats later wrote, 'As we came into the open the weight of our boat seemed imponderable; our feet sank deep in the sand. We must have caught the Krauts by surprise because for the first 100 yards there wasn't a shot fired from the enemy side of the river. Then all of a sudden all hell broke loose... Jerry opened up with everything he had... As if in a rage at our trying anything so drastic, he was pouring everything he possessed at us. And behind us our second battalion and the ten tanks were blasting away for all they were worth.' The British tank battalion commander wrote that when the boats finally made it to the opposite shore, 'Nobody paused. Men got out and began running towards the embankment. My God what a courageous sight it was! They just moved steadily across the open ground. I never saw a single man lie down until he was hit. I didn't think more than half the fleet made it across.' Boy Browning said of that day, 'I have never seen a more gallant action.' Jim Gavin recalled, 'Well, the praise of the gallantry by the British soldiers, who were themselves very gallant. The bravest of the brave and they made the crossing.'

With the first wave landed, the troopers from the 307th engineers turned their craft about and went back to pick up the second wave. Of the twenty-six boats on the initial wave only eleven were able to return for the next run. The troopers who made the far shore was described by the same young officer: 'Many times I have seen troops who are driven to a fever pitch - troops who, for a brief interval of combat, are lifted out of themselves - fanatics rendered crazy by rage and the lust for killing - men who forget temporarily the meaning of fear... However, I have never witnessed this human metamorphosis so acutely displayed as on this day. The men were beside themselves. They continued to plough across that field in spite of all the Kraut could do, cursing savagely, their guns spitting fire. Troopers charged Germans wherever they saw them. In less than a half an hour, the dyke road was secured and the Germans who had survived fell back to their next line of defences. Frenzied troopers ploughed in right behind them. After the torment of the boat passage, nothing could stop them; rage and fear joined forces. With brutal efficiency they dug the Germans out and without stopping to rest or regroup continued their rampaging assault. They fought through fields, orchards and houses back of the embankment under the fire of machine guns and anti-aircraft batteries hammering at them...'

Bill Downs, CBS War Correspondent, wrote: 'Twenty-six assault boats were in the water. Two hundred sixty men would make the first assault. Waiting for them on the other bank were 400 to 600 Germans... the shelling continued. A smoke screen was laid, but it wasn't very effective because of the wind... Men slumped in their seats... of those 260 men, half were wounded or killed... only 13 of 26 boats came back... Others didn't wait for boats. Some stripped off equipment, took a bandolier of ammunition and swam the river, rifles on their backs. There was bitter bayonet fighting and Americans died, but more Germans died.' [22]

By late afternoon, the attackers had reached the railway bridge and secured one end of it. Yet it seemed the attack had finally lost its momentum. Exhausted troopers found the road bridge too heavily defended. Then the Germans collapsed first on the Nijmegen side and then on the steep embankments leading to the bridge. The 504th fired repeatedly

22 With only nine boats still available, the sixth and final crossing was made at 1900 hours. Captain Wesley D. Harris, commander of Company 'C', 307th Airborne Engineer Battalion was awarded the Distinguished Service Cross. The citation for the medal reads, in part: "Captain Harris, while under heavy enemy fire, personally directed the loading and movement of assault boats which enabled the 504th Parachute Infantry to successfully cross the Waal River and establish the vital Nijmegen bridgehead. 'Crossing the river in the face of heavy enemy machine gun, 20-mm and artillery fire in one of the first assault boats of the initial assault wave, Captain Harris was painfully wounded in the back and arm but continued to supervise the movement and unloading of the boats. After returning to the south bank of the river he refused medical evacuation but effected rapid and thorough reorganization of the remaining boats and engineer personnel for the crossing of the second wave. While leading the second wave, a pontoon near his boat was hit by enemy fire and capsized, but Captain Harris plunged into the river and, despite his wounded condition, assisted three men to other boats. Captain Harris then returned to the south bank and while supervising loading of the third wave, fainted for the loss of blood.'

at the retreating enemy. By dusk the 82nd finally had the Nijmegen Bridge. Martha Gellhorn later wrote:

'One paratrooper, who made that trip, recalled how they walked across the sandy flat bank of the river to their boats, while bullets kicked up the dirt around them. He was next to a new man who kept saying 'What is that? Say, are those bullets, for God's sake?' To which the veteran replied, 'You'll find out soon enough, bud.' The end of this battle found paratroopers fighting in the huge steel girders of the bridge, trying to pick off Germans before they could blow themselves and the bridge sky-high. The British tanks were rolling across below them. It is a pity that the movie do not do these things right, for this battle was as sensational as it was photogenic. The dynamite charges to blow this bridge were cemented into the structure and, to give you some idea of the size and intricacy of the steel construction, eighty Germans were captured from their hiding places in the under girders, after the bridge was taken. The approaches to this bridge were hopelessly exposed to machine-gun fire on both banks, as well as artillery and mortar fire. Some time later, in a thoroughly unlikable little piece of Germany which they were then holding, I met some of the paratroopers who made that river crossing. One of them said the final words about it: 'There were three men paddling and the prow of that boat just stood up straight in the water. I wasn't even scared; I just gave up hope.'

'The regiment did cross the river and climbed a steep bank on which the Germans were well and truly ensconced and they fought their way down along the shore to secure the north end of the bridge. The Irish Guards tanks lined up and became artillery, lobbing shells over to cover this amazing operation. Meantime, the Guards Armoured Division fought in Nijmegen to clear the southern entry to the bridge. Elements of the 508th Regiment had been in Nijmegen on the evening of D-Day but were withdrawn to secure the landing fields for the Glider Field Artillery Units coming in on D+1. The 2nd Battalion of the 505th Parachute Regiment fought with the Guards. The men of the 505, to the delight and admiration of the British, fought over roof-tops and blasted their way through houses, to take the near end of the Bridge. A Guards officer said: 'You could see them fighting from the housetops, just swarming over them. They were absolutely splendid; wonderful sightseeing all those chaps swarming over the roofs.' James Gavin said that 'It was a very gallant action, but I must say for history's sake, they suggested we do it. We thought we could do it and the troopers were the ones who did the job that had to be done. They were very, very brave men. I myself have never seen anything more gallant and I saw a lot of good fighting especially with American Parachute troops.

Lieutenant Jack Dube, Company G, 508th PIR, had crept towards the bridge when his unit was stopped by heavy machine-gun and 88mm fire and fought back with a bazooka, 60mm mortar and rifles. 'We were soon pinned down and fragmented as an effective combat unit,' he said. 'I was kneeling behind shrubs in the yard of a structure I thought was a dental or medical office building. Several shell bursts near my location restricted my movement. A shell hit the building behind me and shrapnel from that explosion hit me in the back of the head, left shoulder and left forearm. The shrapnel had penetrated through my helmet and helmet liner, leaving a jagged three-inch hole. A medic applied sulfa powder to my gaping and profusely bleeding head wound. Continued enemy shelling completely dispersed our small group and I soon found myself alone with no weapon and much confusion due to my injury. Weakness, dizziness, and disorientation convinced me to seek cover and medical assistance.'

Dube was taken to a hospital, which he said was soon was hit by incendiaries and set on fire. He was then evacuated by members of the Dutch underground and carried to the basement of a private home where he remained for three or four days before being taken to a US Army field hospital near Nijmegen.

Captain Thomas Moffat Burriss, the CO of Company 'I', Lieutenant James 'Maggie' Megellas of Company 'H' and his Platoon Sergeant named Richmond, one Private and another trooper, having reached the bank ran to the railway crossing, saw that they were all right there and then ran to the road crossing. They noticed wires on the ground and they decided to cut them, wherever they could find them. They were trained to do that and they cut any wire that was on the ground, whether it was a telephone or something else to be sure to get the explosives. They got the explosives and when the Germans went to fire them, nothing fired.' [23]

Paul Jansen was one of those plain, ordinary people, the kind one meets every day in the street without really seeing them. We know the Paul Jansens of the world exist all right; there are thousands of them about. He might be the chap next to you in the bus, the one in the cheap, crumpled suit and dirty raincoat with the collar turned up, all greasy where it met his brilliantined hair. He might be the conductor who takes your fare and punches the ticket. Maybe he is the driver.

Paul could be anyone of these young men. The decent, honest, God-fearing chap struggling for existence and trying hard to build himself a home and security for his young wife and baby girl. Paul Jansen was like that, a plumber by trade. Through sheer hard work and a willing nature he had, at the age of twenty-eight, built up a small but thriving business that enabled him to keep his wife and baby in reasonable comfort. He had plans for the future, too. He wanted to save enough money to open a shop, expand the business and perhaps one day he would be able to afford a really nice house in the country where he could indulge in his favourite hobby of growing flowers. Although he did not speak much about his ambitions, the people of his little town knew that go-ahead Paul would be 'somebody.' Well - Paul is somebody now - somebody of whom the Dutch town of

23 Many years' later, at a ceremony in Holland, Gavin said: 'They look upon it now with dry humour. And one of them recently wrote to me and signed and verified his name, 'Survivor of the Waal River Regatta'. That's the way they saw it, a regatta that had to be run.' *Put On Your Boots and Parachutes!: The United States 82nd Airborne Division* written and edited by Deryk Wills (self published, March 1992). Gavin died on 23 February 1990.

Nijmegen is indeed proud. Paul was the man who saved the bridge over the River Waal and, in so doing he saved the lives of hundreds of allied soldiers and probably shortened the war by a few weeks as well.

The Battle of Arnhem was nearly finished. Those gallant men of the 1st Airborne Division had dropped into the very jaws of a tigerish enemy. They held their ground and fought as only Britons know how, until, weak and exhausted from lack of sleep and food, outnumbered in men and fire-power, they were driven back and forced to give up the fierce, unequal struggle. The position was perilous and the threat to the allied invasion of Europe a very grave one indeed. If the Arnhem drop failed, then we would lose valuable ground, precious time and skilled, highly-trained troops difficult to replace.

From Arnhem to Nijmegen the distance is only ten miles. If our troop were successful in capturing the Arnhem bridge an advance through to Nijmegen was a probability, but as the world now knows the Arnhem attack failed and we were all but lost. One consequence of this attack was that the Germans rushed reinforcements to all vital bridgeheads, amongst them the Waal Bridge. From his home across the river Paul could see the heavily-armed German troops guarding the bridge night and day. All civilian traffic was banned, only German military vehicles were allowed to cross and these were subjected to a close search in case the very active Dutch resistance movement attempted to blow up this vital link with Arnhem. No such attempt was made, however and gradually conditions settled. Paul would kiss his wife, Dora, good-bye every morning and trudge off to work, his heart heavy and his belly empty. Food was scarce in those hard days, and he knew Dora and his little girl were as hungry as he was himself. Still, he did what he could for them. A little black-marketing with German soldiers brought him an occasional loaf of bread or a few potatoes. Once he got six tins of condensed milk in exchange for his wristwatch. That was a wonderful day indeed, and while Dora watched him with anxious eyes he opened up the first tin - it was bad. Feverishly Paul ripped open the remainder; but it was the same story; all were bad.

Paul said nothing; He did not rant or rage or swear vengeance against the Germans. Instead, a quiet, cold, deadly hatred burned within him, a hatred that brooded ill for any German should Paul get a chance at one. That was all he waited for in those days, an opportunity to do something that would help throw the accursed enemy right out of his good, clean Holland and back into the evil blackness that was Germany. He knew that his day was not far off. Daily the allied armies crept nearer to Nijmegen and daily Paul awaited their coming. When the time came he and his comrades in the underground army would be ready - and the Germans would feel their teeth.

As the British forces advanced so the Germans prepared to retreat; but while the main body of German troops were ready to move out it soon became apparent to Paul that a strong rearguard force would remain, their job being to delay the allied advance as long as possible. Paul knew something of these rearguard troops. They were tough, hardened, ruthless, fanatical SS troops capable of putting up a tremendous fight and slowing down our advance while allowing their own troops a clear withdrawal. This meant that the town would become another Arnhem, another battle for a bridge. It meant bombing and shelling, perhaps another airborne drop and, with it, the lovely town would be reduced to a shattered, blazing mass of wrecked houses and torn streets.

As Paul trudged wearily home one evening the first British shell came screaming across the river to land with a sickening roar near the town centre. When he arrived he started to make his cellar as strong and safe as possible. He shored up the roof and walls with timber, laid mattresses on the floor and draped blankets on the walls to minimize the effects of blast, Dora carried down buckets and tins of water and all the scraps of food she could find. Her treasured possessions, the small pieces of jewellery, photograph album, Paul's camera and his best suit, were all carefully stored in a battered tin trunk along with her own clothes. The baby's cot was carried down and all three of them sat huddled close together as shell after shell tore into the town and exploded. The Germans fought back and the crash of their heavy guns smashed every window for miles around. They had the advantage of high ground and could effectively control the bridge without exposing themselves. It was a serious problem because as long as the bridge remained in- German hands no allied soldier would get across the river.

All day the battle raged and all night long the flashes from the guns lighted up the-nightmarish scene. Parts of the town were in ruins and burned fiercely despite the brave efforts of the local fire brigades. There was no sleep for Paul and his family that night, and as the grey dawn broke through the smoke-laden air Paul left the cellar and went upstairs to have a look around. From the top window he could see the Germans manning the bridge and, away on the opposite bank, the heavy German artillery guns. Then he saw something else. The Germans were mining the bridge with high-explosive charges and preparing to withdraw.

Paul went down to the cellar again and told Dora he was going out to try to find his friends. If the Germans succeeded in blowing up the bridge the battle would be prolonged for days, maybe weeks. Dora didn't argue; she knew Paul. Quickly he made his way down to the river, stumbling over debris, skirting fires and bomb damage. For three hours he searched for his friends, but could not find them. Something had to be done and quickly if the bridge was to be saved. British troops were on the opposite bank now and the enemy were only holding them long enough to set the charges. Paul did not trouble to search farther. Slipping off his coat and boots he dived into the river and swam downstream to the bridge. By a feat of superhuman strength he managed to clamber up the inside of a steel supporting stanchion, finally working his way right underneath the bridge itself. The Germans saw him, but in the excitement must have thought he was one of their own men who had fallen in the river while working on the charges. But whatever they thought, no one tried to shoot him.

Swiftly Paul grabbed the first charge of explosive hanging over the side, and with a heave sent it flying into the water below. This time he was seen and the Germans opened fire, but Paul was lucky and being beneath the bridge presented a difficult target to hit. Bullets spattered against the steel girders as he made his way toward the next charge and threw that also into the river. There were four more charges to destroy before the bridge would be safe. On he went and over went a third charge. The Germans were firing like mad at him, but from the opposite bank I gave him covering fire and forced the enemy to keep their heads down.

Another dash forward and then I saw Paul stagger and fall. For a moment I thought he would drop into the river, but no - he climbed slowly to his feet and staggered painfully toward the explosive and sent it over the side to join the others. Again I ordered covering fire to help him and again Paul went forward, clinging to the girders like a monkey. Once he stopped, half turned and waved to me. I waved back and shouted something, but he was too far away to hear. Paul waved again and then went for the next charge. He reached it safely and broke off the fuse wire. I saw him tug at the box, but it was securely jammed and this time he hadn't the strength to move it. The Germans were falling back and Paul knew that any moment now they would explode the remaining charge. He crawled from under the bridge, got up on top and made a wild sprint toward the charge. I saw him fall as a stream of bullets ripped into his poor, frail body and as he fell the charge exploded not five yards from where he dropped.

The explosion tore a twenty-foot gap in the bridge, which was quickly repaired by our Engineers, who threw a Bailey Bridge across the hole. Within an hour our heavy vehicles and tanks were rolling into the town. The Germans fled, leaving behind the wounded and dead. The battle was over, the bridge saved, thanks to Paul Jansen.

I never met Paul or knew him personally, but I feel as though I do. When he turned and waved to me out there on the bridge as though saying: "Thank you," for the covering fire, I felt that here was a person I had known all my life. Paul was a very brave man, a brave Dutch patriot; and I can only hope that when I have to die I shall be able to face death with the same tremendous courage as Paul Jansen.'[24]

Julian Aaron Cook was awarded the nation's second highest award for bravery, the Distinguished Service Cross, for his and his Battalion's actions in crossing the Waal River. [25] Robert 'Doc' Franco recalled: 'We lost quite a number of men in that little footage in front of four 88s, two of them being my Aid men. Shortly after, I saw General Browning who had come to see Colonel Ben Vandervoort and the war correspondent Cornelius Ryan. It was an exciting time for me. I ducked into a small apartment at street level during the fighting and a nice old couple let me use it as an Aid Station. After it became clear that Arnhem would not be ours, we stayed in the Nijmegen area as occupation troops with some patrol responsibilities. We made many friends. What was sad was the information that after the battle the Dutch people in the German held territory were brutally treated, even more so than before.'

When the troopers inspected the bridge they discovered that it had been defended by 34 machine guns, two 20mm anti-aircraft guns and an 88mm cannon. The 504 casualties in this action totalled forty men killed or died of wounds. On the rail bridge alone the German dead numbered 267 with many others lost in the fast flowing river below, plus wounded and prisoners. Now British armour poured across. Exuberant 504 men greeted them with whoops and leaps. 'The tanks of the Grenadier Guards engaged two 88mms dug in on the northern shore, destroyed them and continued across the bridge' recalls Gavin. 'The first people to greet them were the paratroopers of the 504th. So enthusiastic were they that one of them actually kissed the leading British tank.[26]'

Arnhem lay eleven miles distant. But the column stopped because they could go no further until their infantry caught up from Nijmegen. The Coldstream Guards Group were repulsing an attack on the Groesbeek position, the Irish Guards Group had gone back to Eindhoven to meet

24 *Over My Dead Body* by F. Farrow, writing in 70 True Stories of the Second World War (Odhams Press Ltd). Alternatively, there is another name involved in clearing the bridge, that of 22-year old Jan van Hoof. Before the war van Hoof was a Boy Scout with the Katholieke Verkenners (Catholic Scouts). But during World War II Scouting was forbidden in most occupied countries. All the Scouting organization were to be integrated into the Nationale Jeugdstorm (NJS), the Dutch version ofthe Hitler Youth. However, the Dutch Scouting organisations did not agree with the terms of the NJS and as a result went underground or even joined the resistance. Jan van Hoof in particular joined the resistance. Shortly after the start of the occupation of the Netherlands by the Nazis, he became member of a Rover crew and in the spring of 1943 he was secretly installed as full Rover Scout. During the occupation he made observations and drawings of his environment, especially the Waal Bridges. During 'Market Garden' he used his expertise by guiding the Allies through Nijmegen. It was said that on 18 September he crept beneath the Waal Bridge during the fighting and with his knife cut the cables that were connected to the explosives on the bridge, though no-one saw him do it. After this heroic deed he went home and told his sister 'the bridge is saved'; he then returned to the American unit and resumed guiding them through the city. Enquiries after the war could not positively identify Van Hoof as the individual who cut the wires to the bridge, however circumstancial evidence backs up the claim and when the Germans eventually tried to blow the bridge, just before its capture, their attempts failed. The Dutch resistance members wore distinguishing clothing so they could be recognised as soldiers. The Germans however did not recognize them as combatants but rather as traitors. On 19 September, van Hoof was riding on the top of a Guards Armoured Division Humber Scout Car, guiding the vehicle from the allied column located at the central post office to the American soldiers and Guards Armoured Division tanks attacking the railway bridge, when Germans opened fire with a 2 cm gun on the vehicle, which caught fire. The British soldiers were already dead when the German troops arrived, but van Hoof was still alive. They took his gun, identity papers and his armband which identified him officially an allied soldier. He was beaten and then shot through the head. During a lull in the fighting, the men were buried by Dutch civilians in the garden of a house at the corner of Lange Hezelstraat-Kronenburgersingel Nijmegen, about 60 yards from the rail bridge. After the war, a statue honouring Jan van Hoof was erected on the roundabout next to the Hunnerpark. An official investigation into van Hoof's role in saving the bridge was held. By Royal Decree, Jan was posthumously awarded the Militaire Willemsorde, fourth class, the highest Dutch military award. See *Nijmegen: The Bridges to Nowhere* by Jan Bos writing in WWII Quarterly, Winter 2011.

25 He died on 19 June 1990 at a VA Hospital in Columbia, South Carolina, aged 73. *Put On Your Boots and Parachutes!: The United States 82nd Airborne Division* written and edited by Deryk Wills (self published, March 1992).

another attack, the Grenadiers had just captured the approaches to the bridge with the US paratroops and got five tanks over it to support the Airborne bridgehead and the Welsh Guards were in 82nd Airborne reserve. The Guards Armoured Division was scattered over twenty-five square miles of the south bank of the Waal. The Division resumed its advance about 18 hours later, at noon. 'Arnhem and those paratroopers were just up ahead' wrote Lieutenant John Gorman of the Guards Armoured Division 'and almost within sight of that last bloody bridge, we were stopped. I never felt such morbid despair.' [27]

It was during the battle for Nijmegen that Jim Gavin first met General Brian Horrocks and instantly they became firm, lifelong friends. Horrocks later wrote: 'Without Jim Gavin's 82nd Airborne, we should never have captured the two great bridges over the River Waal. While the road bridge was being assaulted and ultimately captured intact by the Grenadier Guards and the 505th and the 504th Parachute Regiments, supported by the fire of the Irish Guards' tanks, crossed the swift-running 400-yards-wide Waal River in British assault boats, which they had never seen before, in the face of vicious German rifle, machine-gun and artillery fire from the far bank... This operation, suggested by General Gavin, was the best and most gallant attack I have ever seen carried out in my life. No wonder the leading paratroopers, when they contacted the Guards' tanks, which had captured the road bridges, were furious that we did not push straight on for Arnhem. They felt they had risked their lives for nothing, but it was impossible, owing to the confusion which existed in Nijmegen, with houses burning and the British and United States forces all mixed up.'

Bill Kingsey's Squadron was given the task of going forward to Arnhem. 'Consequently, we raced over the Nijmegen Bridge and half way up the road to that other famous bridge at Arnhem but we met with fierce resistance from the 88mm armoured-piercing shells directed from the German self-propelled guns. As we travelled along the elevated dyke road, we were sitting ducks! The AP shells went through the tanks like hot knives through butter. Of the 21 tanks in the Squadron, initially, only a few were left, mobile and active. Our vehicle,

26 On the morning of 21 September German tanks approached the American lines in the western part of the Waal bridgehead. Bazooka gunner Private John Towle, Company 'C', 504th, managed to disable the Panzers on the Oosterhoutsedijk. The remaining tanks were pulled back and the German attack was stopped, but Towle was wounded by shrapnel from enemy mortar fire and died on the spot. He was posthumously awarded the Medal of Honor.

27 The US Official History said '[even after the Nijmegen Bridge had finally been taken] The Guards Armoured Coldstream Guards Group still was needed as a reserve for the Airborne Division. This left but two armoured groups to go across the Waal. Even those did not make it until next day, D+4, 21 September, primarily because of diehard German defenders who had to be ferreted out from the superstructure and bridge underpinnings. Once on the north bank, much of the British armour and infantry had to be used to help hold and improve the bridgehead that the two battalions of the 504th Parachute Infantry had forged. By the time the Nijmegen Bridge fell on D+3, it was early evening and it would be dark before an armoured column could be assembled to march on Arnhem. North of Nijmegen the enemy had tanks and guns and infantry of two SS Panzer divisions, in unknown but growing strength, established in country ideal for defence.' At the village of Ressen, less than 3 miles north of Nijmegen, the Germans had erected an effective screen composed of an SS battalion reinforced by 11 tanks, another infantry battalion, two batteries of 88mm guns, 20 20mm anti-aircraft guns and survivors of earlier fighting in Nijmegen.'

'MUNSTER', managed to shelter in the lee of a farmhouse. During darkness, we took shelter in an orchard along with two others. On trying to go forward at dawn, we found ourselves pinned down again by the enemy's guns and the incessant mortar fire. We lived in the tank, virtually, for three days until ordered to withdraw. As the air support had failed to arrive, the Squadron (or what was left of it) could not operate effectively.

'So near and yet so far!' [28]

28 Quoted in *The Words of War* by Marcus Cowper (Mainstream 2009).

Chapter 3

The Devil's Work

'Throughout the day wounded were filling the dressing stations. There now began a remarkable situation as officers and men went for attention to a dressing station guarded by Germans and then returned to their own lines to continue the fight. This strange state of affairs was to exist for days. On this fateful Wednesday, however, some of the walking wounded were taken away as prisoners. Surgery went on all day long. A soldier with a badly shattered foot was prepared for an amputation when it was discovered that the only amputation saws were with other surgeons at the Hotel Tafelburg, another dressing station still within our own lines. It was decided to use an escape file. This was cleaned and sterilized and a piece of wire was run through one end. Forceps were used to grip the other end and the instrument was worked like a two-handed saw. In a few minutes they had cut through the tibia.'

Major General Roy Urquhart CB DSO, CO, 1st Airborne Division

The Dreyeroord Hotel, known as the White House to the defenders, was at the northern most point of the Oosterbeek defence. On Tuesday 19th the 7th Battalion of the King's Own Scottish Borderers was ordered to hold the area around the hotel. Lieutenant Colonel Robert Payton-Reid, a little surprised at how tranquil the area was at the time, knocked on the door of the hotel at about 9pm and was joyfully received by the guests. He later wrote: 'I do not think that any who were there will forget the 'White House' and its surroundings. When I knocked at its door all was peace and quiet. Had I dropped from Mars I could scarcely have aroused more interest and I was immediately greeted as a liberator by the numerous occupants, it was, I found, a small hotel. Never have I felt such a hypocrite. I had come to announce my intention of placing soldiers in the grounds and vicinity and the delight with which this news was received was most touching - but at the same time most pathetic, as I knew I was bringing them only danger and destruction. By the next night the building was reduced to a shell and its inmates were crouching uncomfortably in the cellar. It was then garrisoned by a section of men who were living in the eerie atmosphere of a haunted house. The moon shone through shot-holes in the walls, casting weird shadows, prowling footsteps could be heard on the enemy side and one felt that faces were peering through every window.'

The quietness was not to last for long. In the early hours of Wednesday General Urquhart received a signal from Corps HQ requesting a fresh dropping zone for the main force of Major General Stanislav Sosabowski's Polish Brigade. The only possible one now was south of the river near Driel and this was duly passed to Corps. With the drizzling dawn the 1st Airborne Division in Oosterbeek suffered the heaviest shelling and mortar bombardment yet. Many buildings were flattened and several others were set alight by self-propelled guns firing phosphorous shells.

An account of Brigadier 'Shan' Hackett's Brigade HQ recalled: 'The final location of our Brigade HQ was in a little wood close to a small lake. It was always under fire and we lived very much underground; In fact, in those circumstances, it is advisable to arrange for everything to be underground. Our cookhouse wasn't, to our great regret. Food was something of a problem towards the end of the week and there were some ducks on the lake, It is surprising how difficult it is to kill a duck, even with a Sten and even when they are dead they remain afloat with their legs up out in the middle and you aren't much better off. But the wind gradually carried some of the bodies ashore. We had found a hip-bath and some potatoes and apples and if it was not to be roast duck and apple sauce it was to be a stew with the same ingredients. It was a nice stew and just when it was ready a mortar bomb burst on the cookhouse roof and precipitated the roof into the stew. Fortunately no one was hurt on that occasion. But as a HQ we were unlucky. On the morning of the 20th at 0830 hours they dropped a mortar bomb on a conference and killed the Staff Captain, the Brigade IO, Signals Officer and defence platoon command. Two days afterwards the Brigade RASC Officer and the acting G.3 were wounded and later that day a major from the Light Regiment RA was killed while he was visiting me.

'It is not easy to give a picture of life in the perimeter during the operation. Once we were closed in it was very different from a normal operation. For one thing there was no movement to plan or organise. It was a case of everyone staying put. Nor was there much opportunity of building up any reserves. There was a continual drain on every section of the front and we became, even within our small perimeter, very thin on the ground. You had to adjust your mind to the fact that when you thought of a Battalion you might in fact be thinking of no more than 50 men of all ranks, sometimes even less.

'Even when things looked very bad somehow miracles seemed to happen. A company of Borders was overrun at Heveadorp. The 2 i/c organised an immediate counter-attack with the stragglers of the over-run company and one fairly fresh platoon of the South Staffs and, with that force only, succeeded in re-establishing a position which a company could not hold a short time before. But try as we would, we could not keep the Germans from infiltrating into our positions. They established an SP gun about 150 yards from Brigade HQ. If they had come on further they would have inevitably have mopped us up, but they did not and we had not the strength to push them out. For two days we lived on those terms of proximity. The snipers were as difficult. HQ lost a JLO and several very good NCOs in attempts to clean up the area, but again we had not sufficient men to hold what we could temporarily win back. Without the support of the mediums from south of the river, I do not think we could have held on as long as we did. I think that greater resolution on the part of the Germans could have finished us off completely. They could fire into us from the three sides of the oblong. They had all the space around in which to assemble their strength at anyone point and they had great tank and artillery support. Yet they never broke the perimeter.'

A JLO recalled: 'We took some Dutch liaison soldiers with us and they were immensely useful in the early stages in contacting the civilians in the area, all of whom were anxious to be as helpful as possible. There was one Dutch civilian, too, whom I particularly remember. He was a big man, very noticeable because he wore throughout a gent's natty summer suiting of impeccable cut. He looked like something out of a spy story, of the more sophisticated kind. He stayed with us while he could be useful and then he just vanished. To tell all that he did might still be harmful, but he was a very good man to work with.'

'A Sergeant in the Intelligence Section, Brigade HQ recalled: 'By this time there were only about 100/120 of the whole Brigade left. We had been reinforced with glider pilots, who fought magnificently, anti-tank gunners, whose guns had gone and RASC from Div HQ. The Battalions had suffered terribly. For example, one Battalion was down to a strength which could only hold three houses and, one night, the centre house was overrun and the CO captured. That left the Battalion with no officers at all and for some of the time it was commanded by an anti-tank gunner sergeant, assisted by a gunner captain with a badly broken arm and finally by a HQ LO.

'We were in weapon pits in the gardens of the houses as the houses themselves were badly knocked about. We stayed there during the day and at night posted sentries and moved the remaining men into the ruins of the houses to try and get some rest. Food and men were now very short and water was quite a problem. We found a well, but with all the calls on it, the water was drained in about two hours and we had to wait till the next day for it to fill up. We got one or two of the tanks and SP guns that were shelling us with PIATs and grenades, but, on the whole, they kept their distance. The RSM of one of our Battalions was wounded when killing a tank.

'At the end of the time all our Sten ammunition had gone and the rest was very short. But we were still on top. The Germans never attempted a large-scale attack in our sector but relied on wearing us down. On our night patrols we had the better of him every time. He didn't like fighting at night.

'Signals worked desperately the whole time, maintaining the lines where they could. I don't think the linemen had any rest, for as soon as they came in from one job there would be another line broken by mortar or shell fire and they would have to go out on that, One lineman went out to lay a line and found that he had not enough line to complete it into the house. He moved into the enemy area and found some of their line and cut enough of it for his needs under their very noses.'

A Captain in the Royal Engineers adds:

'We had a strong point in one corner of the position in the grounds of a big house and armed it with two PIATS and three Brens. The rest of us were in weapon pits, except that we maintained plenty of patrols. During that day we had nine attacks, all of which were beaten off before the enemy could reach our position. One attack was supported by an 88 mm SP gun, but a corporal knocked it out with his sixth shot from his PIAT. He was lucky. They were firing back and one bullet struck the PIAT projectile in its rest before it was fired, knocking the weapon out of his hand and chipping a piece out of the bomb without setting it off.

'Later the enemy called on us to surrender and brought up a propaganda machine. It must have been a recently recorded speech, for it started off by saying: 'Gentlemen of the First Airborne Division; remember your wives and sweethearts at home. If you surrender now it will be an honourable surrender.' It then went on for another four minutes to tell us how bad our position was; and how many of our senior officers had already been taken prisoner. It did quite a lot of good. The men were furious with it and answered back with catcalls and worse. Their morale went bounding up as a result.

'Six of our men had been killed there and before we left we buried them. The man who lived in the house was very good. I asked him where we might put the graves and he showed me a place in the grounds. He promised that the men would not be disturbed there.'

In the Hartenstein area fragments flew and the trees were smashed into a web of branches that littered the damp grounds where men kept their heads low in slit trenches covered with earth-filled re-supply containers. An American wireless operator was badly hurt in the stomach and Colonel Graeme Warrack, the brave and resourceful officer in command of the Division's Medical Services, personally conveyed him to the dressing station at the Hotel Schoonoord which was already full when he arrived. He also found himself in the midst of a battle. Mortar bombs fell among the medical transport, a Dutch civilian car was hit on the road and a six-pounder was contesting the issue with a German self-propelled gun. [29]

Warrack and his colleagues soon learned that it was unsafe to venture too near the windows because of somewhat trigger happy snipers. When he heard German orders being given in the street Warrack ripped off his badges of rank and went upstairs to tend the wounded. He was hard at work when a shell crashed into the roof and several wounded soldiers in the room that he was in were injured again as the timbers and tiles crashed down upon them. As the men were being moved in the still swirling dust, two more shells hit the hotel and again the plaster and timbers fell into the makeshift wards. At length the hotel was draped with Red Cross flags and inside its battered walls, for the rest of that day and the next, British and German wounded were treated side by side by British and German surgeons alike.

A very nervous German soldier with an automatic was left to stand guard and a British lance-corporal who had once been runner-up in the Army middleweight championships was detailed to keep an eye on him. Wounded men walked in past the guard for treatment and were even allowed to go back to their units when their wounds had been cleaned and bandaged. A British officer who arrived to have an arm wound dressed was told by the sentry that he must consider himself a prisoner of war. 'Nonsense', he said curtly and walked away from the sentry who made no effort to prevent him leaving. Soon, those who could walk were marched off with some RAMC personnel. Then the dressing station got a direct hit and Warrack and others found themselves

29 Warrack was at the Main Dressing Station at the Schoonoord Hotel when a case was brought to his attention of a soldier of the 21st Independent Company who had been caught having sex with a Dutch auxiliary, while they thought everyone else had been distracted by a bout of mortar fire. The girl was dismissed by a Dutch doctor, but Warrack took no action against the soldier, concluding that it was an 'emotional release'.

removing wounded men who had now been wounded a second time. As the dust began to settle, two more shells crashed into the building, which later was festooned with Red Cross flags with a particularly large one on the roof. A German officer called to inquire about the German wounded being treated there, one of whom, a young Nazi, refused treatment for a shattered knee for four hours until the pain became too great and he consented to the British tending him.

Following his capture on 18 September 21-year old Private John Bernard Corless of No.17 Platoon, 'C' Company, 1st Battalion The Border Regiment escaped to his own company after killing his guard during the confusion created by an Allied counter-attack. On the 20th Corless, who was employed at the Wigan Corporation Electricity Works before he joined the Forces and who served in the operations in Sicily and Italy, was wounded and taken to the Regimental Aid Post. Whilst he was still receiving treatment, Germans overran the hospital and evacuated all patients to Arnhem. Although Corless escaped the same night, he was recaptured when he collapsed from loss of blood. On 24 September Corless was entrained for Germany and in spite of his previous failure he jumped from the train. He contacted Dutch underground resistance workers and they hid him for two months until arrangements were made to ferry him over the Rhine. Unfortunately on the night the crossing was to be made he was captured once more by the Germans, at midnight, on the banks of the river and taken to Ede, a small town north of the Rhine. After a stay of four days he was taken to a Stalag at Enschelde on the German-Dutch border. He escaped from this camp during a mass break, but was re-captured by the Germans and sent to Limberg by train. The occupants of his truck cut the ventilation wires and four escaped before a guard discovered their departure. Corless was to have been the fifth man to jump. This time the Germans transported him to Oflag XIIB at Limberg. (In 1945 The 'London Gazette' announced that Private Corless was awarded the Military Medal).

Not all the wounded made it the RAP. Private 'Denny' Keen in 'A' Company, 10th Battalion, The Parachute Regiment went into nearby woods towards Oosterbeek to destroy a German tank. He was badly wounded, losing a leg and was brought back to be evacuated to the RAP. He was laid across the front of the Colonel's jeep but as it pulled away the jeep received a direct hit from an enemy tank and the occupants were all killed. When Urquhart heard that the dressing station at the Hotel Schoonoord had been overrun, he sent Major John Royle, second-in-command of a wing of the Glider Pilot Regiment, to find out what was happening. He was killed in the middle of the road at the dressing station. At one time before the war, Royle had been a regular subaltern in the Highland Light Infantry. On the outbreak of war he joined up in the ranks and became a warrant officer in the Scots Guards. Later, he was commissioned into the Glider Pilot Regiment.

Having been held up by heavy opposition at dusk, the 156th Parachute Battalion made ready to assault the German positions along the Dreijenseweg at first light on Tuesday. Twenty-four year old Captain Peter Chard commanding 'C' Troop, No.2 Battery, 1st Airlanding Light Regiment, hoped to support their advance by directing the fire of his Battery's guns. However, due to the densely wooded terrain, observation of the enemy positions was impossible and so no fire could be brought to bear. The 4th Parachute Brigade lost much of its strength attacking this Sperrverband (blocking line) and when they fell back, Chard, together with Major J. E. F. 'Jef' Linton and Lieutenant Halliday of 'B' Troop, decided to return to 4th Brigade HQ in the hope of calling artillery support down upon any enemy targets that presented themselves. Not only were they unable to observe any enemy movement to accomplish this, but they also could not discover where Brigade HQ had relocated. Chard eventually found his way into the Oosterbeek Perimeter. During the later stages of the battle, he was making his way to Brigadier Hackett's Headquarters once again when he stumbled into an attack on British positions by German infantry supported by a Renault tank mounting a flame-thrower. The troops defending the area soon dealt with the enemy infantry, whilst Chard went out alone to stalk the tank with a PIAT. He found a good firing position just twenty yards off the road and waited until the tank came forward to enable him to destroy it at point-blank range. The tank duly obliged. however Chard's PIAT misfired and his position was spotted. Armed with several grenades, he abandoned the PIAT and attempted to run around the back of the tank in the hope of dropping a bomb inside its turret, but unfortunately the flame-thrower caught him first. Chard, on fire, ran back to the cover of friendly troops and called on them to shoot him to end his suffering. The troops, however, tried to save his life by rolling him in sand and eventually succeeded in extinguishing the flames. Chard was still alive and he continued to bear his severe burns with a reported great cheerfulness until he died on 9 October. Peter Chard was Mentioned in Despatches as a result of this act of great courage.

Colonel Warrack was allowed to leave to attend to his duties and to visit the other doctors in the dressing stations within the British perimeter, at the Hotel Tafelberg and Mevrouw Kate ter Horst's white house near Oosterbeek Laag church. When Warrack arrived at her house, having visited other houses where the tirelessly working Medical Services under his command were operating in quite as appalling conditions, he found both Kate ter Horst and Captain Randall 'Morph' Martin dealing with several new cases that had recently been brought in, crowding the already congested rooms so tightly that some of the wounded had to be treated in the boiler house. Warrack decided that he must relieve the appalling congestion. He sent several men who were still able to walk to the Tafelberg Hotel and, strapping two men across the bonnet of Martin's jeep and putting two more in the back, he drove to the Tafelberg himself. Elsewhere at this time other wounded men who could do so were also making their way back to less exposed buildings.

During the night 'Shan' Hackett had been reorganising his battalions for a fresh advance at first light into Arnhem. He had wanted to move on the night before but Urquhart deprecated such a move and instead told him to send reconnaissance parties in by night and follow at first light. Hackett saw nothing to be gained by recce parties in the dark and it was agreed in the end that he should move the brigade at first light.' But by 0730 all his units were engaged.

The enemy were pressing forward strongly in front from across the railway line, on his left south of Wolfheze and on his right from Johanna Hoeve. Urquhart now knew that, except for the 2nd Battalion at the Bridge, the 1st Parachute Brigade had to all intents and purposes been wiped out. The South Staffords had ceased to exist as a unit and the 11th Battalion had disintegrated and that whatever prospects there had been of reaching Frost at the Bridge were now gone. Over the R/T Urquhart he therefore told Hackett to abandon his plans for advancing into Arnhem and to close in on the north-east corner of the Oosterbeek perimeter and try to reach Divisional HQ as soon as he could. Hackett explained to Urquhart that he would be delayed as his entire brigade was engaged. 'We have a certain number of tanks among us,' he said. Most of his troops had little ammunition left, others had none; some had neither ammunition nor weapons but using captured German rifles they fought their way back with determination and skill through the open fields and woods. Although completely surrounded by greatly superior numbers of the enemy Hackett managed to get his men back towards the rest of the Division. The brigade, in his own phrase, 'handled beautifully'.

In a bid to increase the pace Hackett changed the line of advance from a south-easterly direction to an easterly one, bringing the 10th Battalion through to spearhead the advance while the 156th Battalion, which had been stopped, took up the rearguard. They formed up at the edge of the woods, where the two battalions were subjected to substantial small-arms fire which raked the rides between the tall trees. The 156th Battalion suffered the worst of the German infantry and tank attacks, while mortars rained down over the whole area. However it is a great tribute to these men that the Germans never realized that they were fighting a foe in retreat - attacks were beaten off and then the paratroopers mounted counter-attacks to push their enemy back. Lieutenant C. Silvester the Brigade Liaison Officer led three attacks on a strong enemy position. Private Gerald Flamberg of the Mortar Platoon, Support Company was sent out into the open with a recognition triangle. He was met by a German tank which immediately opened up and put a bullet through his shoulder and remaining there in action, pinned the Company at about 200 yards. Flamberg crawled back and asked and obtained permission to attack the tank with a Gammon bomb. He then stalked the tank, working up to within ten yards of it, in great pain with one arm useless. He threw the bomb and damaged the tank so that it hastily withdrew, opening the way for the Company. Flamberg was awarded the Military Medal.

A terrible toll was taken in terms of casualties and very few men made it into the Perimeter. Lieutenant Colonel Sir Richard de Bacquencourt Des Voeux and his 35-year old second in command, Major Ernest Vivian Ritson were not among them. Sergeant Andy Thorburn discovered his fatally wounded commander, leaning against a tree. He asked if he could help him, but Des Voeux said 'No. Move forward. The enemy is in front of you; they need you there'. It is believed that Sir Richard died shortly after.

Initially the Battalion had made good but cautious progress towards Oosterbeek until 'A' Company encountered a solid German defence. 'C' Company were ordered to make an attack over their right flank and coming on to some high ground they were afforded a view of a number of German half tracks on the road below them which they quickly dealt with. However, when the Company pushed forward it was discovered that German infantry were holding a strong position on the opposite side of the road and little more progress was made and a number of men were killed, including Lieutenant Donaldson, the only remaining officer in the Company besides Powell. Low on ammunition, the Company dug in whilst Geoffrey Powell returned to Battalion HQ to arrange for supplies to be brought forward and also to visit his commander, who ordered him to withdraw as the Battalion was preparing to push in another direction. On the way here he had passed the Regimental Aid Post which had no shortage of casualties to attend and a solitary doctor was at the centre of them, his forearms coated in blood. Powell carried on to find some ammunition from RSM Robert Dennis Gay, a man who would normally leap to his feet whenever an officer approached but on this occasion he was on his back, slumped against a jeep. Under a degree of pressure at this time Powell demanded 'Bloody hell, can't you get to your feet and find us the ammunition we want?' and the RSM replied 'I'm very sorry, Sir, I've been shot through both legs.' An enemy AFV had harassed him on a road covered by flanking fire from a Spandau. Ignoring intense fire from the machine gun Gay had charged the tank, attracting its attention away from Battalion HQ and trying to put it out of action with a grenade but he was severely wounded in the legs by the tank's machine gun. Feeling somewhat embarrassed, Powell collected the ammunition and returned to 'C' Company. [30]

Lieutenant Colonel Kenneth Smyth of the 10th was wounded. Hackett's brigade major, Major Bruce Dawson, shot a German with a rifle and soon afterwards Hackett followed suit. Then Dawson was shot through the head and killed. In the woods more men of the 10th Battalion were killed by Spandaus firing down the rides and by snipers shooting from the trees. Lieutenant Colonel Derek Heathcoat-Amory, commanding one of the two sections of 'Phantom' had a broken leg and was strapped to a stretcher on a jeep which was carrying mortar bombs. He was untied just before he was enveloped in the flames that had been shot at the jeep by a German flame-thrower. The rate of withdrawal slowed down and Hackett, impatient about the rate of progress, now sent orders to the 10th Battalion for Colonel Smyth to 'pull the plug out'. Nearing the edge of the Oosterbeek Perimeter Smyth said to Lieutenant 'Pat' Glover 'There are not many Germans between us and headquarters and those that are we're going to charge.' What was left of the 10th Battalion fixed bayonets, surged forward and successfully broke into the Perimeter. As Smyth reported to Major General Urquhart that only 60 men remained of his Battalion, Glover sat down and propped himself up against a

30 For RSM Gay's conduct at Arnhem and as a PoW, he was awarded the Distinguished Conduct Medal. In part his citation said: 'Once recovered from his wounds he determined that imprisonment would not affect his own standards nor anyone else. The high state of health, spirits and discipline which he assisted RSM Lord to produce in a prison camp is now well known and reflects most adequately the tradition of a regular Grenadier Guardsman and a member of the 1st Airborne Division which RSM Gay represents.' He was later made a Member of the British Empire.

tree. To his left, also propped against a tree, were two dead Glider Pilots, but Glover was too tired to pay them more than a courteous glance. Also both of his feet were badly blistered in spite of having two pairs of socks on.

At approximately 1500 Lieutenant 'Pat' Glover was at Battalion HQ with Lieutenant Colonel Smyth and Major Ashworth of HQ Company. By this time the Germans were all around their positions and the Battalion had become fragmented and no longer functioned as an organized unit. Smyth said 'Look, I think we've had it. I've lost my command and I don't know where we are. I think you'd better get in pairs and decide if you want to stick with me or go it on your own.' As instructed by their commander, Glover and Ashworth went away to discuss this but were both determined to stick with the Colonel.

As he rested outside the Hartenstein, Glover heard the rumble of aircraft approaching and thought 'Oh, my God, what next?', but it only turned out to be the RAF bringing in supplies. Once they had completed their run and dropped their cargo Lieutenant Colonel Packe of the RASC asked Glover and three other men to retrieve what supply canisters they could find that had been dropped locally, however as he was about to leave Major Ashworth came back and told Glover that Smyth wanted him to visit the Oosterbeek crossroads, at the centre of the eastern side of the Perimeter and report back on what 1st Airborne positions were in the area. Having conducted a reconnaissance and returned to the Hartenstein he was told to go back with as many men as he could gather. He found half a dozen and set himself up in a house with Lieutenant Saunders of No.18 Platoon, but was later moved further forward and into a large building, a former restaurant, situated on the corner of a lane. Along the lane was a German self-propelled gun that had been knocked out. After he had led the depleted Battalion in a bayonet charge through strongly held woodland to open a way for the remnants of the Brigade into the Divisional perimeter and with his Battalion now down to about 50 men Major Peter Warr had then been ordered to take and hold some houses in Oosterbeek on the critical North Eastern edge of the Divisional perimeter. He led the attack on each house in turn himself and in stiff hand to hand fighting in which he was wounded in the face, drove the enemy out. During these attacks he surprised and captured intact a Mk IV tank, finding the crew outside of it and killing or wounding them all with his Sten gun.

Major Peter Warr was based in the building on the opposite side of the road behind Lieutenant 'Pat' Glover's position and he shouted across to him to have a look at the tank to see if he could do anything with it, having previously been a cavalry officer. The machine's interior was smothered with blood, the breech block was missing and there was a strong smell of diesel. Glover knew immediately that the vehicle's chief ailment was a hit to its fuel tank, but in spite of this he was able to start the engine and allowed it 10 minutes to warm up. Unfortunately in so doing he made himself a target for both sides, because the British saw a functioning German tank and the Germans knew that they had abandoned it and so presumed that it was about to be used against them. Explosions went off around the tank and rocked it so much that it knocked Glover's false teeth out. It was a terrible time for him and his brave efforts were followed by much disappointment that he would not be able to use the tank to attack German positions as it only managed 10 yards of movement before the engine gave way and packed up.

Sergeant Tom Bentley, who had already shown conspicuous bravery in much hard fighting since he was dropped on 18 September, was in charge of a detachment of mortars using the top floor of a house as an Observation Post in the hard pressed north eastern corner of the divisional perimeter. The position was held by the remnants of the Battalion about 50 strong, constantly under fire and frequently heavily attacked. From his Observation Post he not only directed telling heavy fire upon the enemy but also obtained information vital to the defence which he was obliged to take back personally to his CO under fire from close range on each occasion. When the side of his house was blown in by a self-propelled gun at point blank range he fell from top floor to basement but crawled out and carried on from another. He was located and shot out more than once that day but set a magnificent example of determination to carry on and during the operation was responsible for the discovery and repulse of a dangerous infiltrating movement from an unexpected quarter. The CO was wounded and a few men in the Battalion Headquarters house were captured and the mortars lost. That night Sergeant Bentley led a patrol into enemy occupied area and brought the mortars out operating them from then on under heavy fire under the personal direction of the brigadier, for whom they were the last two mortars in the brigade. [31]

That night Major Peter Warr encouraged and grimly drove exhausted men in defensive preparations so that on the morning of 21 September he was able to meet and drive off strong attacks by tanks, self-propelled guns and infantry, with mortar and machine gun support during which he moved fearlessly from house to house and kept the men constantly inspired by his own magnificent example.

Corporal Walter Collings of 'A' Company, 1st Battalion, The Border Regiment recalled that their battle position for the last six days of the Battle of Arnhem was north of the Hartenstein Hotel. 'The KOSB was to the right of this position. Of those left from our platoon I was senior NCO with sixteen men not all from my own 10th Platoon. We came under a heavy barrage of mortar fire that was exploding on contact with the trees and causing shrapnel casualties, myself included. Andy Hannah, of Newton Stewart, Wigtownshire, Scotland, one of my best friends, was hit in his head and eye and lost two fingers. One finger was sewn back on and his injured eye was removed, both without anaesthetic. My other great friend, Jack Crawford of Bishop Briggs, Glasgow, came through without a scratch. How, I just do not know! We were the advanced section covering two paths through the woods at Westerbouwing when Andy came and told me that a tank was coming towards us. We soon realised it was on the path to the left and coming very fast, so I got the PIAT anti-tank gun and positioned myself on the corner of a small cottage and then all hell was let loose. Unknown to me, my platoon sergeant and officer were on their way to my section and before I could fire they came around the corner at the same time as the tank came into view. It opened fire killing Sergeant J.

31 Bentley was awarded the Distinguished Conduct Medal.

Hunter who fell right beside me. The officer lost his mind and was running all over the place, the tank still firing. Jack stood up out of his trench firing his Bren gun from the hip giving me time to move position and then I saw a red flash and Jack falling back into his trench. By this time the tank was away and being engaged by another platoon. The engagement had lasted about two minutes. I ran over to Jack's trench, looked in and there he was without a mark; a piece out of his flying smock and a grin on his face. I said 'What the hell did you do that for?' All he said was 'I don't know'. What a friend to have in a tight spot and we had many more before the end. Andy later told me he saw Jack actually kill the German tank commander and with this brave act certainly saved my life.

'We were guarding a path in a different part of the woods when three truck loads of Germans started coming down, we engaged them, then all was quiet, then they felled a couple of trees across the path. I had my binoculars and could see them crawling behind the fallen trees, so I got Jack sighted on the spot from which they had emerged and every time one came out I'd call to Jack and he would let go with his replacement Bren gun and the Germans soon gave up that idea. They then brought up a loudspeaker and asked us to give ourselves up saying our task was hopeless and for us to think about our mothers, wives and sweethearts. They then played some records of Vera Lynn songs to touch our hearts but it would not stop us from trying to do the job we all came to do, in fact it gave our spirits a boost.

'Later on that day Sergeant Burton from another company came and asked if we would go into a bayonet charge to clear a patch of Germans who were giving his group, about twelve men, a rough time. We agreed that he would move his men into line with us and on his command we would all take off, hell for leather, shouting and cheering. The Germans did not wait for us to reach them; they took to their heels and ran. I do not blame them; the noise we were making was enough without the bayonets.

'We took some other German trenches and I helped Jack to clear a couple dead Germans out of his trench so he could position his machine gun ready for action. All the positions we had were either in woods or on the edge of woods; this particular one being on the edge with a view over an open field with woods on three sides and a road about eight hundred yards away facing our positions at the end of the field. While we were there the Germans moved up into the wood on our left. We could hear a lot of movement but kept quiet awaiting our chance to surprise them. After about an hour we could plainly hear them talking and their mess tins rattling. They were about to have a meal and that was a bit much for us, having had very little to eat ourselves, so we gave the area a good burst of fire and all went dead quiet.

'All was quiet for a couple of hours then four German trucks stopped at the top of the road. Troops got out and took up positions to advance down the field towards us. I decided to wait for them to get nearer to us before we opened fire so we would get as many as possible, also before their mortar section was able to locate our positions. There were about sixty to our seventeen. They were about half way down the field when suddenly a Vickers machine gun from lads on our side, opened up on our right. They had waited until the German troops were in line with them and were able to kill them all without us firing a shot. Within seconds the German mortar section got back on the trucks while a couple of Germans carrying a red cross flag ran down the field to their troops, but as there was nothing they could do they went back to the trucks and moved off. Jack and I went to check on the Vickers crew but found them all dead. We had no idea that they were there - we were very lucky.

'We moved our position to a ditch in the woods. I thought it would give us the advantage over the advancing German troops. We decided to have a brew up; you know the old saying 'when in doubt, brew up' - it was very welcome. I will always remember one of our Bren gunners who I asked to reconnoitre lower down the ditch coming face to face with a German doing the same, both so surprised they turned and rushed back to their group, it was one of the lighter times during the battle. Later we came under fire and returned it. I remember Johnnie Brett a few feet from me suddenly pulling his red beret off, looking at it, putting it quickly back on and firing like mad at the Germans, he showed me his beret after this engagement - a bullet had made a hole in it just over his right ear.

'In this same position an officer from another regiment came and ordered me to go with him and take the PIAT anti-tank gun and one man to destroy a German mobile gun which was causing a lot of havoc at a crossroads in the village of Oosterbeek. I brought it to his notice that being the only NCO with the men my priority was to stay with the men. My words fell on deaf ears and I was told that if I refused, I would be on open arrest. Naturally I did go and Private Pilling, 18 years of age offered to go with me - who, I'm sorry to say, later lost his life. He was from my home town of Liverpool and we used to go on leave together. We did our job and then found our way back, moving in and out of gardens and over fences. We were glad to be back with our group. Most of the houses had holes knocked through the walls to the next house and you could walk through a row of houses without being picked off by German snipers who were very good at their job. Being a sniper for a couple of years I knew how to be careful of them. An instance came to us very soon after a glider pilot came and told me he knew where a sniper was and asked if we would help him to flush him out. I told him it was a fool's errand and what the consequences would be, but he was set in his mind. Three of us started with him but he was brave and foolish. Waving his revolver he rushed ahead about twenty feet instead of moving forward together. One shot rang out and he was dead. Although we opened fire, we had no idea just where the sniper was. Sadly we had to return without him.

'Whilst we were in these positions an NCO came and told me to report to a road junction about half a mile away from our position. I informed the men what we were going to do and off we went moving in single file. When we reached this position we found it devastated, the German mortars had got there before us and had destroyed the two heavy guns and crews. I talked over the situation with Jack and decided to move back to our old position again, so I called out to the men to follow Andy back to our old positions, at the double, with Jack and I bringing up the rear. We looked back and it was being very heavily mortared and I felt relieved that we had got out in time without any casualties. We got back to our old positions without any further trouble and awaited the next attack having by this time very little ammunition left, or food or drink. Our only food was Compo rations which we chewed on during the battle and all of us were very tired and weary; days and nights were just as one.

'On the next day a glider pilot came and asked if we would cover their withdrawal to new positions as the perimeter, now known as the cauldron, was getting smaller. I agreed with him that on his whistle we would move back to the trenches that they had left. I know now that it was a mistake as no sooner had we taken up positions, the German mortar bombs started to rain down on us and we suffered a lot of casualties. Andy and I were two of them. Lance Corporal Halliday from another platoon was killed in the same trench as me and from that moment on we ceased to be a fighting unit and became separated. For the last three days or so our heavy guns across the other side of the Rhine had been engaging the German positions in front of our perimeter. It was a great boost to our morale to hear these heavy shells whistle over our heads and landing about a thousand yards away. We all thought that at last we were going to be relieved from this sheer hell but it was not to be. We did our best; the tanks were our downfall and I was glad it was all over.'

When dawn came on Thursday 21st, Lieutenant 'Pat' Glover took hold of a rifle and shot at German snipers that he could see in the vicinity and believed he had hit three or four of them. As is the danger with sniping, his position was eventually spotted and a shell was directed at his building which resulted in Glover falling from the first floor and into the room below. He was not injured as a result of this, though one private was with a shell splinter through the bridge of his nose, which Glover obligingly pulled out with a pair of pliers. Immediately after Glover went to the side door in the house in time to see a German moving across the road and he promptly shot him. A German tank then appeared and began to fire into the house occupied by Major Warr and Colonel Smyth. Glover overheard a debate between the two men as to whether they should stay or abandon and in the end they retreated to Lieutenant Saunders' building under cover of smoke and covering fire provided from Glover's position. Later in the day German soldiers occupied the position that Warr and Smyth had abandoned, thus cutting Glover off and proceeded to put a great deal of machine-gun fire down on his building, but the parachutists put an end to this by charging across the road and driving them out. With the situation stabilized for the moment, Glover turned his attention back to sniping and he was about to shoot a German moving across the green to the north of his position when a bullet hit his right hand and severed two veins. This caused a great deal of blood and in spite of a tourniquet he could not stop the flow, so he left Sergeant Hughes in charge and made his way back through the rain to the Schoonoord dressing station a few hundred yards away. Moving from house to house he was shot at several times by snipers and received a further wound to his right calf when he was caught in a mortar explosion. However he otherwise reached the station intact.

He was helped into the back room which had become the operating theatre, the whole room literally covered in blood and he was lifted onto the makeshift operating table, made out of a stretcher laid across two tables. The doctor informed him that morphia was in short supply but that they would give him a shot if the pain proved too great, but Glover declined the offer and waved them on to continue. As the doctor was examining his leg he said to Glover with a grim smile 'Don't look now, but we've got company'. Glover looked behind him and saw a German soldier holding a Schmeisser which was pointed straight at him. The doctor said 'Keep quiet and he'll go away', but although the German did turn his back to the operating room, he did not leave but instead stood in the doorway. Glover lost consciousness shortly after.

That afternoon a still stronger attack overran the Battalion position. Major Warr collected a handful of men and savagely counter-attacked, driving out the enemy and re-establishing the 20 men, who were now left out of the Battalion, in the same houses. With his little band of weary men, some of them wounded, he held the position against repeated attack and continuous fire at close range, with neither food nor water, often cut off and with ammunition almost exhausted.

Before the defence collapsed on Thursday Warr was brought down into the cellar of the house belonging to Mrs Bertje Voskuil. She remembers 'buoyant' Peter Warr: 'They brought him down and laid him on the ground in front of me. He had been hit in the thigh; it was very painful. Sometimes he was unconscious and at others he was awake and grumbling and swearing - he had every reason to. I remember him saying, 'Oh for a pint of beer.' Then I heard them fighting in the house above us - shots and screams; they made all sorts of noises when they were fighting, sometimes just like animals. Then the door burst open and the Germans came in. A tall British soldier jumped in front of me and Peter Warr, with his back to the Germans. I don't know whether he was trying to protect us. There were two terrific explosions then - German grenades. The British soldier was hit in the back and fell forward over me. He was dead. Many of the people in the cellar were wounded. I was hit in both legs and my hearing was affected. Major Warr was badly hurt again, in the shoulder. He had been hit when he reared himself up on his elbow when the Germans came in and called out to them that he and his men were surrendering.'

For his actions throughout the preceding 48 hours, Warr was awarded the DSO. [32] Those that remained of the 10th Battalion marched down towards Divisional Headquarters, led by Colonel Smyth, the blood staining the bandages of his wounded arm.

32 Major Warr was sent to the Luidina Hospital in Apeldoorn. After several months of treatment, he had teamed up with Major Gordon Sherriff of the 7th King's Own Scottish Borderers and the two planned their escape. They intended to seek the assistance of the Dutch Resistance and, thanks to the nurses in the Hospital, this was arranged. However their escape would undoubtedly bring suspicion down upon the hospital staff and the local population and so to avoid this they arranged to be transferred to the German-controlled St. Joseph Hospital. They arrived on 7 January 1945 and awaited further contact with the Resistance. Before this could take place they were informed that they were to be removed from the Hospital and taken to Germany. If they were to escape then it was essential that it should be as soon as possible, However Major Warr felt that he was not fit enough for such a venture and so resigned himself to life as a prisoner of war, leaving Major Sherriff free to complete his escape in the company of others.

Hackett's group consisted of about 30 tired and hungry men of the 156th Battalion led by 24-year old Lieutenant (later Captain) Oliver Piers St. Aubyn, a modest aristocrat with a languid, deprecating manner of speech and a reputation for leading from the front, [33] about a dozen from the 10th, twelve from his Brigade Headquarters and 20 or 30 others - less than 100 men in all, with seven officers. They had only the ammunition that they carried and that was not much; many were using German weapons. Food and water - there was none. Snipers were a constant menace. Presently, others found their way to the hollow where now Hackett decided he could not hope to get them out till dark and he resolved to stay until dusk. And so, for nearly three hours, they fought the Germans off from the lip of the hollow. Being low on ammunition, Piers St. Aubyn, who had been appointed battalion intelligence officer, told the Germans with a mixture of hand signals and choice Anglo-Saxon to put down their arms and 'fuck off'; which, to his relief, they did. After clearing a neighbouring wood, he brought the Germans' weapons to Hackett, half of whose men were killed or wounded in the next four hours. Hackett then called together all those who could walk and led them in a wild dash through the astonished Germans to his division's defensive position several hundred yards away. It was 'a beautiful little charge and chase' by the men of 156, Hackett commented in his battlefield diary. By now the battalion consisted of little more than two platoons under St Aubyn and Major Geoffrey Powell, Commanding 'C' Company, who took possession of two empty houses. St. Aubyn's building had strong walls, but it was clear that the platoon could not survive there long. When Powell went to ask General Urquhart for permission to withdraw, the shock in the general's face indicated that he had forgotten all about them. After resisting two fierce attacks, in which he lost eight more men, St. Aubyn decided not to await Powell's return and he joined the rest of the battalion holed up in three nearby houses. By now his men had only boiled sweets to eat. On visiting brigade HQ to obtain rations he found no food, but happily fell into conversation with his cousin, Lord Buckhurst, until Hackett told them sharply to get into a trench before they were killed.

Back in his house, St. Aubyn dispatched a foraging party and then settled down to read *Barchester Towers*, reasoning that if he seemed relaxed it would have the same effect on his men. When a private started to run from window

33 Oliver Piers St. Aubyn was born on 12 July 1920 into a military family of St Michael's Mount, Cornwall. The island had been the last Royalist fortress in England to hold out for Charles I in the Civil War. His father, Major-General the 3rd Lord St. Levan, had been twice wounded in the First World War; Piers' elder brother, John, was awarded a DSC serving with the Royal Navy in the Second World War, in which the youngest brother, Giles, the historian, served as an ordinary seaman. Young Piers went to Wellington and St James's, Maryland and had begun to study architecture when he joined the King's Royal Rifle Corps on the outbreak of war. He spent a week at El Alamein in 1942 and then was posted to the Turkish-Syrian border, where he transferred to the new Parachute Regiment. After making trainee drops on the Sea of Galilee, St. Aubyn arrived on the Italian coast at Taranto by cruiser because there were no aircraft available and immediately commandeered a bus. He earned a mention in dispatches for the way he fought through olive trees and farm buildings. Later he demonstrated his marksmanship on night patrol by bringing down a German officer with two pistol shots before leading a charge on a machine-gun post. Before moving on the platoon paused to eat grapes they discovered in an upturned German helmet.

to window, shouting 'I'll get you, you bastard' at a German sniper, St. Aubyn told him to be quiet and returned to the reassuring story of Victorian clerical squabbles. At dawn enemy infantry were beaten off with grenades and two paras ran across the street to drop bombs from the first floor of a building opposite on to a self-propelled gun. St. Aubyn withdrew from his house only just before a tank reduced it to rubble. The following day, as his men were digging trenches, the enemy tried a new tack, using a loudspeaker to play the Teddy Bears' Picnic and to relay a female voice telling them to surrender if they wanted to see their wives and sweethearts again. Some Typhoons swept low to make a rocket attack, but they did not stop the enemy drawing closer. As a private was about to fire his Bren through a hedge, St Aubyn placed a hand over the barrel, coolly saying that they did not want to give away their position. St. Aubyn, one of only three officers of 156 Parachute Battalion to emerge unscathed from the battle of Arnhem and Powell, were each awarded the Military Cross.

German armour continued to harass the paratroopers as they moved along their new route and they eventually succeeded in getting in amongst them, making the position of the Brigade rather perilous. Major Geoffrey Powell got a message informing him that the Brigadier wanted to see him. Geoffrey Powell recalled, 'in a clearing I saw three jeeps of Brigade HQ: two close together and on the trailer of one a wounded man lay motionless on a stretcher. Germans could be seen darting through the trees; and then the squat barrel of a SP gun appeared; it fired and hit one of the jeeps, which burst into flames. A driver ran from it shouting a warning that it was loaded with ammunition. All of us watched in horror, waiting for the explosion. Then out of the trees a short, spare figure ran to the burning vehicle - it was the Brigadier! Springing into the driver's seat of the jeep with the wounded man and shielding his face against the flames, he gunned the engine into life; and the jeep and trailer roared across the clearing to safety... The Brigadier called for me. He was not lying down, but standing upright behind a small bush, seemingly unaware of all this danger and I had to stand up with him. He pointed out a clump of tall trees (around the battle marker) about 150 yards away around a hollow, which was on our line of withdrawal. There was a large number of Boche in the hollow. He said that I had the only formed body of men left and that I was to clear the enemy out of the hollow, after which the rest of the group would join. 'I gathered my men together and gave them the straightforward orders - we would charge the enemy - adding that it would be better to be killed going for the bastards than lying in a ditch. I led my men out of the shelter of the trees. No one hesitated. The Boche started to run. The sight of savage, screaming parachutists had been too much for them. We cleared the hollow; only their wounded were left. Quickly I organized the defence and soon the Brigadier joined, with the other men of the battalion and of his HQ and some of the 10th.'

Brigadier Hackett described Powell thus:

'This was a great fighting man in a great tradition, that of the company officer in a British county battalion of the line, competent, courageous and self-effacing. I saw a good deal of Geoffrey Powell in the last stages of that grim battle in the battered houses and sad groves of Oosterbeek, when he was commanding a little mixed force which included the few men still in action of his own battalion. I rather think I irritated him a little once, though he was too courteous to suggest it at the time, when I protracted a conversation conducted in the open rather longer than the enemy's fire made healthy. But we had each other's confidence and that is what makes battle fighting possible. His was a splendid performance which I shall always admire.'

Captain David Allsop, the Second-in-Command of 1st Reconnaissance Squadron who had taken command after Major Gough left his men on 17 September, never to return also experienced Hackett's seemingly unperturbed attitude to the Germans. During the fighting at Oosterbeek, the Squadron was placed under Hackett's command. Allsop recalls: 'He seemed to have the idea that it was good for the chaps in the slit trenches to see him walking about and so he tended to ignore the firing. When Hackett came and talked to you, it wasn't crouched down in a hole in the ground - you got out and strolled around, as if you were at Henley!'

Throughout the afternoon the enemy kept up their harrying tactics. Some Mark I tanks were brought up to harass the British who stalked them with plastic bombs only to find German infantrymen in wait. Whenever they approached within grenade throwing distance of the hollow, they were seen off by fire or by the bayonet. 'They were' said Hackett, a 'splendid lot - particularly splendid in view of the normal work of some of them. For there were clerks and signallers there and men from the Intelligence Section and Sergeant Dudley Pearson, his chief clerk, turned out to be 'one of the bravest men at really hand-to-hand fighting' that Hackett had ever known. On one occasion, Hackett led out his men in a daring counter-attack on a Spandau post about 30 yards away and killed the enemy with the exception of one German who was cowering in terror in his slit trench nearby, his head pressed down in the sandy soil. Hackett paused. He saw the cloth of the German's tunic stretched tight between two sharp, thin shoulder-blades; the pathetic helplessness of the man was too much for Hackett. He could not bring himself to use his bayonet. Leaving the now apparently unattended Spandau where it was, the men withdrew under fire to the hollow to await the next attack. Almost as soon as they had got back to their position there was more German activity and Hackett had to recall his party. Within three minutes, the gun they had overrun and whose crew-member Hackett had spared, was firing again.

Major Geoffery Powell was sent for by Hackett. 'The Brigadier was standing up in the middle of all this' recalled Powell. 'There was nothing for it but to stand up too, I felt very exposed. He said: 'Geoffrey, you've got the only formed body I've got left. Two hundred yards over there is a hollow full of Germans. That's our only way out. I want you to capture that hollow.' I had no means of covering fire and one platoon of chaps. I gathered them round. There was only one thing to do, go at it hard. We screamed and yelled firing from the hip. The Germans did not wait for us. My Sten jammed, so I picked up a German Mauser, which I carried for the rest of the battle. Joined by the others and now about one hundred strong, we held the hollow for the rest of the day. Luckily most of the German armour was pulled off.'

Captain R. R. Temple, GSO1H to the 4th Parachute Brigade fought for most of the time one-handed, his right arm having been smashed on the morning of the 20th. His shooting with a revolver held in his left hand was 'most accurate.' 'We spent,' he says, 'most of the day in the hollow south of the railway being attacked all the time... At one stage we thought the Germans wanted to surrender and they thought that we did... By Wednesday evening the strength of the Brigade was about 259. We were practically out of ammunition and the Germans were still attacking.'

In the hollow Hackett decided that he could not wait for darkness to get away. He would have to charge out now if he was ever to escape. The German attacks were becoming stronger and more frequent, ammunition had dwindled to almost nothing, the German snipers became bolder and took their toll of the defenders and he must surely soon be overwhelmed. At 1700 Hackett called the few remaining officers and senior NCOs into a small group under the lip of the hollow near this marker. He told them that they would have to 'make a break for it'. Hackett, who had been using a German weapon, now exchanged it for a British rifle with an officer who had been hit in the hand. Thirty-four year old Captain Hubert Brian 'Jasper' Booty, the 4th Parachute Brigade Medical Officer [34] recalled: 'We had been in this dell for 4-5 hours under constant sniper fire when the Brigadier called us into a tight circle. The heavy fire had abated to some extent and there was a lull when he gave out his orders. They were simple and to the point. In 15 minutes' time all of us who could still stand would collect here and on his orders charge through the enemy in one mass to reach the nearest airborne troops thought to be about 250 yards due east. The breakout would be covered by our smoke grenades and by men firing from the lip of the dell up to the last moment. The wounded had to be left behind and the Brigadier went to say a quick farewell to them.'

Major Geoffrey Powell recalled: 'The Brigadier said: 'We can't stay here any longer. The rest of the Division is only a few yards away. I will gather you all down one end of the hollow. When I say go, you will all go. I will lead and you, Geoffrey, will bring up the rear.'

'With a huge shout from all, the Brigadier led us out in this wild charge' recalled Jasper Booty. 'The sheer speed of the breakout completely surprised the Germans and we hardly had any casualties. The pace slackened after about 100 yards as we reached an orchard, where we could see airborne positions ahead.'

'It was a repeat on a bigger scale of what happened before. We broke straight through. I passed one German lying on the ground, screaming in terror' recalled Major Powell. 'I came to rest in the neatly dug positions of 'A' Company of the Border Regiment, who up to then had not seen much action. They were all clean, tidy, shaved, etc. Suddenly this mob flopped down, with

34 Booty was born on 27 August 1910 at Portalloch, Argyll and was educated at Clifton College; Peterhouse, Cambridge. He became the Resident Assistant Physician at the Hospital for Sick Children, Great Ormond Street in 1938. On 15 August 1942 he was commissioned on joining the Royal Army Medical Corps. He was later taken prisoner. On 20 December 1945 he received a Mention in Despatches. After the war Booty resumed his duties as Physician to the Hospital for Sick Children, Great Ormond Street, from 1947 to 1975 and the University College Hospital, 1948-66. He died on 18 December 1994 in Hertfordshire.

two day's growth of beard, bloodstained bandages and odd weapons. A young captain appeared and said, 'Would you mind taking this shower out of my position.'

Hackett walked down to report to Division HQ, followed by the others to be re-equipped with weapons and ammunition before being allocated to positions in the perimeter around Oosterbeek, which was now being formed. Eventually what remained of the Brigade reached the area of Divisional Headquarters; but by then it was not more than 150 strong. There were only 90 men left and they were soon reorganized into unit groups, the 50 men of 156 Battalion into two platoons. Major Powell recalled that 'we were refitted, given ammunition, weapons for those who needed them and a meal. The perimeter was in the process of being formed. We assumed that at any moment XXX Corps would arrive and that for us the battle was over; we had done our share.'

Urquhart, however, with great reluctance, was forced to take a decision which meant the abandonment of all the troops near the bridge, the seizure of which had been the main object of the operation. The virtual destruction of the 4th Parachute Brigade in, the woods north and north-west of Arnhem, the virtual disappearance of the 1st Parachute Brigade in the town itself and the heavy losses sustained by the Air Landing Brigade left him no choice. He decided to form a perimeter round the suburb of Oosterbeek and there hold out until the long expected relief from the 2nd Army arrived, using for this purpose the remains of the 4th Brigade together with any other troops available.

Earlier on in the day Major Wilson had ordered one of the several German-speaking Jews in his squadron to call back that they were too frightened to surrender but that they would come out if the Germans sent a party to take them back, In a few moments about 60 Germans came out of the woods opposite them and the men of the Independent Company obeyed with pleasure Wilson's order to fire.

The 21st Independent Parachute Company was involved in a controversial incident on Wednesday 20th. The Germans had been in the habit of calling upon the British to surrender and though the details are not clear it does appear that the Independent Company lured their opponents into a ruse de guerre. After a period of mortaring a German shouted out 'surrender'. It was not clear whether they intended to surrender or were calling upon the Independent Company to surrender. One of No.1 Platoon's German Jews, Corporal John Peter Rodley (real name Hans Rosenfeld) a University mathematics student who came to England from Düsseldorf in 1939 [35] was told by Major Wilson to call upon them to come out into the open to come and get them. As many as 50 Germans came forward, all armed and none displaying the slightest sign of submission. Lieutenant David Eastwood said to Rodley, who was calling upon them to lay down their arms, 'Tell them we'll give them a minute'. When they were within point blank range the glider pilots on the left flank of the Independent Company opened up with their Brens on this group and No.1

35 Hans Rosenfeld was KIA on 23 September, aged 29, by a ricochet in the neck defending his trench in the garden of the house at Stationweg 8 His parents, Mr and Mrs Richard and Minna Rosenfeld, were murdered in The Holocaust. The 21st Independent Parachute Company included at least 26 Austrian, German, Polish and Czech anti-Nazi Refugees, who volunteered from the Pioneer Corps.

Platoon quickly added their weight to the slaughter. Few Germans escaped. Almost as soon as the firing started, Eastwood, whose face went white and grim, called for a cease fire. [36]

Wilson said, 'They died screaming.' The Germans, too, adopted these tactics and groups of them came forward with their hands in the air calling, 'We surrender! We surrender!' as the British came up towards them, they threw themselves to the ground and machine-guns opened up behind them.

At The Hartenstein at around 1330 Urquhart saw the remains of the 10th Battalion as it turned off the main road, following the line of trees into the HQ area. The 4th Brigade had begun to move towards the comparative safety of the Oosterbeek Perimeter that morning, with what remained of the 10th Battalion leading their way. German infantry and tanks harassed the Brigade every step of the way, though the fast moving 10th Battalion was not as severely affected by this as the 156th. Sometime during the morning, Smyth was wounded when a bullet hit his right arm, but with a final determined charge, he led his men into the Divisional area. 'They were exhausted, filthy and bleeding; their discipline was immaculate' said Urquhart. 'The memory of their arrival has remained strongly with me. Lieutenant Colonel Ken Smyth, his right arm bandaged where a bullet had struck, reported breathlessly: 'We have been heavily taken .on, sir. I have sixty men left.' Aside from himself, the only other remaining officer of the 10th Battalion was his Second-in-Command, Major Peter Warr. There were others who were able to rejoin the Brigade, especially the 4th Parachute Squadron RE which had got through in two parts, one of which was now holding ground near Ommershof under command of the Independent Parachute Company.

'What has happened to Hackett?' Urquhart asked Smyth.

'He'll be here as soon as they can disengage,' he replied. 'They were in rather a mess in the woods up there.'

Urquhart could no longer contemplate putting Smyth and the survivors into the original position. He told Smyth to take his troops to the Utrechtseweg-Stationsweg crossroads on the east side of the perimeter and occupy the houses there, just in front of one of the Main Dressing Stations. But first they had to attack and drive out the German SS troops. Many of the 10th Battalion were killed and Smyth was wounded again. They would give no ground to the end. Urquhart's wireless communications with the outside world and especially with Browning's HQ were still practically non-existent but the BBC war correspondent's set and the Independent Phantom reporting unit were still functioning well. Working one of the powerful long-distance sets in his square yard of cellar space next to Urquhart shortly after 1400, the Phantom officer suddenly laid down his headphones and came up with the exciting information that the Guards Armoured Division was fighting in the Nijmegen area and preparing to rush the bridge over the Waal. His men needed a tonic and Urquhart joyfully gave orders that the news should be made known to every man in the Division. Also, he went out to spread the word to some units

36 For his actions at Arnhem, Lieutenant David Eastwood was awarded the Military Cross.

himself. 'He looked as cheerful as anything, the General did', a soldier he spoke to said. 'I even thought we should be joining up with the blokes at the bridge before morning.'

Sergeant Roy Hatch, a Glider Pilot, described the six foot Scot as 'a bloody general who didn't mind doing the job of a Sergeant.' This was proved during the battle when he helped a signalman drag a heavy spare radio battery out of a storage trench and to the command trench. Not realizing that his helper was an officer, the man asked Urquhart to help him bring another, which he did without hesitation. It wasn't until they had finished their task that the signalman realized that his assistant was no less a man than the General. He offered his thanks, to which Urquhart modestly replied 'That's all right, son'. His unassuming and confident attitude won the respect of any doubters.

Tales of heroism and self-sacrifice abounded. Sergeant J. N. Smith kept his Bren gun in action after an enemy shell had knocked down the house on top of him. Signalman R. M. Duguid had two jeeps shot under him, the second of which he repaired under heavy fire. Private J. Steele of the Border Regiment became a purveyor of gammon bombs, retrieving these dangerous and useful weapons from a container which had been seen to fall in a sniper-haunted wood, just before an enemy tank attack developed. The non-combatants vied with the fighting men in gallantry and devotion to duty. Private J. C. Proudfoot, a stretcher-bearer, 'repeatedly went out into the open in full view to dress the casualties and drag them to safety'.

Thirty year old Private Ernest Hamlett from Manchester was one of four signallers in The Border Regiment's 19th Signals Platoon led by Corporal Larry Cowan which landed at Arnhem without any problems and moved to the positions at Borsselweg where there was a farmhouse and a gate keeper's cottage. At the age of 11 Hamlett had joined the Boys Brigade of the 27th Manchester Division. It was here that his life-long passion for music began, being particularly fond of military music, brass bands and the pipes, he learned to play the cornet, euphonium, piano and percussion. Hamlett would go camping with the Brigade and developed an interest in outdoor pursuits, such as hiking, cycling and sports, especially cricket. Leaving school at 14, he furthered his education by taking several night school courses. Having become an officer in the Boys Brigade, he remained with them until his call up came at the age of 26. He was posted to the Durham Light Infantry and based at Palace Barracks in Belfast for six months before being transferred to the 1st Border, at Carlisle. Hamlett was described by fellow Signaller, 23-year old Private Ron Graydon, as being as fine a fighting partner as a man could wish for, because he always did his best to find a cheerful perspective, no matter what the situation. The other two members of the Signals Platoon were Joe Maguire and Reg Mawdsley. On Tuesday their commander, Lieutenant John Bainbridge, had been ordered to move his men to a crossroads north of Heveadorp to observe and report upon any enemy movement heading eastwards towards lower Oosterbeek. Bainbridge, Sergeant Northgate, Ernie Hamlett and Ron Graydon reached their objective in the evening, but due to the densely wooded terrain Hamlett was unable to contact Company HQ, based only a mile away, to confirm that they had arrived at their destination.

On Wednesday afternoon a German armoured car supported by infantry was spotted making its way toward 19 Platoon's position from a westerly direction along the Oosterbeekscheweg, unaware that British opposition was dug in ahead of them. Once within range a PIAT destroyed the armoured car with a single shot, while a Bren gun dispersed the infantry into the woods on either side of the main road. Ron Graydon remembered clearly that the wounded driver refused his field dressing just before 'all hell let loose'. As this action had exposed the platoon they could no longer observe enemy movements on the road. 'Lieutenant Bainbridge said that we should make our way back through the woods' Graydon recalled. 'I thought that this was dangerous and I had a discussion with Ernie and he agreed that we had come up the main road we should go down it. I approached Bainbridge and he agreed that splitting the platoon was a good idea. So we set off running down the road. I was carrying the wireless set and Ernie still had the headphones on. We ran through 'C' Company when they were in the middle of a ferocious attack. We got back in about 30 minutes. We tried again to make contact with HQ but failed. Ernie suggested it might be the batteries.'

'We were pinned down in hastily dug trenches' recalled Hamlett. 'I was in a forward trench and the radio battery was failing and I asked Corporal Larry Cowan for a relief. He changed places and an hour later he was hit with a mortar bomb. Private Joe Maguire and I dashed forward, carried him to the first aid post, where he died within the hour.'

'Ernie was inconsolable' says Graydon. 'We tried to assure him that he wasn't to blame but he never got over it.' The death of Corporal Cowan was an incident that haunted Hamlett for the rest of his life. He had met the man's family only two weeks earlier and could not help but recall his two children.

'Shortly after a mortar bomb fell on Ernie's foot, or ankle, I recalled him shouting 'It hasn't gone off'. He was in considerable pain but refused to be taken to a first aid centre.[36] Then Captain Hodgson sent for me. There was an RA Officer with a jeep. I was told to go with him with my 18 set. He had the idea that we should climb the top of the lunatic asylum at Wolfheze and we could make contact with an RA unit on the other side of the river. The map references would pinpoint German positions to be fired on from the guns over the river. I climbed to the top. The officer actually climbed on to the roof. I hung out the window. For the first time I got through, probably because I was about 300 feet above the ground. We drove back to the Company. It was hell going on. We dodged a self-propelled gun, both of us practically lying face down in the jeep. I didn't realize it but we passed Major Costelloe on the way to his MC for saving two of his unit. When I got back to 'D' Company it was a hell of a

36 Hamlett and Maguire were captured later. 'We had no ammo; nowhere to run and we were surrounded' recalled Hamlett. 'Maguire and I vowed we would stay together; it was not to be, when the Germans came they separated us. I had a fractured ankle and they put me with wounded and taken to a hospital.' Hamlett was sent to Stalag XIB at Fallingbostel in a cattle truck, where men became so thirsty that they resorted to drinking their own urine. The ankle which had been struck by an unexploded mortar received no treatment and despite the injury he was made to work down a lead mine for the next 7 and a half months. Thanks are due to Jean James for all of her help.

mess. The platoon in the gamekeeper's cottage had been decimated by mortar attacks on the building. Across from the farm we had trenches and we had lost two officers dead and one wounded. I think this would be about the 24th (but I really don't know). I think there would only be about seven fit men and two officers left. When I got back Hodgson asked if I had got through. I said yes but he never allowed me time to say I had been about 300 feet. 'You must try again', he said. We were stood in an outhouse. They went out, Hodgson and Bainbridge and a load of mortar shells fell. It killed Hodgson, although I think it took him five days to die. Bainbridge was badly injured. If I hadn't had to stoop to pick up my 18 set I wouldn't be here today. I decided then that the role of signaller was dead. I went across the road and went into a slit trench facing the wood. We had some success. I was in the trench with a lad called Charlie Nixon who had been one of the survivors from 19 Platoon.

'One morning I woke up (this must have been the 27th). There was a deadly silence. No self propelled guns no mortars. Just the sound of spasmodic machine gun fire, this must have been down by the river. The thing was we didn't in 'D' Company know anything about the withdrawal. Then through the woods came a Feldwebel and about ten soldiers and he told us that we were 'Kaput'. End of 'Market-Garden'; we were PoWs.' [37]

About seventy Dakotas came into sight from the north and slowly droned across the battlefield dropping supply panniers. As on the 19th, smoke signals were sent up, troops held out parachutes and waved frantically, squares were burned in the turf by trails of petrol. Signals had been repeatedly sent from Divisional HQ that this Dropping Zone was in enemy hands and co-ordinates of the places where they should try to drop were given out but not one of them had been received and the aircraft dropped almost all their panniers to the Germans, who had by now captured the orders setting out the directions for marking the dropping places and had had them copied and distributed to all units, one of which was operating a captured 'Eureka' beacon. Although 30 of the 33 aircraft despatched (91%) reported successful drops and two aircraft that were missing may have dropped, the effort was largely wasted only the overs reached the men. Some crews, overshooting, came round in face of most appalling flak. Some aircraft were on fire. Hundreds saw one man in the doorway of a blazing Dakota refusing to release its pannier until he had found the exact spot, though the machine was a flaming torch now and he had no hope of escape. [38]

Late that afternoon Father Bruggeman saw a group of about 50 English prisoners, some of them needed help walking. 'It was so sad to see' he wrote,

37 Ron Graydon and about 40 others went into Stalag IVb and then in cattle trucks through the Ruhr, while the bombs were falling into Sudetenland where they were put to work in the Betty Shaft pit. 'My philosophy after Arnhem was to make something of every minute of my life because I was lucky, but there were many lovely mates who didn't come back and I owe it to them not to waste time because they didn't get that time.'

38 The RAF, for understandable reasons, had always refused to consider soldiers on the ground communicating with supply dropping aircraft. At the Rhine crossing so as to avoid the mistakes of Arnhem, RAF teams wearing maroon berets and smocks went in with the airborne troops. Hibbert.

'our liberators passing by in that way. Our dreams were so different. Also all of the supplies dropped from the sky for those men fell in the hands of the enemy. Father Ammerlaan spoke to two English patrols which were sneaking around the back of the villa, asking for the name of the road and if we knew where the Germans were and if there were any in the house.'

During the hectic and confused afternoon, Urquhart tried to maintain physical contact with as many of the units in the perimeter as he could, partly in the hope that his presence might help morale and also because he wanted 'to get the picture absolutely right'. One of his trips was to the northern sector to see 'Boy' Wilson and his Independent Company who held a number of houses in a heavily wooded district. Urquhart wanted to see how he was doing and also to warn him of Hackett's possible appearance in the Independent Company's area from the north. He took his ADC, Captain Graham Roberts and they were given directions by some troops which led them along a wooded ride. Suddenly they found themselves in the middle of a battle between the Independent Company and a number of SS. From slit trenches on the roadside, faces appeared and men shouted and gesticulated. Urquhart braked hard and, with Roberts, made an undignified dive into a ditch. They were in No Man's Land. Urquhart decided to make a run for it to the house occupied by Wilson fifty yards away on a slight wooded rise. He told Roberts of his intention and told him to collect the jeep if he could. The two men ventured out simultaneously. Urquhart reached the house unharmed but Roberts attracted some enemy attention when he climbed into the jeep. The ride was too narrow to allow him to turn round, so he decided to drive on towards a right-hand turn which looped round close to the house. Going fast, he negotiated the corner and swerved to avoid a burned-out German half-track. Suddenly the steering wheel swung round in his hand and the jeep crashed into a tree. The jeep was wrecked but Roberts was thrown clear and he rolled into a ditch. Warned of snipers and despite a severe pain in his leg, he managed to jump over a four-and-a-half-feet high wire-mesh fence. When he arrived at the house, he had a large swelling on his forehead as well as a leg injury and Urquhart sent him to the RAP for attention. More than anything he was worried about the jeep. 'I'm afraid, sir,' he said, 'it's a complete write off.' Roberts went off and was presently tended by Graeme Warrack, who was having a hectic time. In mid-afternoon, as the attrition continued and the supply situation worsened, Urquhart sent off a signal saying:

Enemy attacking main bridge in strength. Situation serious for 1 Para Brigade. Enemy also attacking position. east from Heelsum and west from Arnhem. Situation serious but am forming close perimeter defence round Hartenstein with remainder of Div. Relief essential both areas earliest possible. Still retain ferry crossing Heveadorp.' [39]

On the 20th September a party was ordered to defend Heveadorp ferry. During the night of the 20/21st the ferry was heavily attacked and the protective party forced to withdraw. Twenty-nine year old Lance Sergeant

39 There is some evidence that this signal did not finally get through until the following morning, Thursday 21 September.

Herbert Mallet Lake of No.3 Platoon, 9th (Airborne) Field Company, however, lay up near the ferry on the water edge, half submerged. He loosened the cables and prepared to disable the ferry should the enemy attempt to use it. He remained on his own under fire within 200 yards of the enemy without food or water until the early morning of 22nd September, when he rejoined the unit, wounded and exhausted with detailed information of the enemy's movements and disposition on the river bank. When the unit ran short of food and water, on his own initiative Lance-Sergeant Lake organised a foraging party and with two sappers carried water through intense mortar fire to the company positions. On the night of 24/25th September Lake led a party of RE which fought its way through enemy positions to the river bank. Though badly wounded a third time in the shoulder and back, he saw all his party safely into boats before he allowed himself to be carried aboard. His actions earned Bert Lake the Distinguished Conduct Medal. [40]

By now, the overpopulated hotel and its grounds were filled with men living and sleeping in the same clothes they had worn since the landings and as the Germans had long since cut off the water supplies, the lack of washing facilities meant a good deal of body odour. There were only two toilets in the hotel, both of which were blocked. As they could not be flushed either, men were forced to use the grounds where proper latrines were out of the question because one could easily be caught in the open on such occasions by the odd shell and mortar bomb.

As this bitter day dragged on, with its numbing mortar and artillery attacks, Colonel John Frost continued to hold out at Arnhem Bridge, Dickie Lonsdale and his scratch garrison kept up their guerrilla activities in the south-east, the Border Regiment was preoccupied to the west and Hackett, fighting his way out with the 4th Brigade, lost contact with us. For a time, Urquhart knew nothing of the fate of this force.

Hackett reported to Urquhart at 1850. He had seventy officers and men. Urquhart said to him: 'Take a night's rest.' There was some food and water. A few hours' sleep was all that they could grab before the next battle started. Urquhart knew that he was now in no condition to attempt any kind of offensive towards the town. He told Hackett that they must at all costs now hold the perimeter on the northern bank and not allow themselves to be destroyed. Naturally, his first request was for information about the progress of XXX Corps. Together with sixty sappers of the 4th Parachute Squadron who had been fighting on a different approach, Hackett's men took up position south of the 10th Battalion. Hackett set up his Brigade HQ in the wooded part of the hotel grounds, fifty yards from the Hartenstein.

'The Boche had pressed very hard all day' recalled Captain Harry Faulkner-Brown of 4th Parachute Squadron, the Royal Engineers whose section was dug in at the corner of some woods, under the command of the Independent Company 'but were repulsed every time'. 'Towards evening there was a great shout from the enemy in front and a German officer, with a grenade in his hand, came forward calling out 'Hande hoch', I shouted at my men to cease fire and

40 Bert Lake died on 5 October 1990.

I hurled abuse at the German, but he insisted on our surrender. A short burst of Bren fire sent him scurrying behind some trees and we let them have all we had. Later that evening, after we had beaten off another attack we heard the strains of 'In the Mood', which seemed incongruous with the surroundings. The Germans had brought up a loudspeaker which first played jazz music; mostly by Glenn Miller. Then the music stopped and very clearly we heard a voice, which sounded English urging the 'Gentlemen of the 1st Airborne Division to remember your wives and sweethearts at home. 'It is better you should give yourselves up, Tommies; your General is our prisoner. You are surrounded. The rest of the Division has surrendered. If you do not surrender, you will die. Panzer units are about to attack you. Are you hungry, Tommies? Would you like to share the food your aeroplanes have dropped to us. Give up, Tommies. Why die? You are beaten anyway.' It went on to list the names of senior officers, including our General, who had been captured and told us to surrender now and that it would be an honourable surrender. 'This monologue' recalled Captain Harry Faulkner-Brown 'was not allowed to be heard for long, for it was greeted by abuse, catcalls, whistles and the odd burst of Bren fire and Major Wilson's men fired a PIAT bomb in the direction of the loudspeaker. There was a big bang and it stopped and some men of the 1st and 3rd Battalions shouted back, 'You cheeky bastard.' We all thought it was a great joke.'

On Wednesday night Lieutenant Colonel Robert Payton-Reid was walking around the position with a company commander, Major Gordon Sherriff and they were inside their own perimeter when somebody walked up to them. He spoke German. Before Payton-Reid had recovered from his surprise Sherriff jumped at his throat. After a struggle while Payton-Reid tried to shoot him but was frightened of hitting Sherriff, he, Sherriff, strangled him. Sherriff was wounded. In the midst of this a friend of the German threw a stick grenade. Then they heard a frightful wailing and found it was a goat that had been hit.

Chapter 4
The Bridge

Wednesday's first light saw me sharing a fry-up of bacon with a gunner-officer. A cooked meal, my first since early Sunday in England. Especially welcome. Welcome because I had left my pack at one of the woodland halts. I had since lived off the land, pears and tomatoes, scrounged on the way. One of the lads began to shave. To shave in his meagre supply of water - precious water. 'What the hell are you shaving for? When we get back they will think you have been to a bloody party'. When we get back - if we get back. From windows overlooking the Rhine and the low-lying fields between, with Bren gun I waited, waited with aggressive, war-like Jock Clements. Below us, an anti-tank gun, camouflaged. Beyond this, skirting the field, were remnants of our unit, under Lieutenant Williams, a well respected officer. Further ahead lay a scattering of dead cattle and a deserted German 'Flak' position. Time slipped by, the Germans were late. Suddenly from nine o'clock left, over the railway, poured a fast moving arrowhead formation of troops. Our forward unit called 'Enemy' and we fired our Brens. The Germans never knew we were there. They never knew what hit them. At 300 yards they were wiped out - one man flailing his arms above his head. Quiet again. At the broken bridge beyond, a German tank sneaked through. Before it could gain advantage the anti-tank gun fired. A direct hit. An explosion, flame bursts and scurrying figures. Another danger dealt with. As the 'Perimeter' closed we withdrew again, under fire, to new positions, dug in along the edge of a dyke. Spasmodic mortar fire punctured the night. In one flare up we suffered a great loss - Sergeant McKnight - one of the boys.'

Private Walter 'Bol' Boldock, 1st Battalion, The Parachute Regiment.

On Wednesday 20th September it was still raining. At the Arnhem Bridge, soon after first light, the shelling began again. German snipers and machine-gunners had so well covered the entire area that the positions on either side of the Bridge had become isolated from each other. Stretcher-bearers were allowed to go about their work unimpeded, but all other movement was fraught with danger. Relocating troops from one building to another was scarcely possible and so the men in each building had to defend it until their position became untenable, whereupon they either had to surrender, run the gauntlet of mortars and machine-guns to reach a neighbouring building or, if possible, continue to hold the line by digging themselves into the rubble. 'In the early morning' wrote Captain Eric Mackay 'there was another half-hearted infantry attack, supported by a Mark III tank, but the enemy's major preoccupation during the morning was clearing out the remaining infantry from under the Bridge. They succeeded in this by midday. We were then left as the only force east of the bridge. This time they started to reduce our building by artillery fire, systematically.' The German artillery gunners south of the river began to demolish every church steeple protruding from the Arnhem landscape. Clearly they suspected that the British were using these 18th Century towers as observation posts, though throughout the battle Tony Hibbert had believed that the enemy were using them for just such a purpose and as such it was a relief to him to see them go, but at the same time sad that such beautiful buildings should have to be destroyed.

'Suddenly from a house about 250 yards up the road' recalled Major Tony Hibbert 'emerged a very dishevelled-looking woman pushing a brand-new, immaculate pram, presumably with a baby in it. With her free hand she was waving frantically and I could see she was screaming hysterically as she weaved her way through the rubble. The small-arms fire around her stopped instantly, but the heavy guns continued. Miraculously she survived and when she got to about 100 yards from our HQ, one of our platoons managed to get a Dutch-speaker to call her over and we got her under cover. The poor woman had completely lost her mind.'

By now Frost's gritty band of defenders had been burnt out of its original positions on or near the bridge and was fighting in the ruins close to and beneath it. Presently German tanks were able to move across the bridge from north to south, for the six-pounders, sighted to cover it, were under small arms fire and could not be manned. Aircraft also played a part in the German attacks and a Messerschmitt 109, diving on the position, hit the steeple of a nearby church and crashed. Nevertheless, the defence was still maintained and hopes were still high, for news had been received that the 2nd Army would attack the south end of the bridge that afternoon at five pm.

'Now that the buildings on either side of the bridge had been destroyed and their rubble was still smouldering' recalled John Frost, 'the bulk of what remained of the force was concentrated round the headquarters buildings. From here we could still control the bridge. We had found a limited water supply in one of the houses, sufficient for one more day at any rate. At last divisional headquarters came on the air and I was able to speak to the General. It was very cheering to hear him, but he could tell me nothing more than I knew already about XXX Corps and not anything really encouraging about the ability of the Division to get through to us. They were obviously having great difficulties themselves.

'As I was talking to Doug Crawley outside his headquarters about arranging a fighting patrol to give us more elbow-room to the north, there was a sudden savage crash beside us. I was thrown several feet and I found myself lying face downwards on the ground with pain in both legs. Doug was lying on his back not far away and he started to drag himself into the house. Stunned and bemused I did likewise and Wicks my batman came to drag me in under cover. I could not resist the groans which seemed to force themselves out of me and I felt ashamed, more particularly as Doug never made a sound. After we were hit with the same bomb, Crawley alleges that I said, 'There you go again. Always getting wounded. What a silly ass I was to come and talk to you in the middle of a battle.'

Crawley recalled: 'We were discussing our positions not long after

The view from a glider cockpit of a Stirling tug.

Ted Wood, a Stirling navigator on 570 Squadron, who had flown an Albemarle on D-Day, also flew four supply flights over Arnhem. He had taken off from Harwell on the re-supply mission on 17 September. 'We went in Vics of three until we reached the Dutch coast, where we met two other streams of Vics of three. We were then nine abreast as we went in, and it was estimated that there were 2,500 aircraft in the sky at that moment, at 2,000 feet. So what it sounded like on the ground, God alone knows.

Amongst that lot were 25 squadrons of fighter escort, and any fool who opened up on the ground, you would see the Tiffies go down - and they never missed. They just aimed the aircraft at the target and let the rockets go. That went well and we reached Arnhem and dropped our gliders in the fields outside Arnhem town. I don't think we lost an aircraft at all. Then the next day we went with resupply - the usual 20 containers and two panniers. We dropped them on the same place that we had dropped the gliders - it seemed alright again. We got a bit of flak, mainly after we'd dropped the supplies, because we were flying at 500 feet with bomb doors open and flap down throttle back at 140 mph.

'The fourth day we went and we led 40 aircraft over France, this time, not over the North Sea. Over the battle zone you had to fly above 3,500 feet, because of your own troops and we met cloud. We stayed above the cloud and got higher up at the rendezvous for the start of the run-in, at about 6,500 feet above 10/10 cloud. We'd got to get down to 500 feet and make fairly quick decisions. I said to the old man that we'd better go underneath it - Holland is pretty flat and there are no large lumps sticking up - so we waggled our wings at the rest of the 40 and stuck our nose down. We broke cloud at about 1,000 feet and I said to the old man that I didn't like flying at 1,000 under that lot - you were a sitting duck. I suggested we got down on the deck. The Dutch maps were very good, with every duck-pond and tree marked, so we went down to nought feet for this run-in. We climbed up to 500 feet as we crossed the Rhine. We were obviously the first in, and when we arrived at the new dropping zone, it turned out to be a field the size of a football pitch, completely surrounded by woods. I could see all this, lying in the nose, ready to drop the containers. Now, because the blokes the day before had had some casualties over the dropping zone, we had agreed it would be suicide to pull up after you had dropped, because you had no speed, and you were offering the whole of this damn great aircraft to a gunner. So we arranged that, as soon as the last container was away, we were going to go down.

We'd slam open all four motors and go down on the treetops - you'd offer no target then. 'I was having a good look round as we were dropping the containers, and I could see our blokes in one corner of this dropping zone, burning smoke flares for us. I could see a couple of jeeps with a red cross on them - but it was obvious by the flashes, that Jerry had got the other three sides. It was like someone kicking the side of the aircraft in with hob-nailed boots, they were so close. The old man was a lunatic pilot at the best of times - he was doing rate-four turns over the treetops in this damn great thing and I could have picked leaves.

'We were due to go again on the Friday, with a brand new aircraft because one of the flight commanders had borrowed our aircraft and pranged it. We were literally waiting to go when they cancelled it and said they were going to pull out what was left. Totting it up, we started the week with 34 aircraft and crews on the squadron and I had twelve new aircraft delivered. By Friday I hadn't twelve fit to fly.'

Stirlings lined up for a re-supply mission

R
315317
W
315671
X

The German commanders: Left to right: Field Marshal Model, commander of Army Group B; General Student, commander of the 1st Parachute Army; General Bittrich, commander of II SS Panzer Corps; Major Knaust; General Harmel.

Opposite page: Amercan parachutists 'suit up' in preparation for the flight to Holland.

Stirlings depart on another mission, towing Horsa gliders

B-24 Liberator skirts the drop zone near Son. The crews flew so low that even the smallest details such as the clock faces on church towers could be seen. (USAF)B-24 Liberators of the 491st Bomb Group, Second Bomb Division, drop supplies at LZ.N Knapheide-Klein Amerika (Little America) near Groesbeek on 18 September. Allied gliders can be seen littering the fields. (USAF)

B-24 Liberators of the 68th Bomb Squadron, 44th Bomb Group, 2nd Bomb Division flying at very low level drop their supplies to the ground troops in Holland. Aircraft left is WQ-E Corky. (USAF)

A Horsa with Polish troops about to land on the LZ.

Men of the Polish Brigade on the runway in England. Finally, on Thursday 21 September (D+4) at about 1715 two of the Polish Parachute Brigade's three battalions were dropped amidst heavy German fire, opposite the 1st Airborne Division's position on a new drop zone south of the Rhine near the village of Driel. Of the 1,511 Polish troops and around 100 tons of supplies and equipment carried, 998 troops and 69 tons of supplies are dropped in the vicinity of the prescribed zone. About 750 paratroops, three-quarters of those who had been dropped, are able to assemble that evening. Statistically speaking, the mission was only about 50 per cent effective.

The St. Elizabeth Hospital is surrounded by the wreckage of war, flying a huge Red Cross flag from the windows.

A British mortar platoon stop to pose with Dutch civilians.

A column of British vehicles stopped at Eindhoven while soldiers light up watched by Dutch children.

British troops dug in at Oosterbeek.

Sherman tanks of the Irish Guards on Hell's Highway.

Mass parachute drop.

Sherman tanks of XXX Corps crossing Nijmegen Bridge.

Arnhem from 20,000 feet on 19 September, as smoke from burning buildings drifts around the St Elizabeth hospital and museum.

British troops fight from house to house, street to street.

A German tank on fire.

British paratroopers take a quick cigarette break during the fighting.

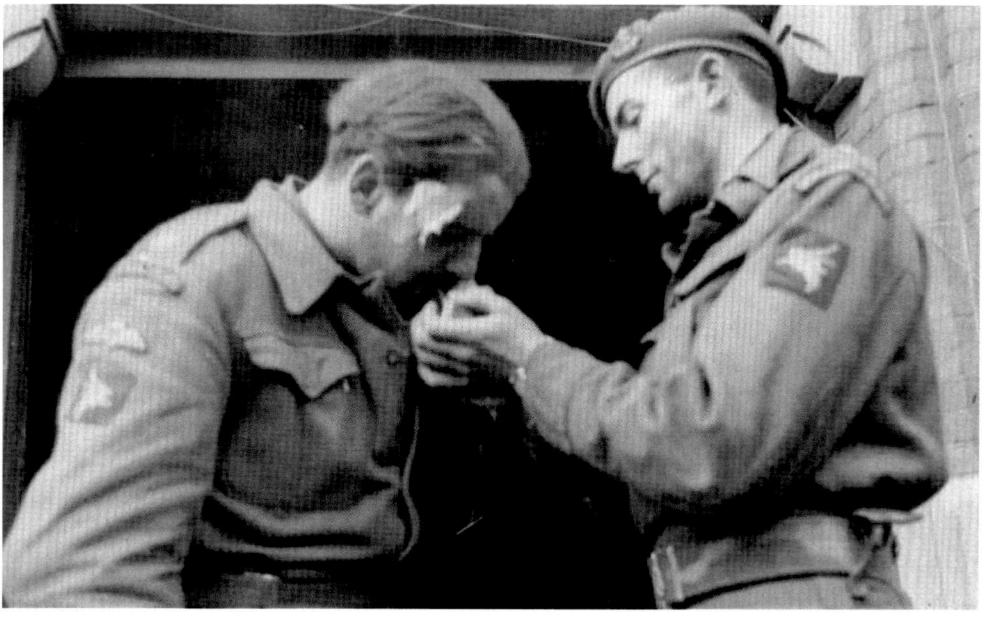

British soldiers fighting in the streets of Eindhoven.

British soldiers shrouded in smoke from burning houses in Eindhoven.

A column of British soldiers patrolling a Dutch street.

MEN OF ARNHEM

Wounded British soldiers smoking cigarettes under the watchful eye of a German guard as they are marched off into captivity.

A German soldier with his helmet covered in camouflage netting.

A Corporal in a mortar platoon loads his mortar before firing.

A captured wounded German soldier under guard.

A wireless operator and a Corporal try to decipher messages received over the net.

General Montgomery meets with some of his troops. From left to right: Major General A H S Adair, commander of the Guards Armoured Division, Montgomery, Lieutenant General B G Horrocks, commander of XXX Corps, and Major General G P B Roberts, commander of 11th Armoured Division.

German prisoners are put to work near the Hartenstein Hotel.

Defiance is etched on the face of a British soldier as the gallant defence at Oosterbeek nears the final outcome.

General Stanislav Sosabowsi and General Frederick Arthur Montague Browning, who typically is immaculately dressed.

British airborne troops stop to speak with Dutch civilians.

British soldiers are marched off into captivity.

A British soldier with his Lee Enfield rifle at the ready.

A British soldier listens in on his walkie-talkie.

Two British soldiers holed up in a Dutch street show the strain and fatigue of battle.

Troops suiting up before boarding their C-47.

A British soldier with his Sten gun perched on a shattered window sill in a narrow Dutch street.

Men of the Glider Pilot Regiment, one armed with a Sten gun, the other a revolver, emerge from a rubble strewn house in Arnhem.

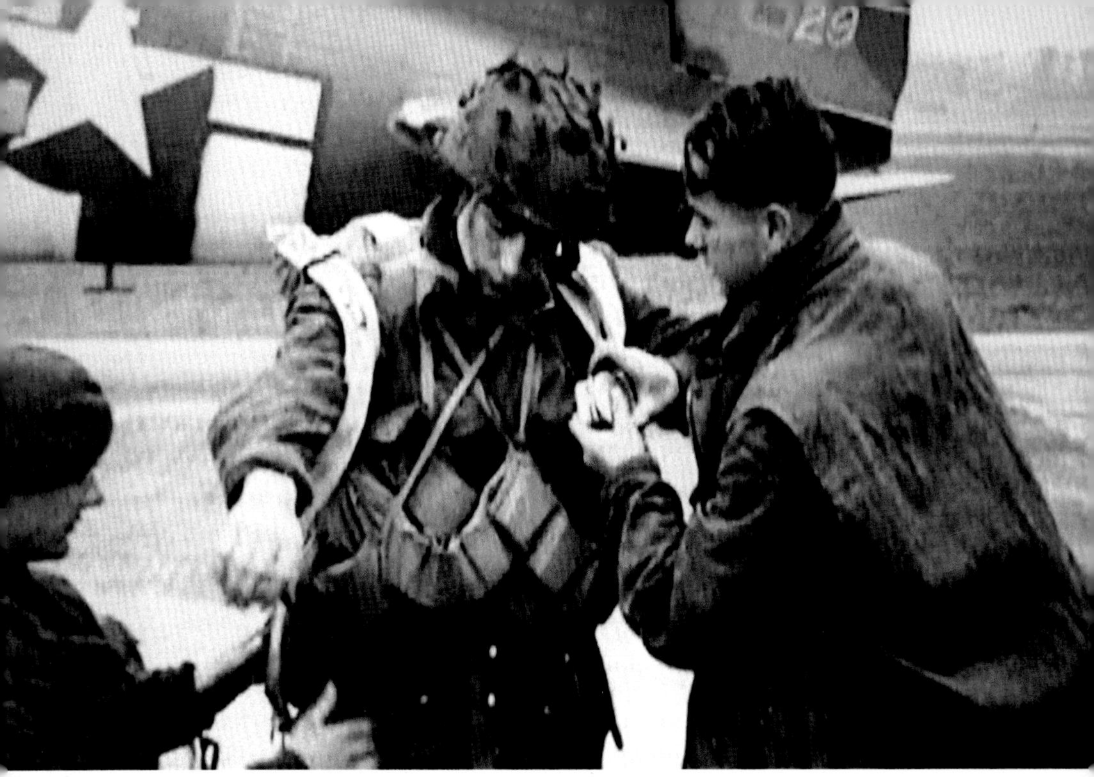

A British paratrooper gets suited up prior to take off for Holland.

A German officer with a captured British officer.

Captured Waffen SS snipers.

Glider Pilot Regiment personnel advance through a wrecked building.

German prisoners being marched off led by an unarmed Tommy.

British soldiers with arms raised in surrender after capture.

Above: A column of British paras are marched off with their arms on their heads in surrender.

Opposite page: Defiance in the face of defeat. Left to right: Sapper J. Dunney; Sapper C. Grier and Sapper R. Robb of the 1st Parachute Squadron Royal Engineers just after vacating the burning von Lunburgstirum School.

Below: German wounded being carried away from the fighting at Nijmegen Bridge on a stretcher.

Bowed but unbroken.

daybreak, 20 September. We were in a back garden behind the houses occupied by our men, when a small mortar bomb exploded beside us. We both bought it in the ankles and I had an extra bit in the right arm. We were bandaged up by the medical officer, Captain Jimmy Logan and put into the cellar of the Brigade HQ house.'

'Before long' continues Frost 'stretcher-bearers carried me to the RAP where Jimmy Logan made light of my wounds and I felt that after I rest I should be able to carry on. I sat on a box in the doorway of headquarters and vainly tried to pull myself together. I tried to swallow the whiskey that remained in my flask, but this made me feel like vomiting. After a bit I got some men to carry me on to a litter in one of the cellars and tried to rest. By now the pain had localized itself to my left ankle and right shinbone. I lay there rather dazed, hoping that the worst of the pain would lessen. Now I was given morphia and most of the pain went, enabling me to sleep.

'When I woke some bomb-happy cases were gibbering in the room. In the evening the Germans began to pound the building again. The doctors came to see me about the evacuation of the building in case of fire. The doctors said it would take an hour to get everybody out from the cellars and so I told him to be prepared to move with all those still able to fight from new positions. The building took fire several times and they fought the flames as best they could, but gradually the fire began to spread. One of the doctors came again to say that we would have to do something fairly quickly. I sent for Freddie Gough once more and told him to move. I gave him my own belt with revolver and compass and we wished each other luck.

'Later I heard shouts from above of: 'Don't shoot! Only wounded are here.' George Murray suddenly appeared, wanting to know what on earth was happening. Scarcely had he gone when I heard German voices in the passage outside and the sounds of the stretcher cases being moved out. Then Wicks came in. He said he was going to stay with me till they took me out and I was very glad to see him. He went away to get a stretcher, but while he was gone a German NCO rushed in intimating that we must get out as soon as possible. With the help of one of the bomb-happy cases he dragged me up the stairs to the door. I sat down among the stretcher-cases on the embankment leading to the bridge. Both sides laboured together to bring the wounded out and I saw that the Germans were driving off in our jeeps full of bandaged men. The prisoners we had taken were standing in a group nearby, not seemingly overjoyed at their liberation. Wicks found me again and put me on a stretcher, at the same time moving me alongside Doug Crawley. As one of the orderlies was giving me an injection of morphia for the journey, I said good-bye to Wicks and thanked him for all he had done for me. He was going to get back to our people as soon as the opportunity arose. The SS men were very polite and complimentary about the battle we had fought, but the bitterness I felt was unassuaged. No living enemy had beaten us. The battalion was unbeaten yet, but they could not have much chance with no ammunition, no rest and with no positions from which to fight. No body of men could have fought more courageously and tenaciously than the officers and men of the 1st Parachute Brigade at Arnhem Bridge. I remember saying to Douglas: 'Well, Doug, I'm afraid we haven't got away with it this time.'

'No, sir,' he replied, 'But we gave 'em a damn good run for their money.' 'We still could not believe that XXX Corps would fail to come to our rescue. It was difficult to feel that there was enough genuine opposition to stop them. It was desperately disappointing that having done everything we had been asked to do we were now prisoners. It was shaming, like being a malefactor, no longer free. For the moment all this was alleviated by the sympathy and even admiration of our captors. I could remember saying to someone when it did seem inevitable that we would fall into the hands of Hitler's SS, 'I don't think that this is going to be much of a pleasure.' We had all heard stories of them shooting their prisoners or herding them into burning buildings, but these men were kind, chivalrous and even comforting.' [41]

The active defence was taken over by 'Freddie' Gough's Reconnaissance Squadron, though Frost continued to do all he could to bear a share in the fighting. To report his presence and the situation at the bridge, Gough spoke to the Divisional Commander, using not wireless, for all the sets were out of order, but the Arnhem telephone system. The exchange was held and operated by Dutch patriots, but to make sure that any German who might be listening in would not be able to identify him, Gough referred to himself throughout as 'the man who goes in for funny weapons.' Like many other officers at the bridge, Gough inspired those around him with his confidence and humour.

With the death or capture of the last remaining troops on the eastern side of the ramp and with the loss of the school which dominated it, the collapse of the whole position, Frost now knew the end was near. For a time there was hope that a last stand might be made in a warehouse further to the

41 Doug Crawley received a bar to his Military Cross. Following his release from captivity in 1945 he met Doreen Specht, a Canadian and Red Cross ambulance driver, the two would later marry. After serving in Palestine, he spent four years as an instructor at Sandhurst, followed by three years at Staff College before renewing his acquaintance, in Trieste in 1954, with the Loyal Regiment. Crawley then served in the Korean War as a staff officer and later was Second-in-Command of the 1st Loyals in Malaya, where he was Mentioned in Despatches. Promoted to Lieutenant Colonel, he continued to lead this Battalion in Germany. Douglas Crawley retired from the army in 1975. He died in 1986. In tribute to him, John Frost wrote, 'His decorations for gallantry only barely reflect his conduct in battle. He was imperturbable in trouble and great fun to be with at all times. His old friends and comrades will miss him greatly but will always be thankful that we knew him.'

Frost spent the remainder of the war in captivity at Oflag IX-A/H at Spangenburg, near Kassel, but after his ankle wound had opened up again he was transferred to the PoW hospital at Obermassfeldt. It was here in March that the spearheads of General Patton's 3rd US Army arrived and Frost was freed and returned home. For his part in Arnhem he received a Bar to his DSO. Shortly after resuming command of the 2nd Battalion, before he led them to Palestine, Frost met Jean MacGregor Lyle, a widow and YMCA worker who had been driving tea vans for the 1st Airborne Division and they married on 31 December 1947, Frost's 35th birthday. Later they had a son and daughter. Frost attended the Staff College at Camberley and became GSO-2 of the 52nd Lowland Division. He spent two years in Malaya during the emergency, acting as GSO-1 of the 17th Ghurkha Division. From 1955-1957 he commanded the Support Weapons Wing of the School of Infantry at Netheravon, after which north; but at dusk this building was set alight and within a few minutes was burning fiercely. An hour or so afterwards the wireless operator in Major Dennis Munford's observation post, which he had had to move twice already that day, signalled to the 1st Light Regiment's Headquarters at Oosterbeek: 'We have been blown off the top storey. We are quite OK. We have killed three or four hundred Germans for the loss of thirty. We need more small arms ammunition.' It was the last signal which the regiment's operator at Oosterbeek received from Arnhem.

As resistance began to fail on Wednesday the defence concentrated their last gasp at Brigade HQ. The building had over 200 wounded men crammed into the cellar attended by two Royal Army Medical Corps doctors, Captains Jimmy Logan DSO and D. Wright MC who did particularly fine work in dreadful conditions and remained with them to the end, which came quickly after the house was set on fire and the flames threatened to engulf the building. The structure was so badly damaged that it was in danger of collapsing. Men 'were almost lying on top of each other' as the suffocating smoke poured down the steps. The two Medical Officers advised Gough that unless a truce could be arranged for the wounded to be evacuated into German care they would be burned alive. Staff Sergeant Godfrey Freeman wrote: 'We no longer have any means to put it out. In our cellar there is an all-pervading stench of blood, faeces and urine, the only latrine being an oil drum brim full, with faeces floating on top. Upstairs small arms ammunition is exploding in the fire. From time to time I caught glimpses of Colonel Frost as he lay, white as wax, issuing orders and instructions. A visit from a German interpreter to enquire whether he was prepared to surrender proved fruitless. He was sent back with a message that Colonel Frost would accept unconditional surrender from the other side. From then on it was only a matter of time. Some while later he acknowledged defeat and the bitterness in his voice was unmistakable.'

With Frost's consent Gough arranged a ceasefire, but before doing so, he ordered the non-2nd Battalion members of the bridge defence to scatter

he commanded the 44th Parachute Brigade (TA) in London. He then returned to the 52nd Lowland Division as their commander, before being appointed to the post of GOC in Malta and Libya and later Commander Malta Land Forces. In 1968 Major-General Frost retired from the military. He settled down to rear beef cattle at Northend Farm at Liphook, Hampshire. The farm was initially derelict, but John and Jean set about restoring it and were eventually able to preside over a good herd. Frost was encouraged by his old friend Freddie Gough, who had since become an MP, to take up a career in local politics. In 1976 during the filming of 'A Bridge Too Far' Frost acted as a military consultant. When he was asked if he would like Arnhem bridge being named after him, he was unsure whether he should accept, but made up his mind when Gough told him 'Unless you have your name put on the plaque, it will not mean anything to anybody and will be ignored and forgotten in no time. It is the same with all memorials'. In 1977 the reconstructed Bridge was christened the John Frost Brug in honour of those who had participated in its defence. Frost was appointed Deputy Lieutenant for West Sussex in 1982. Two years' earlier his novel 'A Drop Too Many' was published. This was followed in 1983 by '2 PARA Falklands: The Battalion At War'. In it Frost was highly critical of the way that the operation had been planned; his principal argument being, that the operation, not unlike Arnhem, relied upon an outstanding performance by the troops to make up for numerous gaping holes in the tactical and logistical elements. In 1991 he wrote his autobiography, *'Nearly There'*. John Frost died in 1993.

north into Arnhem and try to make their way back to the rest of the Division at Oosterbeek. Almost everyone was captured in the attempt, however Sergeant Eric Simpson succeeded. For the remainder of the battle he fought near to Divisional HQ at the Hartenstein Hotel, but when the withdrawal across the Rhine began he was positioned too far forward to be evacuated and so became a prisoner of war. [42]

Two orderlies carrying a Red Cross flag walked out of the cellars towards the Germans to ask for a few hours' truce. The enemy immediately agreed; and for the first time in nearly three days there was a momentary release from the fear of pain or death as the Germans took the wounded to captivity.

'An officer carrying a white flag came out of the school' recalled Gefreiter Alfred Ringsdorf. 'He wanted a truce just for the school. I ordered the firing to cease. All units were given this order and gradually all firing stopped completely. I stood up and went forward to meet this man and he gave me cigarettes. He asked me to take him to our commander. I had him taken to the Battalion Command Post by one of my men. There it was agreed that all the dead and the wounded would be handed over to us but on condition that the German prisoners also be surrendered to us. In fact the English had requested that the artillery fire be stopped because they had German prisoners in the school. They agreed to our terms, however. It was then that I went inside the school and brought out all these old veterans, paymasters, administration soldiers etc. I spoke with some of the English soldiers. They seemed very depressed which was not surprising. During the truce we joked a bit with the English. We laughed and we said: 'Prima, Tommies, prima gekampft!' (Great, Tommies, great fighting!) After all we were all soldiers and had no reason to be unfriendly.'

'Down the cellar steps comes the first SS soldier, sub-machine-gun at the ready' wrote Staff Sergeant Godfrey Freeman. 'In English he enquires, 'Are you British or American?' Unknown to us, the American Airborne had sworn to avenge the massacre of their comrades at Ste-Mere-Église and were reputed [incorrectly] to have taken no prisoners. 'We're British' came the reply. 'Tommy' he cried with a huge grin of combined relief and apparent affection, 'Tommy, Tommy.' Doors were ripped off to make stretchers. Mixed pairs of SS men and Airborne struggled together to lug the wounded from certain death. A British

42 Thereafter he was imprisoned at Stalag XIIA, Limburg, Stalag VIIIC at Sagan and finally, Stalag IXC at Bad Orb. Though the end of the war was near, their fate appeared to be very much in the balance. After a week at this camp, amidst rumours that Germans had executed prisoners and that their present meagre rations may not be enough to keep them alive, Eric and a few colleagues decided to escape over the wire. The attempt was a success and travelling by night he began to make his way towards the American lines. Desperately short of provisions, Simpson broke into a Burgermeister's house in the hope of finding some food, but instead stole a signed copy of *Mein Kampf*, which is presently on display at the Airborne Forces Museum, in Aldershot. He succeeded in reaching American troops, but by this time he was very weak, suffering from lack of food, lice and dysentery. He admitted that he would have been better advised to have remained in the camp rather than to have escaped. When he left for Arnhem on 17 September, he weighed 10½ stone, but this was reduced to just 6 by the time of his liberation. Eric Simpson died on 6 August 2001. He was father to four daughters and a son, Nigel to whom thanks are due for this story.

medical officer was directing operations with a vehemence that struck even the SS with awe.' [43]

Gough stayed behind with the paratroopers who would carry on the fight until the bitter end. When German infantry entered the remains of Brigade HQ to carry off the wounded, the British stood aside, however some German elements did not fully appreciate the definition of a truce and proceeded to use it to locate their men in positions closer to and even cutting into the much shrunk perimeter. Some German soldiers approached the British jeeps, which had somehow escape the battle largely unscathed and though Gough ordered them to back away he was powerless to argue with their assertion, truthful or not, that the vehicles were needed to take the wounded to the St. Elizabeth Hospital. When the fighting resumed and the defence was finally broken during the night, the defenders tried to scatter into Arnhem, though with very little success. Gough made for the local waterworks and upon hearing German voices in the vicinity he burrowed his way beneath a woodpile, however his left boot remained visible and he was dragged out by it and captured. Completely exhausted, he surveyed the faces of the men who had captured him and found that they were little more than boys, which prompted him to burst out laughing. Shortly after, a German major asked to see Gough, understanding him to be the commander at the bridge. The officer said 'I wish to congratulate you and your men. You are gallant soldiers. I fought at Stalingrad and it is obvious that you British have a great deal of experience in street fighting.' To which Gough simply replied, 'No. This was our first effort. We'll be much better next time.' [44]

During the truce it was seen that German troops were breaking this peace and moving troops to fresh positions, closer to the airborne men. Major Tatham-Warter sent Captain Hoyer-Millar to protest. Hoyer-Millar could speak German and as the battalion's Intelligence Officer in North Africa, he was able to put this skill to good use when interrogating captured troops. In Italy by the time of their departure he had managed to master the local language. Hoyer-Millar located an English speaking German officer dressed in a long dark leather coat and he warned him that if his men continued in that manner then they would be fired on. The officer insisted on only saying that there was no hope of them

43 Quoted in *'Victory In Europe'* by Julian Thompson.

44 Freddie Gough remained in captivity until his escape in 1945. By 1947 he had been promoted to Lieutenant Colonel and had joined the Parachute Regiment where he commanded the 11th (8th Middlesex (DCO)) Parachute Battalion of the Territorial Army, He held the post until the following year, earning the Territorial Efficiency Decoration in 1948. Eventually becoming a full Colonel, he was Honorary Colonel of the Sussex Yeomanry 1959-63 and Honorary Colonel of the 16th (Volunteer) Independent Company The Parachute Regiment 1952-74, with whom he was awarded a Bar to his Territorial Decoration. Whilst maintaining a prominent position within Lloyds up until 1970, he was also the Trustee of Airborne Forces Security Fund, Vice President of the Lloyds Branch of the British Legion, Chairman of the Royal Aero Club from 1958-68 and President of the Federation of Sussex Industries from 1964-70. He took an interest in politics and was President of the South Lewisham Conservative Association and 1951-71 was Chairman of the Horsham Division Conservative Association, before becoming the Member of Parliament for Horsham in 1971. Having briefly occupied the posts of Governor of the Cutty Sark Society, Prime Warden of the Fishmongers Company and becoming a Trustee of the Maritime Trust, Freddie Gough retired from Parliament in 1974. He died on 19 September 1977 aged 76.

being relieved and that they should surrender, but Hoyer-Millar disagreed and informed him that they fully expected their ground forces to arrive at any moment.

When the last wounded soldier was taken away the battle began again - there were only about 150 men capable of fighting - and it was decided to split into two parties which at dawn on Thursday would occupy a group of ruined buildings on the river bank. But by midnight the defence was 'greatly weakened.' The 2nd Battalion, commanded by Major Tatham-Warter, whose conduct was exemplary even amid so much gallantry, had suffered heavy casualties; so had its supporting troops, among whom must be numbered the signallers fighting as infantrymen under Captain Bernard Briggs. Ammunition was running short and the key house commanding the north end of the bridge had been burnt down. The Germans posted in houses further back nearer the town, though making no attempt to infiltrate, kept the whole area of the defence under more or less continuous small arms and automatic fire. By now those of the defenders who were not beneath the bridge were holding slit trenches hastily dug in the gardens of the houses from which they had been driven by fire. The spirit of the defence is best exemplified by the following wireless dialogue which was overheard.

Captain Briggs: The position is untenable. Can I have permission to withdraw?

Frost: If it is untenable you may withdraw to your original position.

Captain Briggs: Everything is comfortable. I am now going in with bayonets and grenades.

The final stand was made, first in a warehouse and then underneath the bridge, the total number still capable of fighting being about 110 men and five or six officers. The position was shelled by a German tank and armoured car, but they were unable to hit that part of the underside of the bridge where the defence was holding out. It was at this juncture that Lieutenant Jack Grayburn commanding No.2 Platoon, 'A' Company, whose valour earned him a Victoria Cross which he did not live to receive, led a series of counter-attacks, in one of which Germans laying charges to blow the bridge were killed and the charges torn out. The day before, when the enemy had renewed its attacks, which increased in intensity, the house that Grayburn's men held was vital to the defence of the bridge. All attacks were repulsed, due to his valour and skill in organising and encouraging his men, until eventually the house was set on fire and had to be evacuated. Grayburn, although the wound in his shoulder was obviously giving him great pain, had then taken command of the elements of all units including the remainder of his company and re-formed them into a fighting force. He spent the night organising a defensive position to cover the approaches to the bridge.

Now, he extended his defence by a series of fighting patrols which prevented the enemy gaining access to the houses in the vicinity, the occupation of which would have prejudiced the defence of the bridge. This forced the enemy to bring up tanks which brought Grayburn's positions under such heavy fire that he was forced to withdraw to an area further north. The enemy now attempted to lay demolition charges under the bridge and the situation was critical. Realising this, Grayburn organised and led a fighting patrol which drove the enemy off temporarily and gave time for the fuses to be removed. He was again wounded, this time in the back, but refused to be evacuated. Finally, an enemy tank, against which Grayburn had no defence, approached so close to his position that it became untenable. He then stood up in full view of the tank and personally directed the withdrawal of his men to the main defensive perimeter to which he had been ordered. He was killed by machine-gun fire from the tank that he had stood in front of. His body fell into the Rhine and was not discovered until 1948. His Victoria Cross citation had these words:

'From the evening of 17th September until the night of 20th September, a period of over three days, Lieutenant Grayburn led his men with supreme gallantry and determination. Although in pain and weakened by his wounds, short of food and without sleep, his courage never flagged. There is no doubt that, had it not been for this Officer's inspiring leadership and personal bravery, the Arnhem Bridge could never have been held for this time.'[45]

Thirty-one year old Sergeant Neville Leonard Ashley MM who commanded 2 Platoon's I Section was dug into the ramp of the bridge, near the steps which led down to street level, when he was shot through the hip by a sniper's bullet. It was not a new experience for Ashley, who had been awarded the Military Medal by King George VI for his action on 14 July 1943 when he manned a Bren gun in a most exposed position, South of Catania in Sicily, in order to allow his section to dig in. During this period he was continually being sniped. On one occasion he located an enemy machine gun post taking up a position from which to engage his comrades. With complete disregard for personal safety he moved his gun wall forward and destroyed the crew. Later having shot a German soldier at short range he went out and brought him into the RAP as he was in danger of being burned alive. This was a world away from the life he had led between the wars. Born in Hale-Barnes, Cheshire on 26 June 1913, he led a typical rural life, working for various farms and small shops in the area. On 5 May 1930, at the age of 16, Neville enlisted in the Territorial Army and was assigned to the 7th Battalion of the Cheshire Regiment, where he achieved the rank of Corporal before being discharged in May 1934. Thereafter he married the sweetheart of his life, Isabella Cottingham of Hale and before the outbreak of hostilities in 1939 was father to two daughters, Margaret and Sheila. On 2 February 1939 Ashley rejoined his old battalion, who were later a part of the British Expeditionary Force when the German attack commenced in May 1940. He was involved in several engagements in Belgium and France during the retreat to Dunkirk and it was from the nearby beaches at La Panne that he and the remainder of his company were evacuated aboard the Dutch

45 Grayburn was promoted to Captain. After hearing of his death his wife Marcelle, who was a secretary at the HQ staff when Jack Grayburn met and married her in 1942 and with whom he had a son, John, returned to her native Scotland where she married again, but her own life was also tragically cut short by leukaemia. Plaques dedicated to Jack Grayburn's memory can be found in the Parish Church at Chalfont St. Giles and on the Hong Kong and Shanghai Banking Corporation war memorial in Queen's Street, Hong Kong. Thanks are due to Chiltern Rugby Club website for the details of this account.

ship, *Horst,* which unloaded its human cargo at Margate. Ashley was discharged from service for a second time, but in January 1943 he re-enlisted in the Army Air Corps Returning to England after the action in Sicily, Ashley was promoted to Sergeant and given command of I Section under the command of the indomitable Jack Grayburn.

Out of ammunition and under heavy fire from all sides Ashley led the remaining five men of his Section, accompanied by one German prisoner, down the side of the ramp and into a chamber beneath and built into the bridge. A Tiger tank arrived and at point blank range proceeded to fire several shells at the door behind which the paratroopers had sought shelter. German engineers equipped with flame-throwers closed in but first threw in smoke grenades to flush out the now blinded men. The prisoner that the Section held offered to go outside offer their surrender if the German troops would hold their fire. This was accepted and the six paratroopers, all of whom now carried wounds, emerged into the open where they were disarmed and told to rest on the grassy side of the ramp. Here the Germans treated their wounds and handed a small barrel of beer around to quench their thirst. [46]

'They used Tiger tanks and 75mm SP guns and positioned them to the south east where we could not get at them' recalls Captain Mackay. 'The building now was considerably weakened, particularly the roof and this time their efforts were successful. More fires were started in the roof and by 1500 hours these fires were out of control. The only place left to us was the basement, particularly as at 1530 hours our store of explosives in the upper floor was exploded when the fire reached it and blew off the whole of the top story. It was obvious that we could not hold out much longer. The situation then was that out of our total strength, at the start of the action, of 50 men, three had been killed and 24 sufficiently wounded to be of no combatant use. Most of the others had been less severely wounded at one time or another.'

'When the two German tanks were brought up onto the bridge' recalls Lance Sergeant Padfield 'and started to blast away with their 88mm guns they had a direct hit on the front of the school and the roof was set alight. Joe Simpson and Paddy Neville were killed, the rest of us were OK and we went into the basement. It was becoming obvious that we should move out. Twiggy Hazelwood was getting worse by the hour and sure enough another direct hit and the school was well alight. We got the wounded downstairs and I went round all the rooms to be sure everyone was out. Joe and Paddy were limbless bodies, otherwise everyone was out. We tore down doors to put the wounded on and went out the way we had come in. As we made across to a wall we came under fire. John Bretherton was killed as he was getting over it. Twiggy got a machine gun burst up the side of his body as we were lifting him over the wall, but he was still clinging on to life. We were all eventually over and the bank gave a little protection. One of the wounded was a Major Lewis. He must have come into the school with the signaller on the first night. I don't know when

46 Like a great many others, Sergeant Ashley was later sent to Stalag XVIIIC at Markt Pongau, in Austria. Two more children, Jenny and Graham were born to the Ashley family. After a short illness, Neville Ashley MM passed away on 17 March 1993. Thanks are due to Robert and Jenny Shaw, Neville Ashley's daughter.

he got wounded but he was the company commander of 'C' Company 3 Battalion. The next 20 minutes were phenomenal! We were caught in an enfilade of fire and airbursts. A stray bullet hit Charlie Grier; it made a hole in his helmet but didn't mark his head. Billy Marr had his pack severed from his back but with no injury. Major Lewis told us that we should surrender and that we should all take pride in our performance. We took the bolts out of our weapons and threw them away; we left the weapons where we were. Sapper Butterworth put a white handkerchief on the end of his rifle and went forward waving it. As he was walking forward a machine gunner opened up and hit him in the legs, his German officer drew his pistol and shot the machine gunner. He then told us to come forward, saying, 'You are very brave, but very foolish'. We considered we were unfortunate.

'We were then led off, with our hands up, through the streets of Arnhem and held in the basement of some house. We were prisoners of war. Our wounded had been taken away from us when we were captured. That night we had a few snatches of sleep. I say snatches because just as you were nicely off, they wanted you to move to another room or another house, just to be bloody-minded.'

In the afternoon Lance Corporal John Baxter was handed a situation report which was to be sent to England by carrier pigeon. 'When I dropped on the Sunday I had a container tied to my chest which contained a pigeon, together with a small bag of grain; its only ration until it got back to England. I then had to rewrite the message on to special thin rice paper and attach it within a small cylinder fixed to the bird's leg. In order to launch the bird successfully I had to go to the upper floor of the house, where the roof had been blown away leaving just broken rafters reaching for the sky. The report gave the situation as it affected us, ending with an optimistic statement 'Our morale is high and we can hold out forever'. I then launched the bird, but instead of flying off it settled on a broken rafter. This attracted enemy machine gun and rifle fire as they tried to shoot the pigeon. Bullets were coming thick and fast, but I had to get the bird on its way, so I picked up a section of copper aerial, about five foot in length and prodded the bird until it flew off. It was with a feeling of envy that I watched it safely head for England. There was an end to this episode, for when I returned home after having been released from the Prisoner of War camp, my wife related to me a radio broadcast from the BBC about our last ditch stand at Arnhem. It was just about word for word that which I had written. It felt good to know that my pigeon had made it back.'

'It was a relief when darkness fell,' recalled Arthur Hendy 'but we were soon under attack again. This time two enemy tanks came along the road. They fired at both sides of the road, although none of the buildings opposite were unoccupied, the tanks continued firing as they moved past us and started firing at the only other building by our forces on the opposite side of the road. Although we didn't know who they were, after each attack we would shout out our old North African battle cry, *'Whoa Mahomet'*. The following enemy infantry were easy targets as burning buildings illuminated the whole area although by now, owing to the involvement of the tanks we were now engaging the enemy from the cellar. When we returned to our position as daylight broke the latest casualties were taken to the cellar. We still expected that we would be relieved; the room which Malley and I had occupied had been completely destroyed by the tanks. 'Boxer' had set up the wireless again on the stairs. Ammunition was now getting short; the extra 'B' Troop had brought on the trolley was nearly exhausted. As I looked into one of the rooms, I saw Major Lewis, his face lathered, having a shave. Later on that day in a minor attack he was wounded and Malley and I carried him down to the cellar.'

During the final day of the fighting Bill Murray of the Medium Machine Gun Platoon, Support Company, 2nd Parachute Battalion was caught in heavy fire and had his leg blown off. Despite coming under intense fire, 27-year old Private William Joseph Ralphs went out to collect his comrade, who was brought under cover and survived. Ralphs was recommended for the Military Medal for this action, but in the event it was refused. [47]

'After quitting the Headquarters building' recalls Lance Corporal John Baxter 'another soldier and I began to look for somewhere we could take cover from the heavy shellfire, some of which was from the guns of the Second Army. Eventually we found an opening to a cellar, which gave us some cover and a place to catch up on some much needed sleep, for I don't remember sleeping since we landed. We were later joined by an officer and a number of men. The next thing I remember was this officer saying, 'It's all over chaps, you'll have to come out with your hands up.' Before I obeyed this order I had enough time to activate a Gammon bomb, which when disturbed would erupt in a violent explosion, my final defiant act. We were led into a square and made to stand facing a wall, with three machine guns trained on us. I honestly thought that we were about to be shot and I said to the fellow next to me: 'What a way to go and we can't do a bloody thing about it.' He must have thought as much as I did, he didn't say anything, but he looked very pale. I just felt very angry that it had to end like this. Surprise, surprise, all they wanted to do was search our rear pockets for any weapons. After the search was over, a group of us were standing together when an English speaking German sergeant major came up to us and said, 'If you would like to give me your number, rank and names I will make it my duty to see that this information reaches the Red Cross.' We then began asking him what his different medal ribbons were for. He told us of each campaign the medal was for and finally he said, 'And this is for the Russian Front.'

'My Liverpool mate then said, 'You dropped a bollock there didn't you?'

'A bollock' he said, 'What is a bollock?'

'The Germans showed us great respect, for we had given them a hard fight, they were not the second class troops we had been told to expect but soldiers of the ninth and tenth SS Panzer Divisions. I subsequently heard that one of their officers had told one of our own officers, that we had inflicted casualties on his men at a ratio of six to one.

'We were held overnight in a church, so we were able to sleep sitting in the pews. The next morning we were herded into closed wagons, but not before they made us remove our boots, which accompanied the guards, yes

47 Thanks are due to Stuart Holdcroft for this account.

you've guessed it; none of us got our own boots back. Our journey into Germany was not the most comfortable that I have known, nor was it the quickest. We were aboard that train for two weeks before reaching our destination, a holding camp. For a few days after our arrival batches of Airborne lads continued to arrive and when they did we crowded as close to the gates as possible in the hope of catching sight of someone we knew. On this occasion, sticking out like a sore thumb amid the red berets was a sailor. After he had been interrogated we asked what he was doing here. 'It's a long story,' he said. 'Actually I'm still on leave, I had a pal in the RAF and he was dropping supplies to you lads so I went along for the ride. We were shot down and here I am with still three more days of my leave to go.' [48]

During the day more tanks appeared which now fired at will at the ruined buildings. Nothing could be done to stop them, but infantry attacks were still repulsed. Three Bren gun carriers tried to break through from the west with supplies and ammunition but two were destroyed and the third forced to turn back. The defenders in one house were forced out but continued in hand to hand fighting under the spans of the bridge. By 1430 they had been driven out but continued to counter-attack to prevent the Germans setting demolition charges on the piers. To the defenders resisting in the school, the 2nd Battalion seemed finished, but then a Tiger Tank and self-propelled gun opened fire on the school itself, which soon caught fire. Captain Mackay finally had to give the order to evacuate it, by then there were only fourteen men left. The 31 wounded were surrendered and the remainder, with Captain Mackay, burst into the open where two tanks and 50 Germans were lined up. Firing from the hip they split into groups and ran into gardens behind ruined walls.

'By midday it was obvious that we could not hold out' wrote Arthur Hendy 'and when armour started to appear Captain Mackay gave the order to pull out and make our way to the 2nd Battalion position. 'A' troop's Bren was still covering the ramp and footpath and was manned by Corporal 'Canadian' Joe Simpson whose large moustache grew up the sides of his face to join his hair. He had already been awarded the American Silver Star and British MiD during the North African Campaign. 'Joe' was not a Canadian; he had been born in Tavistock in Devon but returned to England from Canada at the outbreak of the war. Joe was supported by Sapper Johnny Bretherton from St. Helens, Lancashire. The road was still covered by 'B' Troop's Bren manned by Lance Corporal Danny 'Paddy' Neville who came from Southern Ireland. He was supported by Sapper Steve Carr, a Scot. Getting the badly wounded from the cellar was difficult, so we carried them up on mattresses and then transferred them onto doors. During the evacuation we used side door which was out of view of the enemy. We encountered a problem as there was a high wall covering the side of the school, which with the combined weight of the door and the wounded man made it very hard work. It took four men to get them over the wall. The pull out was quite orderly and Lieutenant Simpson's final orders to Malley and me were to destroy the remaining weapons. The last man to get wounded was the man who had been wounded in the first

48 John Baxter died in 2006. Thanks are due to Tom Manning for this story.

attack. One of the men carrying him was Johnny Bretherton who was killed. He had only nine minutes before come down from his Bren position. Another one of 'B' Troop, Norman Butterworth, was mortally wounded caring for the wounded.

'I could hear the Bren still engaging the enemy when the whole building shook. Malley and I were covered in debris and I was completely deaf and had difficulty in breathing and it took some time to clear. The roof was completely gone. Malley and I made our way through the rubble and we found Steve Carr bleeding from his nose, mouth and ears so we moved him into the garden. We could see two tanks on the ramp and they had now turned their attention to the house opposite. We started pulling the rubbish and found Joe Simpson as we pulled him clear he was still grasping the Bren. I carried his upper body and Malley his feet and laid him on the stairs. I took his helmet off but it was obvious he was dead. We then went to find Danny Neville but there was so much debris we were unable to find him. Whilst we were searching Eric Mackay returned to the building with the news that the main party had been captured. He suggested that we should cross the road and make our own way through the rear garden to 2nd Battalion. First we sheltered in the building previously occupied by 'A' Troop, which was by now just a shell. We had decided to cross the road one at a time and I was the first to cross. As I ran into the rear garden I ran into a party of the enemy. They were engrossed in their tanks destroying the houses and did not see me and I fired a quick burst. They dived for cover and did not return fire. I quickly made my way forward but could see Captain Mackay or Malley and decided not to wait for them and quickly ran in the other direction to make my way out of the garden. I had only gone about 50 yards when I saw a strong force of enemy who were searching the houses. I lay behind the garden wall and the first of the enemy passed me and indicated to me to stand up. As they marched me back towards the building that had been occupied by the unit we had been shouting *'Whoa Mahomet'*. I saw Lieutenant Barnett who was badly wounded being supported by one of his men. They were from Brigade Defence Platoon who we had worked with on many occasions. The other man told me that as well as the Defence Platoon, some of HQ of 1 Squadron fought in the building.

'It was while he was talking to me that one of the escorts hit me with a rifle on the back, he was instantly reprimanded by an officer. He told me to take my hands off of my head and called a man who could speak English. The first words he spoke were 'do you need medical attention?' I was bleeding from the mouth from my old boxing wounds and my clothes were blooded from those we had been carrying apart from a few burns on my legs, I was not wounded. The interpreter indicated for me to stay with the wounded. We were loaded onto lorries, the floors of which were covered with straw and I stayed with them for two days. I was able to help feed the badly wounded then I and a slightly wounded 2nd Battalion man who was able to tell me what had happened to the rest of the Squadron. One section had gone to the railway bridge with the 'C' Company; the remainder of the troop had with our HQ troop, fought on the other side of the ramp and had been responsible for destroying the pill-box on the Bridge. Only the two injured men had failed to reach the Bridge.' [49]

Looking at his men, exhausted and filthy and unshaven, with their shirts cut open revealing blood-soaked field-dressings, but ready even now to go on fighting after more than 72 hours without sleep, after more than 24 hours without food and 12 hours without water, Mackay thought to himself that he would never have to give them the order - 'This position will be held to the last round and the last man'. He felt instinctively it would be. But now there were no other troops left on his side of the bridge and the school was no longer inhabitable. 'It was like a sieve,' he says. 'Wherever you looked you could see daylight... Splattered everywhere was blood; it lay in pools in the rooms, it covered the smocks of the defenders and ran in small rivulets down the stairs... The only clean things in the school were the weapons.' The building had begun to collapse and the heat was intense. And so at last he gave the order to evacuate it. Outside he came face to face with 50 Germans beside two yellow Mk III tanks. He stood in line with his men firing from the hip, 'continuously till the ammunition ran out'. The survivors split up into little groups and ran away into the gardens behind the ruined walls. Of those Sappers the ten who could move made a dash for it, each with a Bren and one magazine, the last left. All were killed or captured. Mackay, himself, removed his badges of rank, destroyed his identity card and fell to the ground completely exhausted. After a few minutes some German soldiers walked up to him. He pretended to be dead. 'They were evidently not satisfied' said Mackay 'and a discussion arose. Suddenly a private ran a bayonet into me which came to rest with a jar against my pelvis. When he withdrew it, the most part, I got to my feet. They were evidently still very frightened of us and I was forced to walk with my hands clasped on top of my head. I was led past the place where we had our last battle a few minutes earlier. I was pleased to see several still, grey forms and two more dying noisily in the gutter. There seemed to be masses of Germans everywhere with tanks and self-propelled guns at every corner. [50]

'We were taken to the nearby church for the night' recalled Len Hoare 'and

49 It took Arthur Hendy over 60 years to record these events. 'Joe 'Canadian' Simpson, 'Paddy' Neville, Johnny Bretherton and Norman Butterworth sacrificed their lives for their comrades. They were in their twenties and three of them had children, which made their sacrifice even greater. I did not return to Arnhem for 15 years. I could not trace the farm or the lad that helped us or any of the Dutch party I took to 2nd Battalion. In 1946 I met Steve Carr who was still serving in the Army. He said the shell burst had hurt his lungs but otherwise he had not been wounded. I also met Joe Malley and I asked him why he did not follow me across the road. He said both he and Eric Mackay only heard one burst of fire and thought that I had been hit and decided to cross at a different point. The bodies of Danny and those buried in the remainder of the school and have never been found. Their names are not shown at Oosterbeek or Arnhem but are miles way at Nijmegen. In 1963 I met Major Lewis when we were invited to the War Office in London. Amongst those present were Lieutenant Colonel John Frost and General Wilhelm Bittrich.' Arthur Hendy died on 19 February 2007.

50 Captain Mackay was taken with Captain Simpson of the Royal Engineers and two corporals to a prison camp at Emmerich just inside the German border. At 1000 the next day, Friday, with the silk map Mackay had managed to retain, they planned their escape. The corporals prised loose the bars of the cookhouse and that evening they got out, followed by fourteen other prisoners. The party travelled across country towards the Rhine. The next day was spent in a hut on the river bank and that night they stole a boat from a barge and set off down the river towards Nijmegen which they hoped had been captured by the British and Americans advancing from the south. They reached Nijmegen in the early hours of Saturday the 23rd and a few hours later were at XXX Corps HQ.

treated as well as could be expected. Next day the walking wounded were marched to the hospital, all very cheerful, singing *'Lili Marlene'* with the German guards joining in and the Dutch women clapping. That is until an SS Officer appeared with a camera team. He threatened to shoot the guards as well as us if we didn't stop. He was greeted with raspberries and two fingers from those that could. We reached the hospital and joined a queue, hundreds of yards long. Eventually reached a temporary operating theatre with about six tables, it was like a barber's shop. Six on the tables being put out with ether by British doctors, German and Dutch doctors doing the operating, British medical orderlies doing the dressing and the next six customers sitting on chairs waiting their turn. It was a gruesome sight as some of the wounded had gangrene and had to have a lot of flesh cut away.' [51]

In the end the gallant remnant at the Bridge were dispersed or captured. Every time a patrol went out it suffered casualties and with each hour the situation became more and more hopeless. There was no more ammunition, there had been no food for a long time and hardly a man but was wounded. The very ground on which the defenders stood or crouched was constantly seared by flames from the burning houses about it and no man could remain there and live. A group of men tried to break out to the west to get back to Oosterbeek but most of them were killed or wounded as they ran through the smoking streets and the rest turned back. Every street was 'well-covered by machine-gun fire and almost every building in the neighbourhood seemed to be held by the enemy' who, during the cease-fire, had infiltrated three complete companies of Panzer grenadiers into the British position. By then only about 150 men were still capable of fighting and it was decided that these should be split up into two parties which, at dawn the following morning, would concentrate in a group of ruined buildings by the river bank. There was no food at all in the area now and no water. There seemed no longer any hope of relief, no chance of escape or victory.

Captain Hoyer-Millar said that on that final night, with the battalion crammed into a tiny perimeter and flanked by burning buildings and being constantly shelled, he was as scared at that time than at any other in his life. However he said that a strange feeling prevailed of 'exhilaration mingled with pride and bitterness'. In spite of everything, they had held out for three whole days and four nights and yet they remained unbroken and alive. But Hoyer-Millar knew that this would not last long and, though they could withstand the night's shelling in their slit trenches, daylight would see an onslaught of infantry and armour that their hopelessly low ammunition could not hold at

51 When it was his turn Len Hoare was examined by the medics who enquired about his wounds. He convinced them the bullets had gone straight through, so he had the wounds redressed and was on his way to Stalag XIIA, Limburg. When he reported sick the Doctor informed him that the bullet was still in his wrist. He was told to sit in a chair look out of the window and think of home. He felt a needle in his arm and thought he had screwed it to the table. After a while he felt warm blood at the tips of his fingers and the Doctor handed him the bullet. His wounds were dressed and he returned to the hut where he had met friends taken prisoner in Sicily and Italy. Thanks are due to Bob Hilton for this account.

bay for long. The thought that British tanks may come to their rescue did seem quite unlikely, however he and the many other veterans of Sicily knew that they had been in dire straits before and yet friendly tanks still broke through. During the final hours of the defence of the Bridge, Hoyer-Millar thought 'of those of us who had taken part in the Primosole Bridge operation in Sicily' and recalled how, 'twenty-four hours overdue, the first troop of Eighth Army tanks had finally reached us when we were hanging on by our fingernails; might it not happen again? I recall clearly, during those final hours, one line of A. H. Clough's poems: *'If hopes were dupes, fears may be liars'*... but deep down there was the feeling, 'They've just written us off'.' Hoyer-Millar was awarded the Military Cross for his deeds at Arnhem Bridge. With the cessation of hostilities in 1945 he returned to the airborne fold with the divisional Battle School, which was posted to Norway with the 1st Airborne Division. Here he acted as John Frost's Adjutant, much to the pleasure of his unshakeable commander. Now with an eye to seeking a career with the Foreign Office, Hoyer-Millar became one of only a small number of British officers to begin the process of learning to speak Norwegian.

'When we finished on the Thursday night' summed up Major Tony Hibbert; 'out of our 350 men; 280 were so badly wounded that they could not move and I do not think it was physically possible for the remainder to have fought any more. Their morale, however, remained as it had been on the Sunday.'

Colonel John Frost concluded: 'We had been ordered to capture Arnhem Bridge and then, reinforced by the rest of the division, to hold it for about 48 hours until relieved by 2nd Army. We had held it for three days and nights, but on our own. Our Force, my own 2nd Battalion and men from units of the 1st Parachute Brigade, never more than 700 strong, had fought on, isolated and surrounded, until, finally, we were blown out and burnt out of our positions by a strong enemy continually reinforced with heavy tanks, artillery and mortars. The SS soldiers were polite and complimentary about the battle that we had fought, but I felt bitter: no living enemy had defeated us. We were not defeated, but there was little chance, with no ammunition, no rest and eventually no positions from which to fight. No body of men could have fought more courageously and tenaciously than the officers and men of the 1st Parachute Brigade at Arnhem Bridge.

'The anti-tank gunners never hesitated for a moment to engage at close range enemy armour. They were a fine example of the Royal Regiment giving all to their guns. As usual, the men of the Royal Engineers fought through to the end. We of the Parachute Regiment always thought it a waste to use them as sappers when they were so good at killing the enemy. The Brigade HQ and the signallers never ceased in their efforts to establish communication, despite being under direct fire. The Service Corps on the far side of the ramp proved themselves to be tough fighters. Then there were the soldiers of 'C' Company of the 3rd Battalion and of my own 2nd Battalion - the riflemen, the machine gunners and mortarmen, the tank hunters with PIAT and grenade, who were all magnificent.'

Of the Brigade staff and the attempts of their signallers to make contact with anyone, John Frost wrote: 'The attic in which they laboured was hit repeatedly, but they never flagged. Tony Hibbert and Major [Cecil Distin] Rex Byng-Maddock [the Deputy Assistant Adjutant Quartermaster] had to sit it out with as much cheerful resignation as they could muster, filling in time by taking turns at sniping whenever they had the chance'.

Every hour Hibbert updated his diary and one of his entries for Wednesday reads: 'Two Mark IV tanks suddenly appeared round the corner and under cover, a 15cm gun was unloaded and pointed directly at Brigade HQ.' As contact had been established with the Light Regiment's guns at Oosterbeek it would have been appropriate to request that they put some fire down on this threat, however the radio set in Brigade HQ picked the worst possible moment to break down. Hibbert moved his men out of the attic, which minutes' later was struck by three armour piercing shells fired from the south. Shortly after one of the 2nd Battalion's mortars attached to 'A' Company attacked the gun and put it out of action when one of their bombs struck the ammunition dump beside it, leaving a large crater where it had been.

'The tactic was to fire high explosive into the sides of the building to break the wall down then fire smoke shells through that and of course the smoke shells have got phosphorus in them, the phosphorus sets light to anything inflammable in the house and they then burned the perimeter down bit by bit over the period of the next 48 hours. Once the water ran out and the flames became uncontrollable then you had to get out of the building as quickly as you could and get into another one set that one up for defence.'

Using the Type 22 radio set in the attic of Brigade HQ, Hibbert managed to establish contact with XXX Corps and he informed them that the bridge was still passable but would not be so for much longer. He asked when he could expect a relief force and received the reply that an attempt to take Nijmegen Bridge was imminent and that they hoped to reach Arnhem soon. During the morning contact was made with Divisional HQ and upon learning of their supply problems Major General Urquhart, unaware of how intense the fighting was at the bridge, suggested to Hibbert that he organize groups of Dutch civilians to scour the area for supply canisters from the resupply flights and bring back as much food and ammunition as they could. The Brigade Major quickly put this thought from Urquhart's mind as it was impossible for even the paratroopers to move from one building to another without attracting heavy fire and so the civilians, sensibly sheltering in their cellars, would stand no chance at all. In the afternoon he heard from the General again, who bore the grim news that the vanguard of XXX Corps was stuck north of Nijmegen and with this report Hibbert felt that an end to resistance at the bridge was close.

'We had by this time about 300 wounded in the cellars, but I still believed that XXX Corps would be coming up certainly up to the south bank within a matter of almost hours. And damn it we could hear them! At 8 o'clock I realised that our little battle was finished. We just didn't have the ammunition. When the other side can run tanks right up to your front window with no chance of you retaliating, there comes a moment where you can't go on.'

It was decided that the remnants of the 2nd Battalion would defend the bridge until they were overwhelmed. Meanwhile Major Hibbert set about making a plan to break out the remainder in the hope of getting as many men as possible back to Oosterbeek. In preparation for this he reconnoitred the northern end of the perimeter, where he was almost run down by a British jeep driven by Germans. The break out force of approximately 120 was organized into just two platoons, each consisting of five sections, each under the command of an officer. Though exhausted and woefully short of ammunition, almost all of the men made it out and assembled as planned at a convent school 100 yards to the north of the perimeter. One by one the sections set out, but almost everyone involved was captured before making much progress. Hibbert led the last section away a few hours before dawn, but it quickly became apparent that the Germans had a stranglehold on the town and there was no way through. Having advanced no further than the Cathedral, 300 yards north-west of the bridge, Hibbert halted his group and instructed them to hide in the back garden of a house. Most were barricaded by Hibbert inside a bedroom, two more hid inside a tool shed, Major Dennis Munford of the Light Regiment shut himself inside a wooden crate and Hibbert with Major 'Tony' Cotterell the Army Bureau of Current Affairs Staff Writer installed themselves in a coal shed, 'which' recalled Hibbert 'was so small that we hoped it would seem an unlikely place for anyone to look. Unfortunately someone hiding near us fell asleep and started to snore so loudly that the Germans started ferreting around. Soon Tony and I were hauled out, covered in coal dust, feeling very angry and foolish. They marched us off to the cathedral square where a depressing sight met our eyes. About 20 officers and 130 other ranks were being guarded by a large number of unfriendly SS guards. This probably represented most of the survivors from the bridge. It was a great shock - we'd felt sure some of them would have got away.

'That evening we were told we would be moved to another location; anyone breaking ranks would be shot. Freddie Gough put us through a quarter of an hour's parade drill before we set off. Let's show these bastards what real soldiers look like. This boosted morale and restored our self-confidence, which had been a bit shaken by the events of the last day. We marched very smartly and as we went along we gave the local Dutch the Victory sign. This infuriated our German guards and they threatened to shoot us if we did it again - which we did whenever possible. We hoped by irritating them that we might get it chance to slip away, but there were too many of them around. They marched us to a small house on the outskirts of Arnhem and shoved us into a tiny room. It was here that Tony Deane-Drummond found a cupboard and we reversed the lock and hid him in there with a few bits of bread and a jam-jar of water to keep him going.'

At dawn on Thursday the Germans began an operation to clear out the last 150 men of Colonel Frost's force from the houses which they were still occupying by the bridge at Arnhem. The Panzergrenadiers came up the streets, throwing stick bombs through windows and blasting their way into cellars, firing their automatic rifles from the hip. At the end of Marktstraat they were held up for a few moments by fire from the cellars of a house on the corner. But then the

British troops defending it ran out of ammunition and two paratroopers came out into the street. While one of them tried to draw the Germans' fire, the other worked his way forward with a knife in his hand. For a moment the Panzer grenadiers held their fire as they watched them and then both the British soldiers were shot and through the smoke and dust and the rattle of fire and the crash of exploding bombs the German advance continued. From house to house the Germans pushed through the rubble, surrounding isolated groups of men and forcing them to surrender, missing several who lay hidden in cupboards, under floorboards and in empty water tanks, picking up a few wounded men and leaving others to be collected later. 'The fighting was of an indescribable Fanatismus', a German says. 'When the ground floor was taken, the British defended themselves obstinately on the first floor. The fight raged through ceilings and staircases. Hand grenades flew in every direction. Each house had to be taken in this way. Some of the British offered resistance to their last breath. Their casualties rose.' But by nine o'clock the area was cleared. There was no more resistance and tanks and lorries of infantry were rolling unchecked across the bridge for the south. In the cellars where the wounded lay, the SS troops came down to their enemies and some of them with rough chivalry offered them brandy and chocolate, congratulating them on the battle they had fought.

'All prisoners were formed up' recalls Lance Sergeant Padfield. 'I was surprised and pleased to see Norman Swift, a friend of mine from 'A' Troop so we fell in together. We marched off singing all the old songs, *Tipperary, Pack up Your Troubles* etc., until about a mile up the road we came to a halt at a memorial. To our amazement it had 17th September 1944, emblazoned in beautiful flowers, it was really something. The reason for the halt wasn't to admire the memorial, but to be loaded onto lorries and transported to Appledoorn. Here we were herded into a big railway shed, told to take our boots off, tie them together and mark them. We were then given a black loaf of bread between five of us, the date indentation on it was 16th September. I got my knife out of my haversack and tried to cut it into equal portions, but the blade snapped. Anyway we did eventually get it cut and that was all we were getting. As time went on more and more were arriving, including familiar faces from the Squadron who had their own stories to tell. It appeared that it had been gruesome everywhere.

'As dusk fell we were marched for about a mile up the railway line in our stockinged feet. The first cattle truck we came to we had to throw in our boots. We were then herded fifty to a cattle truck, the door closed to within three inches and the gap was intertwined with barbed wire. Fifty to a truck meant that you were sat shoulder to shoulder, it was most uncomfortable. We moved off during the night and were shunted about all over the Ruhr, for about five days. Relieving oneself was degrading because you had to use one half of your mess tin for bowel movements and nothing to clean yourself or the tin with. On the third day a loaf was handed in to be cut into fifty slices. Poor old Les Ellis was the unfortunate who had to do it, as he was the most senior rank in the party. The only luck we had during this miserable period was that it rained continuously for the whole journey. We took advantage of this by taking it in turns to hold the other half of our mess tins outside the gap to catch the rain drops from the roof of the train, so eventually we all had a drink of water. When we were at last ordered to 'Get out', we had to find our boots. It would have been hilarious if we had been watching on film, but we weren't in that frame of mind. I suppose it took about an hour before we were all ready for our next episode. They formed us up in ranks of five and we marched off, we found the place was Limburg. We marched and marched and with no real food inside us for over a week, it felt as though we had gone about twenty miles, later it was discovered that it was only four. The camp we arrived at was Stalag XIIA.' [52]

The struggle of Frost's band of men holds a place in British history like that occupied in American tradition by the battle of the Alamo. Eighty-one soldiers died defending Arnhem Bridge. German losses cannot be stated with any accuracy, though they were high; 11 units known to have participated in the fighting reported 50% casualties after the battle. Whereas most non-2nd Battalion combatants were ordered to disperse into the town, Lieutenant Harvey Todd remained at the bridge. When the situation was truly hopeless and the order to scatter was given, the American led the first party, consisting of approximately nine men, away from the bridge at 0200 on Thursday. At this time all he had about his person was one grenade and a pistol containing two rounds; he held onto the former, but gave the pistol to another man in his group who did not have a weapon. As they crossed a street a German machine-gun opened up on them at point-blank range and Todd was hit and fell down near to the pavement, but he saw that the machine-gun was very close to him and so destroyed it with the grenade. Todd got to his feet and ran across another street and through several destroyed buildings, drawing more machine-gun fire in the process. He climbed over a wall but on the other side could hear German voices approaching and with nowhere else to go he climbed up a tree where remained undetected as the patrol passed beneath him. It then occurred to Todd that he could no longer feel any pain where he had been hit and investigating as to why this was he discovered that he had not been wounded after all, but instead an empty magazine in his pocket had absorbed the shot; the misshapen bullet was still tangled up in it. Todd stayed up the tree until Thursday evening when any signs of battle had now subsided. Climbing down he crawled beneath a bush, slept and remained here until the following evening when he relocated himself in a burned out factory. He stayed here for the next five days until Wednesday 27th September, when a German soldier discovered

52 Harold Padfield suffered bouts of dysentery and only Red Cross Food Parcels kept him and the other PoWs alive throughout their captivity, much of which was spent at work camps unloading rubble from railway carriages; at least food was more plentiful. Harold returned to the 1st Parachute Squadron in February 1946 and served with them in Palestine. Promoted to Sergeant, he became Troop Sergeant with C Troop, but temporarily left the Squadron to become a Drill Instructor. Having been Mentioned in Despatches for his work in Palestine, Padfield, upon returning to the UK in mid 1948, was posted to the newly formed 9 Independent Parachute Squadron RE, with whom he served in Germany as Platoon Sergeant of 3 Troop. In September 1950, he married Beryl Joy Edwards. In 1952 Padfield was promoted to Staff-Sergeant and in June 1953 was posted to 25 Engineer Regiment, stationed in Egypt. This move saw the end of his days as a parachutist. Thanks are due to Harold and Dave Padfield, his son, for this story.

him hiding behind a large metal plate. [53]

An exhausted British wireless operator sent out his last signal to report their long-delayed surrender. General Urquhart did not receive it but a German interceptor did. He wrote it carefully on his pad. It was short and matter-of-fact and it ended with the words, 'God save the King'.

'Artillery was moved up around the school' says Gefreiter Albert Ringsdorf. 'This was done at dawn and they began firing immediately into the school, without interruption. This did not last long. The white flag went up again and the English surrendered. I think there may have been 150 to 200 soldiers in the school. I saw them again when it was all over and they were being marched away to a gathering place for prisoners. It was just as well that they surrendered when they did. It would have been pointless to go on with this artillery fire battering them. I think the most terrible thing for me in this battle was the fact that it was all close combat. It was one man against another, face to face. Also, you never knew where the enemy would pop up. What most impressed me was the fairness of the English soldier. He fought hard and well. In some ways I felt sorry for the English because they were brave soldiers but they were outnumbered. All they could do was defend themselves until they received the order to give up. The English came out after having surrendered holding their heads high. They looked proud and not at all defeated. I felt a great deal of respect for them and I felt sorry for them too. I respected the way they had fought, it was so fair. I showed them that I respected them. But I felt sorry for them because they looked so worn, haggard and exhausted. We were also tired but we had won. I spoke with one high-ranking officer. I don't think it was Frost but I really don't know. Frost stayed to the very last and never did surrender. He was informed that it was useless to fight any longer, that he should give up and avoid further pointless bloodshed on either side. He answered, however, that he would go on fighting with the rest of his men. This in itself alone commands respect. Actually there was no animosity on either side, no hatred. The English lost after a very hard and fair fight. They were then taken prisoner not by us because we had to go to Elst but a unit from the Wehrmacht took in direction of Germany.

'After everything was over and the prisoners had been marched away, we assembled. I was responsible for assembling the company whose command I had taken over after Vogel fell. I am not really a religious man but I prayed during this battle. I said to myself, 'The good Lord will help me' and then I waited for the next hour to come. I told my mother about this,

53 If captured 'Jedburgh' agents could expect harsh treatment, possibly even execution, but like so many others in his unit, Todd succeeded in passing himself off as a bona-fide soldier. He passed his period in captivity at two camps and remained a prisoner almost until the end of the war, but he escaped on 1 May 1945 and was picked up by American troops three days later. Lieutenant Todd claimed he had killed 16 German soldiers with his Springfield automatic carbine at Arnhem Bridge and for his part in that action he was awarded the DSO and also a Purple Heart for his wound. After the war he became an insurance agent and settled in Illinois with his wife, Amanda. Thanks are due to Jim Ommeren for this story.

my sister too. No one who has lived through such a terrible experience, whose life had hung by a thread, can tell me that he was not afraid. I don't care if he has the Knight's Cross with diamonds I am sure he was afraid. I lived through this battle and everyone was afraid even if they did not always show it. I often asked God just whose side he was on but somehow I was convinced that he was on our side.

'I do not remember seeing any birds, cats or dogs during the fighting. In fact I did not even hear a bird sing until after it was all over. We were then brought to a depot, a sort of park just outside Arnhem, where we were all assembled. That was when I came to myself again. That morning I had handed the company over to another leutnant, after things were wound up. This company was not at full strength. We had a fighting force of about 120 to 130 men at the beginning of the battle. I think that we had had reinforcements, perhaps another company, but I don't know exactly. Rosenbach and Klapdorn were not in my squad but in another one in the same company. They also moved up after our assault squads, mine included, had opened up the way for them. This was on the last day. Paul Rosenbach was lightly wounded. It was a head wound. He had taken his steel helmet off during the night and had forgotten to put it back on. We often took off our helmets at night. They got so heavy after a whole day. I remember the water being cut off but it did not bother me much. My squad and I had tea and coffee in our canteens. It wasn't real coffee or tea but it was liquid. My responsibility was limited to my men so I did not know what was going on in other platoons or squads. All I know is that we were in constant need of reinforcement, that we needed more men all the time and that each time we asked reinforcements were sent.

'It was when we were gathered all together that I consciously heard a bird singing. It was like coming back to life, as if during the battle I had been living in suspension. I was suddenly alive again and realized that I had come through it alive.

'We had only a couple of hours' breathing time before we were loaded on SPWs [Schützenpanzerwagen - armoured scouting car] and sent south of Arnhem to Elst. Before we left, the Battalion Commander addressed us. He thanked us for our courage during the recent action and told us that he regretted not being able to give us any time to rest. There was more fighting to be done, another matter to be cleaned up. I thought to myself: 'Here we go again. Things are going to be hot again.' The casualties were very high. They must have been about 50%. We went over the bridge on which lay burnt-out vehicles. The drivers were still inside. They were burned and charred black.[54]'

'With hardly a chance to catch our breath' wrote Rudi Trapp 'we are already sitting in a personnel carrier and are members of the Battle Group Knaust. We go across the bridge, now free of enemies, to the other bank [and] into the battle area Elst, to drive back the enemy paratroopers who have

54 After the battle Ringsdorf was promoted to corporal (SS-Unterscharführer) and received the Iron Cross, 2nd class. He later received the Iron Cross, 1st class.

landed there. Then I finally get it after all. An infantry shell hits me squarely in the knee. A personnel carrier takes me along to the rear. Sitting next to me is a major of the army, in battle fatigues and with a Knight's Cross at his neck. In response to my groaning he shows me his wooden leg and tries to calm me down, [he says] he can walk again. It was Major Knaust, one of the battle group leaders in the Arnhem Brigade Sonnenstuhl.' [55]

'Market-Garden' Timeline

Wednesday 20 September (D+3)

Although at take-off time ceilings over eastern England are between 1,000 and 2,000 feet visibility is only one or two miles, the first wave of 67 Stirlings depart for Arnhem. Area cover is provided by 46 P-51s of 8th Air Force while ADGB furnish a total of 65 fighters from 3 Spitfire and 3 Mustang squadrons for escort anti-flak operations. Visibility in the Arnhem area is poor, making an already difficult operation even more difficult. One Spitfire and one Mustang are lost. The later missions are given escort and cover to the IP by 17 squadrons of Spitfires, of which one squadron runs into bad weather over the Channel and turn back. The rest make 173 sorties but see no action and have no losses. The 8th Air Force has five P-51 groups on area cover beyond the IP and six flying the perimeter. These fly 430 uneventful sorties, losing only one Mustang and that by accident. Because the 9th Air Force is unable to contribute its quota of fighters, the 8th has to handle all flak suppression beyond the IP. It sends four groups of P-47s and the rocket squadron to do the job. They fly 179 sorties, but, hampered by bad visibility and by lack of briefing in the case of those substituting for 9th Air Force units, they are able to claim only two gun positions destroyed and two others damaged. They have no losses and little damage. (Two P-51s and one P-47 got back but had to be salvaged).

The second-wave of RAF supply aircraft to Arnhem numbers 97 aircraft. Out of 100 Stirlings and 64 Dakotas dispatched only two Stirlings abort. Flak is reported as very heavy, especially in the target area. It brings down 9 aircraft and damages 62. Of the remainder, 30 Stirlings were scheduled to make their drop on DZ 'Z' and their pilots reported doing so. That zone was entirely held by the Germans and all that was dropped on or near it probably fell into their hands. At the Hartenstein drop point a 'Eureka' and visual aids had been set out despite the incessant bombardment and 122 pilots reported dropping supplies there. Although only 13 of them picked up the Eureka

55 - Rudi Trapp died on 27 May 1990. After the battle for the Bridge Knaust was moved south with the task of holding the village of Elst. His force grew in strength with the inclusion of Tiger and Panther tanks as well as infantry. He was awarded the Knight's Cross on 28 September by Field Marshal Model. His Kampfgruppe remained in this section for a further two months being attached to divisions such as the 10th SS Panzer, 116th Panzer and 9th Panzer. Knaust was posted to the 490th Infantry Division in early 1945 as the commander of Regiment 'Knaust'. His regiment was involved in stopping the British advancing through the Teuteburger Forest. It was for this battle he was awarded the Oak Leaves to the Knights Cross. He was also promoted to Oberstleutnant. Knaust was captured on 5 May 1945 by the British and held for 12 months being released in 1946

and 32 sighted visual aids (Very lights being much the most effective, probably because they rose above tree-top level), results are decidedly better than on the day before. Out of 386 tons of supplies dropped, about 300 tons is intended for the Hartenstein drop point and 41 tons or about 14 percent of this is reported as collected. Considering that recovery is possible only within an area of about one square mile and that in the turmoil of battle much that is recovered is never reported, the precision of the drop is greater than the statistics indicate. Assuredly, the rations which are recovered are worth their weight in gold to the airborne, most of whom have had almost nothing to eat for 24 hours or more.

The Polish paratroop mission is again postponed because of fog, which persists until late in the day in the Grantham area. The aircraft are loaded and warmed up, ready to go if there is the slightest break in the overcast, but the opportunity never comes. Finally, five minutes before take-off time the mission is delayed another 24 hours.

After the disastrous pre-planned resupply mission the day before another major effort in the same strength is carried out. Brief wireless contact is made with Rear HQ in England and another DZ is chosen 250 yards NW of the Hartenstein. 164 aircraft take part but 33 Stirlings of 38 Group are ordered to drop their supplies on LZ 'Z' now in German hands. The drop on the perimeter is scattered but a fair proportion of supplies is gathered in. Fifteen aircraft are lost. Over 600 fighters of 8th Fighter Command strafe and bomb ground targets. Intense light flak claims five fighters.

Morning Irish Guards and 504th PIR begin to clear the suburbs of Nijmegen for the river crossing, while the Grenadiers and 505th PIR move towards the bridge. The weather in England again prevents the take-off of the third lift, with 325th Glider Infantry Regiment to land near Groesbeek and the Polish Parachute Brigade to drop at Driel.

1440 Assault crossing begins with an attack by Typhoons of RAF 83 Group, followed by a ten-minute artillery and smoke bombardment from 100 guns of XXX Corps and the tanks of the Irish Guards. **1500** two companies of 3/504th Parachute Infantry cross the Waal west of the bridges in 19 feet assault boats under heavy German artillery fire. Half the boats reach the far shore and six successive journeys bring the rest of 3/504th PIR and 1/504th PIR across. Once ashore, 3/504th PIR attack eastwards, clearing first the railway bridge and then the road bridge at the cost of 107 casualties. (417 German bodies are later recovered from the railway bridge area alone). 505th PIR and the Grenadiers attack through the town towards the road bridge. 1910 First Grenadier Guards' tanks cross.

Uncoordinated German attacks continue all the way around the British perimeter at Oosterbeek.

Main German attack on the Groesbeek heights. At first II Parachute Corps' drive is very successful and by evening has almost reached the bridge at Heumen, threatening to cut the road behind 82nd Airborne but counter-attacks by 508th PIR, supported by the Coldstream Guards, gradually restores the position.

Noon At Arnhem Bridge Frost is badly wounded by a mortar blast. Major Gough takes over command of the remaining troops, who now have water for only one more day. **1800** four PzKpfw IV Tiger tanks crash their way across Arnhem Bridge from north to south, but are unsupported. **2100** Major Gough negotiates a truce enabling the Germans to collect over 200 wounded of both sides from the cellars, including Frost who becomes a prisoner.

Relief of the Arnhem the bridge by Adair's Guards Armoured is now critical. With only three battalions of the 10th SS Panzer Division 'Frundsberg' between Nijmegen and Arnhem, it seems that nothing can stop the Allies reaching Arnhem bridge that night but Guards Armoured, fought to a standstill, will not advance at night into the polder of the 'island' without infantry and Horrocks lets them halt.

SHAEF HQ completes its move from Granville to Versailles, just west of Paris, drastically improving its communications. Montgomery at 21st Army Group HQ receives a message from Eisenhower denying that SHAEF had ever intended a broad front advance and reaffirming priority for the northern thrust.

Chapter 5

The 'Witches Cauldron'

'In The Cauldron there were times when it seemed no living thing could survive above ground. The shelling and mortaring were kept up with a fury designed to bend the will of the little force now remaining. And along the fringe of the perimeter the Germans were attacking vigorously, especially against Lonsdale Force in the south-east and also to the north and north-east where it was seen that many more tanks were in operation. The tactics were the same - to drive the British out of the houses either by demolishing them with high explosives or burning them with incendiary shells... As those still resisting went to ground, the wounded in the dressing stations and other buildings were enduring unspeakable conditions of hardship. By now the Tafelberg Hotel had been hit twice by shellfire and some of the wounded were showered with rusty water from the pipes. Movement about the perimeter was difficult not only because of the amount of splinters flying about but also because of the snipers, more of whom had infiltrated. There were physical obstacles, too. Roads and lanes were blocked with shattered masonry, fallen trees and abandoned vehicles. The few jeeps that were left had only a limited usefulness, mainly to the medical officers. On the faces of the men I could see the cumulative wear of lack of sleep and food and exposure. Dirt-caked and with heavy lidded, reddened eyes, they had not an unlimited endurance before them; but their spirit was magnificent to see.'

Major General Roy Urquhart.

During Wednesday the 20th and during that night there had been some activity by German patrols and tanks were heard, which encouraged further improvement to the defensive positions. 'Dawn on Thursday morning' wrote Private Fred Moore 'found us occupying a position on open ground, to the north of the Arnhem-Oosterbeek Road. Dug in behind a slight rise we had a clear view of the road junction immediately in front of us. Before long we observed two self propelling guns approaching the junction, supported by infantry. We opened fire, together with forward units on our left flank, causing the enemy attack to halt and we were then engaged by the heavy guns firing across open sights. This attack was aborted and comparative peace reigned once more.'

German tanks supported by infantry in considerable strength attacked through the woods and astride the road from the west. This was a training battalion of the Hermann Goering Regiment. There was confused fighting with heavy casualties on both sides. The Germans pressed on through the forward Border positions around the Westerbouwing Restaurant, at the extreme south-west of the Oosterbeek Perimeter; both the Border platoon commanders were killed and their platoons overwhelmed. 'As soon as it was daylight' Lance Corporal 'Ginger' Wilson of 12 Platoon, 1st Borders, recalled 'We heard the tanks coming. They turned off the road and headed straight for the hotel. There seemed to be hundreds of Germans like a football crowd. We opened up with everything... As the Germans overran the top of Westerbouwing, I saw to my left in the trees 24-year old Lieutenant John Wellbelove, a Canadian officer of Eston, Saskatchewan in command of 22 Platoon, standing up firing his Sten gun and shouting, 'Come on you Heiny bastards'; then he too was overrun and killed.' The Borders were driven off the hill. Four tanks, French Renault types captured in 1940, then followed up on to the open fields making for the reserve platoon at the crossroads below, where 20-year old Private George Everington of 12 Platoon manned a PIAT. Moving from position to position, one behind a dead cow, he knocked out three of these tanks. Everington, who was born in Lincoln, the eldest of six children and lived with his wife, Louisa, in Kippax, Yorkshire, was killed the next day. Four days later, his wife gave birth to their son, George.

Major William Armstrong rallied some of his men and led them back in a counter-attack up and on to the hill, where they were met by heavy fire; he was wounded and captured; his Company Sergeant Major, Ernest McGladdery, was killed. The attack petered out. Further counter-attacks, more in the form of fighting patrols, were attempted by men of HQ Company, but without success. The Westerbouwing was lost and with it the Driel ferry. The survivors of 'B' Company - and there were few - regrouped around a large white house called Dennenoord and dug-in in the gardens. The Germans after their heavy casualties did not follow up in strength, but their patrols did occupy the area of the gasometer 200 yards the side of the crossroads. During the night, a fighting patrol of Borders tried to recapture the Driel ferry as Lance Corporal 'Ginger' Wilson recalls:

'The Jerries had it well covered with machine-gun fire and we were driven back. Just before dawn some Poles came running towards us shouting, 'Don't shoot. We are Poles,' and we held our fire. 'We were mortared almost continually and lost more men, especially from bomb bursts in the trees, so we set to, to make head cover for our slit trenches. The Germans launched an attack across the open ground, but we shot the lot; they were allowed to pick up their wounded. 'The cellar in the big house was full of wounded. Every available space was filled and there were bodies laid at the back. A little Dutch girl called Dina was helping to feed our bids, with what little food there was.' The acting 2ic of the battalion, Major Breese, was sent down to take over command of this area. Reinforcements were also sent - some men of 'A' Company, a depleted platoon of South Staffords and, later, some mortarmen from the 11th Parachute Battalion. The task of this ad hoc group, now called 'Breese force', was to hold firm at this vital SW corner of the perimeter, which at this point was little more than 700 yards wide, with the risk that a determined enemy attack could break through and cut off the Division from its base on the river. The Germans, after their unexpected success on Westerbouwing, did not attack again in strength in this sector, but contented themselves with maintaining a steady pressure on these Border positions, with mortar fire and accurate machine gun fire from the slopes above and from the ferry and of course continuing fire from snipers. The Border casualties mounted and those that could not be evacuated filled the cellars and rooms of Dennenoord.

General Bittrich issued orders to 9th SS Panzer to step up their attacks and annihilate the British airborne troops as soon as possible. 'It is particularly important that the remaining British forces north of the Rhine are quickly destroyed and the enemy bridgehead cleared.'

Enemy fire varied in intensity, but never by day or night did it cease, though there was apt to be a lull at sundown. 'The Germans always drew stumps at seven o'clock,' said Major 'Boy' Wilson. But he added, 'They mortared us continuously at all other times.' It was this mortar fire which was especially galling and which accounted for a high proportion of the casualties suffered. Never could anyone feel reasonably safe even in a well-dug and well-sited slit trench. More than one 'looked very like a grave' and more than one became a grave. On one small sector alone five mortar bombs fell every twenty seconds and this rate of fire was often kept up by the enemy for hours at a time.

As day succeeded day and no relief appeared and ammunition ran lower and lower till there was almost none at all, to remain cheerful needed a constant effort of the will. The remedy - one which never failed - was to take some action against the enemy. Sniping became a favourite pastime; and since the standard of marksmanship was high, very few bullets were wasted. 'We built a figure out of a pillow with a helmet stuck on one end of it,' says Sergeant Quinn of the Reconnaissance Squadron, 'and put it on the top of a broom handle. We popped this out now and again, always from a different window, so as to attract German snipers. One of us was watching them from a nearby house - not the house where we were using the dummy. Whenever a sniper showed up, he fired and got him. One of our chaps got fifteen like this and I got two or three. We were using Stens and Brens. For this work it is best to fire single shots.'

Wilson's Independent Parachute Company cut notches on the butts of their rifles for every German killed. One of them returned to England with eighteen. Others stalked tanks and self-propelled guns with PIATs. Others, again, who had orders to issue and plans to make, stuck to their task, not allowing the heavy fire to interfere with its fulfilment and even finding time to note the symptoms which that fire produced.

'I found that under such long periods of mortar fire,' says Lieutenant Colonel Charles Mackenzie 'my mind showed a tendency towards lethargy. It was hard to concentrate and to write anything took a long time.'

Father Bruggeman, however, was still able to write up his diary. 'There is still no reliable news, although we are close to the fighting. Are the English still in Arnhem? Where is the Second Army? Nobody knows and pessimists rule. This morning we saw cows on the lane behind the garden. Theophilus thinks that they belong to Farmer Evers from Johanna Hoeve, who drove them on our meadows. Dick Polman, who helps the Red Cross, came with an English officer with a broken leg. We hid him in the shoemakery and tried to smuggle him to the Diocesan hospital later this day. Later some Germans came by in a stolen car full of bodies. They were covered with plastic but the legs stuck out. They forced us to bury the bodies and after talking to the rector, Fathers Claver and Odulph went with them to the cemetery at the Limburg van Stierumlaan. They went with a lot of aversion but came back rather happy. On the way back they had found a couple of baskets full of food and cigarettes. Like yesterday, supplies had come from the sky. Again many anti-aircraft guns were active. How long will this take?'

The Breman's home in Oosterbeek was taken over by men of the 1st Parachute Battalion's Mortar Platoon, included amongst whom were Sergeant Harold 'Dick' Whittingham, Private Nobby Clarke, Frank McCormick and Reg Curtis. Whittingham had found a jeep trailer loaded with mortar ammunition. The accurate fire of his mortar helped to break up many attacks by the enemy, some at such close range that he fired his mortar with the barrel almost vertical and with the primary charge only. The Bremans' 15 year old daughter recorded in her diary [56] that 'during the morning of the 21st the English soldiers gave us something to eat: meat and vegetables. Last night they almost managed to set the room on fire. They had put a candle on a glass ashtray. The ashtray got so hot that it burst, so that the tablecloth caught fire and a hole was burnt in the table itself. Fortunately they discovered it before it was too late. The shooting has continued all morning and we are not allowed to leave the cellar. At noon we had another English meal which was very nice.

'In the afternoon the Germans suddenly start to fire very heavily. Many English soldiers got into our cellar. Then another came down and told us that a container with ammunition at the other side of the house had been hit and was now burning. Everything would now explode. The soldiers that were in the other cellar now also came and joined us: the container stood just outside the cellar and they were no longer safe there. They all brought axes. Some parts of the wall collapsed but there was no fire. We all sat tight together on our heels in order to make room for all the people. We got very stiff. A couple of soldiers came down with a wounded man. They put him on the ground and covered him with a blanket. I stood up, but suddenly my legs got very wobbly, so I must sit down again. Suddenly Len and Gerald come down. I am very pleased to see some familiar faces. They examine the wounded soldier and say that he has no wounds but that he has a fright, that he has 'shock', because of a grenade exploding near to him. He looks a bit calmer now. They have given him some eau-de-cologne and now he dozes a bit... We call the wounded man 'Uncle John' [Private Nobby Clarke] because he resembles my Mummy's brother who is also called John. He has had something to eat and drink, but he is still very absent-minded and does not recognise me when I ask him how he is. They have put a wet towel on his head. The other soldiers often come to have a look at him. They treat their wounded very differently from the Germans who stayed with the Klaassen family.'

56 From a report compiled by David Clarke, which traces the Arnhem exploits of his father, Nobby Clarke.

On the fourth day' recalled Trooper John William Bateman of the 1st Airborne Reconnaissance Squadron, 'Lieutenant John Christie and I went out to engage a German tank that was causing us a lot of trouble. We proceeded down the road and the tank missed us with his first shot, Lieutenant Christie and I took cover and then he tried to get the jeep under cover and was blown up with the second shot from the tank. It struck him full in the chest and took an arm away as well as part of his shoulder and chest. His jeep was destroyed but I could not believe he actually walked towards me and fell into my arms. The horror of it all remained with me forever. How could he, with such terrible injuries have managed to try to return to his men. I tried to comfort him but he cried out 'My God! My God!' and died in the shelter of my arms.

'I then returned to my own troop position and when I arrived there I was told to take a wounded Dutch boy to the First Aid Post about half a mile away. This I did and then returned to my position by GHQ at the Hartenstein Hotel. The woods in front of us had 300 German soldiers waiting for us to surrender. Around us our dead lay unburied because the shelling was too great. Little Jock Odd my friend suddenly shouted 'I'm Twenty One Today!' and jumped up with joy. A sniper's bullet rang out and hit Jock in the head. The next he lay dead. From that moment memories became hazy. I suffered from back wounds from shrapnel, but still remained in the front line instead of reporting to the First Aid Post. Night followed day and one lost track of time.'

At about 1630 in the afternoon of Thursday 21st an attack in strength by HQ 9th SS Panzer Division came in against the White House. The attack featured a number of probing attacks by German infantry and tanks, occasionally backed up with mortars and when they penetrated the KOSB positions there was fierce hand-to-hand fighting for some time. To counter this, Lieutenant Colonel Payton-Reid ordered that a number of patrols be carried out in the area. The situation was saved by the 44-year old World War One veteran and Lieutenant Jim Taylor, who both independently ordered a savage bayonet charge, that resulted in the battalion regaining all the ground that had been lost. Sergeant George Barton, SP Company, 7th KOSB adds:

'Throughout the day we had been under heavy mortar fire, including the 6-barrelled Nebelwerfer or 'moaning minnie' SP guns set to demolish the White House and snipers were active; our casualties mounted. In the late afternoon, under a heavy mortar 'stonk', Panzergrenadiers in more than company strength charged our positions in a style reminiscent of World War I and we had to give ground. Our CO rallied us, urging us to fix bayonets: the call was taken up and with him in the lead we charged back shouting to vent our wrath at being hammered for two days. The Germans took to their heels and the position was ours again. I reckon that they lost over 100 men. But now the White House was well ablaze and almost in ruins.'

It is believed that near to 100 German soldiers were killed during the fight for the White House, however half of the remaining 7th KOSB became casualties in the process and their numbers were too few to defend the area.

Payton-Reid wrote: 'I had tentative orders to come to a closer position further south. I had no company commanders, no Colour Sergeant Majors and very few senior NCOs. I decided now was the moment to move away while we had the Germans where we wanted them. So I got everything cleared out and all the casualties evacuated. We moved along to the left about 400 yards to connect with the 21st Independent Parachute Company. I got orders to move back into Hartenstein about 2130, connecting up with the glider pilots on the left, the Recce being on my right. We passed the night there peacefully and the Brigadier saw us in the morning.

'Two people who, though not Borderers, had, whilst attached to us became so in spirit, came very much to the fore. These were Captain Walker, our Forward Observation Officer from the gunners and Staff Sergeant Tilley, the glider pilot. The former, who was attached to the Battalion did some very outstanding Infantry work when, owing to the break-down of communications, he could not get in touch with his guns. He acted as 2nd in Command of one of my Companies and took an extremely active part in its operations. Later when he did establish communications with his guns and was looking for a forward observation post, he was shot in the head by a sniper, but was saved from being killed by his steel-helmet. He was taken to the Regimental Aid Post, but after two days there decided that he must get back into action. By this time I was very short of Officers and he acted as my Adjutant, being of the greatest assistance, particularly during the final evacuation.

'Staff Sergeant Tilley, who had found himself attached to the Battalion, became one of its most active members and was to be found everywhere, where there was a useful and dangerous job to be done. When the MO and most of the Medical Staff were captured, he attached himself to the RAP where he did magnificent work in bringing in the wounded and tending to their comfort. Later, when the RSM had been wounded and NCOs were very short he acted as RSM and organised ammunition supplies. When rations were short he organised a central kitchen in which he cooked a hot meal every day, consisting of vegetables dug from the gardens and stores found in the evacuated houses. These are only indications of some of his activities, but he was a great stand-by and maintained extreme optimism even in the most adverse circumstances as a result of which he helped to keep the morale at a very high standard. I understand that he had been awarded the DCM.

'Tilley had, from no known reason, decided to remain with us instead of rejoining his own unit and had appointed himself my 'bodyguard'. On one occasion I was going round the front with him and when we arrived near where I expected to find a platoon he shot ahead round some houses to locate it. He shot back even faster, however, seizing me by the arm, dragged me along with him, whispering: 'there's a trench round there cram full of Bosche'. As he thought they could not have failed to see him we deemed it wise to get out of sight, so leapt through a window of a damaged house nearby. Our leap took us further than anticipated, because the floor had been demolished with the result that we dropped right down into the cellar. And there we were, caught in a trap, expecting at any moment to see Hun faces peering down at us. Only Tilley's strength and agility saved the situation. By standing on my hands he could just reach ground level. With what help I could give him he managed to pull himself out and then, by a stupendous effort, he hauled me up after him.

A few minutes later we reached the proper platoon position [No 12 Platoon 'C' Company] where, now it was safely over, our adventure took the appearance of a huge joke.'

During this escape, Payton-Reid had moved across a vegetable patch stretching across several gardens, crawling amongst the beans and peas he eventually found a lone tank sitting in a vulnerable position on the road. He went back to find the Battalion's only remaining PIAT, but by the time he had returned the tank had wisely moved on.

'It was a great moment when we realized that we could now call on the support of the Corps Artillery of the ground forces' continues Payton-Reid, 'since this made us feel that reinforcement was at hand. The fire itself was most effective and broke up several attempted enemy attacks. It would probably have been considerable more so had not our Forward Observation Officer, Captain Walker, chosen this precise time to get himself hit on the head by a bullet. Having been born under a lucky star and having, according to himself, a thick skull, his life was undoubtedly saved by his steel helmet. Nevertheless the MO insisted on his being admitted to the Regimental Aid Post so we had perforce endeavour, in our own amateurish way, to perform his duties. For Corps artillery this must have been the 'Gunners Nightmare' because our methods were unorthodox in the extreme. As our only wireless set was established in a cellar the officer observing the shoot had to relay his alterations over a human chain extending from roof to basement, a system hardly to be recommended for either speed or accuracy. The astonishing thing is that it seemed to work, even if the Gun Position Officer must have been somewhat startled to receive in lieu of the prosaic 'On Target', some such ejaculation as: 'Marvellous, you're right among them. We can hear the bastards screaming.'

Staff Sergeant Bert Harget had a trench on the edge of a wood facing the German position about 250 metres away. 'I was told that I was wanted at Divisional Headquarters at the Hartenstein Hotel and I made my way there leaving my rucksack at the side of my trench. That was the last I saw of it - when I returned later I found that a German mortar bomb had landed on it and I had lost all my rations, including several bars of chocolate that I had hoarded over the previous weeks. At Div HQ I was asked to take a patrol to a forward area to try to locate the German mortar positions. We found a suitable house for observation and were able to send back messages indicating where the mortars were.'

At the Hartenstein at around 9 o'clock - the same hour that the troops at the bridge surrendered - Urquhart held a conference in the 12-foot-square wine cellar, which was now the operations room. 'It was a tight squeeze' wrote Urquhart. 'Down the aisle running through the main wine cellar, an arched dungeon from which coal was moved to make room for us, we had the ops table laid out with maps. A duty officer sat close up against it in order to make room for others to move between his chair and a roof support. My place was in the right-hand corner of the cellar between one of the blocked-up ground-level window grilles and a wine rack. Next to me was an officer of the phantom Reconnaissance Unit, who had a direct wireless link to the War Office; then the chief clerk. On the far side of the cellar in a four-feet-deep recess leading to the other grille which overlooked the gravel path outside were several strangers, including two RAF officers who had been shot down during the re-supply operations.'

Now that the 2nd Army was on its way Urquhart told the assembled officers the horseshoe-shaped bridgehead around the Hartenstein, North of the Heveadorp ferry must be held at all costs. From the last returns there seemed to be 3,000 men still fit to fight. Urquhart ordered Brigadier Hackett, commanding 4th Para Brigade was to take command in the east and Brigadier 'Pip' Hicks of 1st Airlanding Brigade the west. Hicks would have the remnants of three companies of the Border Regiment, the surviving KOSBs who were holding the northern edge, the Independent Company and some Poles, a number of Royal Engineers and a detachment of glider pilots. Hackett had all that remained of the 156th and 10th Parachute Battalions and the Borderers; Sheriff Thompson's Light Regiment gun batteries, north-east and north-west of Oosterbeek Church on the rising ground, the Reconnaissance Squadron, the 21st Independent Parachute Company, [57] elements of the Royal Army Service Corps who had abandoned the care of vehicles and stores and were fighting stoutly as infantry and the Lonsdale Force under Major Robert 'Dickie' Lonsdale DSO MC and consisting of the survivors of the 1st, 3rd and 11th Parachute Battalions and the 2nd South Staffords; a handful of 2nd Parachute Battalion troops who had never reached the Arnhem Bridge and three glider pilot detachments.

Falling back from Arnhem, Lance Corporal Fred Moughton of the 3rd Battalion's Medium Machine-Gun Platoon was with a group of nine others under the command of a corporal. Awaiting fresh orders, they occupied and fortified two neighbouring terraced houses, knocking the wall down between them so they could move from one to the other. The house afforded them a good view of the road below, along which a company of German infantry and a Tiger tank soon came. Moving forward on either side of the road, their casual manner betrayed that they were not aware that the paratroopers were lying in wait up ahead. Moughton and his comrades took full advantage of this fact and allowed them to approach to within point blank range before they opened fire. When the order was given, at least seven or eight men fell to the ground

57 The 21st Independent Parachute Company, after it had completed its pathfinder tasks for the second lift on Monday, moved to the Graaf Van Rechterenweg area but during the next day, as 4th Parachute Brigade withdrew over the railway, a stronger defensive position was established around the house Ommershof. Later that evening the position was strengthened by a Troop of 4th Parachute Squadron RE and by 60 glider pilots under Major Jackson. No 1 Platoon, which had been marking LZ 'L' for the gliders bringing in the Polish vehicles and guns, was cut off for a time, but rejoined the Company after dark. SS infantry and SP guns crossed the railway during the night and for the next-two days repeatedly attacked this area and also tried to infiltrate through the woods to the south. All these attacks were repulsed with heavy losses to the Germans, including two SP guns knocked out by a PIAT. Late on Thursday as the enemy pressure increased all around the perimeter, Division HQ ordered the northern tip of the perimeter to be drawn in. The Independent Company and the sappers withdrew from this area and moved across to the east flank to take up new positions around the MDS crossroads. The glider pilots pulled back to the woods south of Ommershof. *A Tour of the Arnhem Battlefields* by John Waddy (Pen & Sword 199, 2001).

instantly, but those who were escaped unscathed quickly found cover. The only anti-tank weapon the airborne men had available was a solitary gammon bomb, which exploded harmlessly on the railings bordering the house when it was thrown by a man from an upstairs window. Luckily the tank was so close to the house that it couldn't use its main armament against the airborne men, but its machine-gun riddled the downstairs rooms, firing through doors and windows. All of the British troops, except for one man who remained on the stairs to cover the front door, went upstairs where they took up positions in the bedrooms and bathroom, giving them four windows to fire from.

The Germans did not know how many men were defending the building and so cautiously surrounded the house before opening fire. This fire was returned and Moughton and his comrades were able to hold out for about an hour, by which time the futility of their situation had become obvious. Two men tried to escape out of the back door, hoping to reach the river about 100 yards away, but both were shot before they had covered much ground. Inside the house there were only four men still able to fight, the three others being badly injured from single wounds, one to the shoulder; another to the leg and the other in the stomach.

The commander of the Tiger tank spoke good English and called for the men to surrender, promising them that they would be well treated. Realising that they had no sensible alternative, the men agreed to lay down their arms. Walking out the front door, they had to step over the bodies of two Germans whom they had killed. This act angered their comrades and the man walking in front of Moughton was hit over the head with the butt of a rifle while he himself received a similar blow to his arm, however the tank commander quickly put a stop to this mistreatment. The paratroopers asked for permission to go back into the house to bring out their wounded, but they were told that the Germans would take care of them. The group was taken from this building and held overnight in the cellar of a house which served as their makeshift prison. The night was not spent comfortably as the cellar was submerged beneath two feet of water.[58]

Private David Warden, also of the Medium Machine Gun Platoon, HQ Company was another of the few members of the 3rd Parachute Battalion who made it into the Oosterbeek Perimeter. On Wednesday, when the Lonsdale Force were under heavy attack in their isolated position in Oosterbeek, he and several comrades were fighting from a ditch that was filled with three feet of water, in some fields just north of the river bank. A tank shell had exploded near Warden and left him concussed. Upon recovering he realised that Lance Corporal Walter Stanley had been badly hit and was about to fall face forward. David Warden grabbed hold of him around his waist and kept him above water. Though in a deep state of shock, Stanley was aware that he was about

58 On the following day, Moughton and other prisoners were marched for twenty miles until they reached a railway siding, where they were loaded into cattle trucks for transportation into Germany. Conditions were most unpleasant during this journey, with fifty men held in each truck for the next five days. Moughton was freed from his prisoner of war camp in 1945. He rejoined the Parachute Regiment and was due to leave for Palestine with them during the following year; however he was demobilised before the move could take place.

to die and spoke to Warden about his wife, before singing a few lines of the song 'I'll walk beside you in the years to come'. The brave Lance Corporal died soon after and Warden left his body leaning against the ditch, however despite this, Stanley has no known grave.

In the intense fighting towards the end of the battle, David Warden believed he saw two Germans enter a house near to his position. His suspicions were confirmed when a stick grenade was thrown out of a window into his slit trench. The explosion immediately killed Sergeant Blakeley and wounded Warden in the leg. He returned the favour by throwing a grenade of his own through the window where the other one came from. The two Germans ran out of the back door but were both killed by Warden and Private Tongs who opened fire with their Sten guns. When the grenade he had thrown exploded, the house caught fire and burned to the ground. [59]

The Polish Brigade was expected to fly in later that day which would enable Urquhart to reinforce the weaker parts of his perimeter, especially by the river where the enemy were making constant efforts to break through. Everyone received a morale boost, when later on Wednesday morning, shells fired by XXX Corps's 64th Medium Regiment, commanded by Lieutenant Colonel Hunt, began exploding on the outskirts of the perimeter, sometimes under 100 yards in front of the forward trenches. They were directed against targets in the outlying fields and woods by Robert Loder-Symonds from a distance of rather more than eleven miles. Urquhart was still unable to contact the bridge and was unaware that all resistance had ceased, he reported:

'Enemy attacking main bridge in strength. Situation critical for slender force. Enemy also attacking Divisional position east from HEELSUM vicinity and west from ARNHEM. Situation serious but am forming close perimeter around HARTENSTEIN with remainder of Division. Relief essential both areas earliest possible. Still maintain control ferry-crossing HEVEADORP.

On the second day the HQRE element had joined the main unit at 1600 and an hour later moved down to Oosterbeek, taking up position at the Hartenstein. HQRE remained there throughout the operation until the eventual evacuation. On the morning of the 21st; recalls Sapper V. H. Brimble, whose unit had dug in and obtained additional cover overhead by using four-inch logs that were found, 'after the forces of John Frost were overrun at the bridge area of Arnhem, the Germans concentrated on the Oosterbeek area, mortaring the Hartenstein Hotel area. At about 10.00 the ammunition and petrol dumps at the Hartenstein were hit. Fires were started and these were put out between bursts of fixed trajectory mortaring. A jeep carrying small arms and some six-pounder ammunition were the next casualty causing bullets to shoot in all directions.' Brimble, Sergeant Cooper and Staff Sergeant Brown all had a lucky escape when trying to get this under control by shovelling earth onto it. Incoming

59 In 1950 Warden revisited the area and met an elderly Dutch gentleman, whom he discovered was the owner of the house that his grenade had destroyed. The man was under the impression that the Germans were to blame for the ruin of his home and he was still quite furious about it. David Warden couldn't find it in his heart to reveal the truth of the matter and so merely commented 'Oh dear, how terrible...'

mortars were heard and the three jumped into the same trench, when the six-pounder ammunition blew up, completely destroying the jeep. Later the HQRE Intelligence Officer Lieutenant Sankey left to command a platoon of the 10th Parachute Battalion. Sankey was wounded in the chest by a sniper and died instantly. German mortar fire and bullets from fixed-point machine gun fire bombarded the area frequently. The ground was very sandy which caused the magazines of the airborne troops' Sten guns to become blocked and need constant cleaning.

During the period, there were several incidents, which are recalled by Sapper Brimble. He was ordered to accompany the CRE in two jeeps from the 9th Field Company on a recon to investigate the possibility of using the ferry across the Neder Rijn near Driel. Due to the area not being fully secured the mission was aborted before reaching the river. Later on in the period spent at the Hartenstein Brimble was tasked with accompanying Driver Hill who was to take a message to the forces regrouping at Oosterbeek Church. The journey was damgerous. Going through the woods trees were covered with phosphorous, which glowed eerily in the dark. At the church Brimble saw many dead airborne troops outside. He recalled the church being packed with both able and wounded airborne troops. The return journey was equally dangerous but they arrived safely back at the Hartenstein. During the morning of the 22nd, mortar fire destroyed one of the HQRE jeeps, a motorcycle and much of the unit's equipment and stores. It also set fire to the fuel dump for a second time. The next day 88mm shelling started at 0400 hours, two hours earlier than normal. At 0730 German mortars joined in. The second HQRE jeep and the remainder of the stores and the radio set were blown up. On the 24th the HQRE position was mortared continually during the night to about 0300 and then Spandau MG fire trained on the hotel grounds. Another HQRE motorcycle was destroyed. The Hotel grounds by then were a complete shambles.

Corporal Smithson was dug in close to the divisional HQ in the Hartenstein hotel. Towards the end of the battle their plan was to systematically destroy every house by putting a shell into it. They were moving forward wiping them out one at a time up the road. You can't fight tanks with rifle and bayonet. So you just moved back until there was nowhere to go back. Towards the end there was hardly anything that wasn't burning or smoking or collapsing or falling down. There were so many casualties they were wheeling them in all the time. They'd got nowhere to put them, so they were lying outside and getting wounded again by shellfire. It was always a question of: 'Any news of XXX Corps? No news.' During the night you'd hear the clanking and movement of armour and you'd think, oh, it's XXX Corps, but when it got light - no XXX Corps. It was German armour.'

Lonsdale's men, defending the south-eastern sector of the divisional perimeter along a semi-circular line on Hackett's right east of Oosterbeek Laag church and were in danger of being cut off from the rest of the Division by armoured attacks from the north, east and south as the enemy launched a major attack with infantry, tanks and self-propelled guns. Lance Sergeant John Daniel Baskeyfield of the South Staffordshire Regiment was the NCO in charge of a six-pounder anti-tank gun. Baskeyfield was born in Burslem in November 1922. He became a butcher in 1940 and became the manager of a Co-Op butchers in Pittshull. In February 1942 he received his call up papers and served with the 2nd South Staffords in North Africa, Sicily and Italy.

During the early stage of the action the crew Baskeyfield commanded was responsible for the destruction of two Tiger tanks and at least one self-propelled gun, thanks to the coolness and daring of this NCO who, with complete disregard for his own safety, allowed each tank to come well within 100 yards of his gun before opening fire. In the course of this preliminary engagement Baskeyfield was badly wounded in the leg and the remainder of his crew were either killed or badly wounded. During the brief respite after this engagement Baskeyfield refused to be carried to the regimental aid post and spent his time attending to his gun and shouting encouragement to his comrades in neighbouring trenches. After a short interval the enemy renewed the attack with even greater ferocity than before, under cover of intense mortar and shell fire. Manning his gun quite alone, Baskeyfield continued to fire round after round at the enemy until his gun was put out of action. By this time his activity was the main factor in keeping the enemy tanks at bay. The fact that the surviving men in his vicinity were held together and kept in action was undoubtedly due to his magnificent example and outstanding courage. Time after time enemy attacks were launched and driven off. Finally, when his gun was knocked out, Baskeyfield crawled, under intense enemy fire, to another six-pounder gun nearby, the crew of which had been killed and proceeded to man it single-handed. With his gun he engaged an enemy self-propelled gun which was approaching to attack. Another soldier crawled across the open ground to assist him but was killed almost at once. Baskeyfield succeeded in firing two rounds at the self-propelled gun, scoring one direct hit which rendered it ineffective. Whilst preparing to fire a third shot, however, he was killed by a shell from a supporting enemy tank.

For these deeds he was awarded a posthumous Victoria Cross and his best epitaph is to be found in the words with which the citation ends, 'The superb gallantry of this NCO is beyond praise. During the remaining days at Arnhem stories of his valour were a constant inspiration to all ranks. He spurned danger, ignored pain and, by his supreme fighting spirit, infected all who witnessed his conduct with the same aggressiveness and dogged devotion to duty which characterized his actions throughout.' [60]

As attacks on the British perimeter increased in several sectors, particularly from the west along the river line, the ring was becoming dangerously weak as enemy tanks and infantry inflicted heavy casualties on the defenders. When the Border Regiment was driven off the high ground at Westerbouwing the loss of this commanding position seriously endangered the Division's hold on the waterfront and Urquhart ordered a company of the Border Regiment to retake it. Major Cousens's men, however, were so exhausted that the attack was not put in for fear that, if it were not successful, a disastrous gap would be opened upon that vital

60 John Baskeyfield's body was never found. A memorial statue, depicting him in action, stands at the Festival Heights, in Stoke.

corner of the perimeter. Urquhart did not feel that he could reinforce them by taking units away from the northern lines which were under increasing pressure from hour to hour. And German reinforcements were on their way. At noon 45 of the long-awaited Konigstiger tanks from Panzerabteilung 503 had arrived in Arnhem. Later came units of another Panzergrenadier battalion from Germany under command of Captain Bruhns, several hastily-formed companies of Luftwaffe ground staff fighting as infantry, the 171st Auffrischung liegende artillery regiment with over 30 guns from Zutphen and the Landsturm 'Nederland' of the Dutch SS. By 1600 all of these units were in action. An hour later sixty Luftwaffe aircraft arrived over Arnhem and Nijmegen and all the German anti-aircraft units joined in the attack.

Urquhart's men's most pressing need was for water because the enemy had cut off the main supply to Oosterbeek on the first day of the battle. There was little for drinking, none for washing and precious little for the wounded. Storage tanks, central-heating systems, even fish bowls were drained. One enterprising company filled a bath half full of water before the tap failed and used this for cooking, even after a piece of the ceiling had fallen into it and made it look like thin, unpleasant porridge. When they moved to a new position on the north-side some of Boy Wilson's men had taken over a house belonging to a far-sighted doctor who had taken the precaution of filling his bath before the Germans cut the water supplies. 'We cooked a goat and we have enough water for brewing up for some nights to come' he told Urquhart. 'My God I only just managed to save it though. I found two chaps about to use it for their ablutions'. The daily supply drop on Thursday included canisters of water but most of the supplies landed outside the perimeter and German sniper fire and lack of jeeps made it difficult to recover some of the containers that did land within the defences.

As night fell and the rain added to our discomfort, we moved to a position near a mortar group, with houses in the vicinity. The night passed with very little activity on the part of the enemy and we were able to snatch brief periods of sleep.

Twice in the afternoon the RAF tried to get supplies to the men in the perimeter. The first supply mission, at 1245 was a disaster. 'A new sound intruded on the sound of battle, the throb of approaching aircraft' recalled Fred Moore 'and then the sky was suddenly filled with Dakotas. They started dropping desperately needed supplies, but too far away from us. We stood up, waved our yellow triangles, our arms, anything to attract their attention, but all to no avail. We watched, in horror, as planes were hit, caught fire and spiralled downwards to destruction. Then they were gone. Before long our position was being pounded with mortar shells, from dreaded Nebelwerfers, which were multiple barrelled. We withdrew to the tree lined ditch at the rear of our position to wait for the barrage to cease. I was one of a close group of three, with a 1st Battalion Sergeant in the middle. A salvo straddled our position, two live shells bursting, one to our front, the other to the rear and another landing between the Sergeant and the other guy, which unbelievably failed to detonate.'

The aircraft were shot up by enemy fighters and there was some evidence to suggest that the Germans were using British signals to attract some of the supplies and that they were operating at least one of the Eurekas. Corporal Smithson recalled 'There was no way of saying 'not there, we're down here. We did everything we could, like waving, but it didn't make any difference. I watched one afternoon - seven Dakotas came in slow and low. And the Germans had God knows how many 88mm guns and they shot the first five down - bang, bang, bang. Down they came. Missed the sixth one and shot the seventh one down. They were all dropping their stuff towards what is now the cemetery but you just couldn't get it. So we had no supplies whatsoever.' [61]

'Hell is Thursday' wrote Private Walter Boldock. 'Supply planes were still coming in, dropping their precious supplies into German hands. Sometimes 'Dummy' running, some at tree-top level, in flames from flak, courageous but futile; crashing in flames from concentrated flak pounding like devilish piledrivers. In a hopeful attempt, Lieutenant Clarkson lit a yellow smoke candle. A recognition signal to the planes. Almost immediately he was hit by a well directed mortar bomb. The yellow cloud drifted slowly over our lines. 'Anybody gotta fag? When's the Second Army coming?'Look to your front'. We repelled an advancing company of Germans, reeling and scrambling for cover. The Germans were quick to react. Bombs showered among our positions, spewed by the multi-barrelled mortars, splinters splattered through the stinking smoke. Death stalked two-handed to his harvest. Amid this hell, pinned down, deafened and weary, I dozed off. Asleep in the inferno. When I awoke (a hundred years later?) An astonished comrade exclaimed, 'I thought you were dead'.

'Four pm. we must withdraw. The remnants of our unit fell back along the base of a dry ditch. Me, Corporal Stan Lunt and Private Frankie Thompson covered them with Brens. We went back, through the smoke, eyes peering. An oath. Lunt had been hit. In the thigh from the flank, we couldn't see where. We ran back. 'Nothing serious'. He pushed us on.'

The second mission, at 1600, was much more successful. Because of the bad weather, the later waves of supply aircraft had to fly in without fighter protection and the force of 117 aircraft of RAF 38 Group met heavy flak and for the first time enemy fighters were in full evidence. Some aircraft were intercepted by ten FW 190s which broke through the fighter screen again. They took a heavy toll, shooting down seven out of ten aircraft from one squadron in the third wave. Corporal Clemont Burton Sproston of 253 Company, RASC, 49 Air Despatch Group was a member of a despatch crew of two in a Stirling on the re-supply mission. On approaching the dropping zone the aircraft was hit by Anti-Aircraft fire and caught fire. Sproston was given orders to despatch the load. Although the aircraft was well ablaze and the rear gunner's ammunition was exploding inside the fuselage, Sproston continued to despatch the load, which consisted of high explosives, at the right moment. It was entirely due to his coolness and courage in despatching this extremely dangerous load, that the pilot of the aircraft was able to crash land it without loss of life. He was awarded the Military Medal. [62]

61 Quoted in *'D-Day To Berlin'* by Andrew Williams (Hodder & Stoughton, 2004). Smithson was one of the lucky ones who would later safely cross the Neder Rijn to freedom.

62 After the aircraft had been crash landed Corporal Sproston and the crew of the aircraft eventually reached an Allied HQ from which they were despatched to Brussels in a troop carrying vehicle. On the way the convoy was attacked by four Tiger tanks and a number of vehicles were knocked out. A small party from the convoy took up their positions in a house and Sproston was put in charge of a forward observation post from which, although under heavy enemy fire, he directed with great effect the fire of a Bofors gun.

Ralph Fellows, from Winnipeg, Manitoba was navigator on a DC-3 on 271 Squadron at Down Ampney in Gloucestershire flown by 48-year old Major P. S. 'Joubie' Joubert, a South African who had flown in the 1914-1918 war and wore World War I ribbons.

'We were detailed to drop supplies to our troops on the ground. But, due to faulty communications and unknown to us, the designated drop zone was held by the Germans and our fighter cover, so essential to protect us on the way in and out, was back on the ground in the Brussels area, rearming and refuelling.

'The line of Daks received a terrible battering during the slow low-level drop, but Joubie held on grimly straight and level and eventually we were through. We climbed away and turned for home. Joubie put in the auto-pilot and wandered back to the cargo cabin to speak to our wonderful army despatchers.

I was busy at my navigation table when a shout from our wireless operator caused me to glance outside. FW 190s had got among our unarmed Dakotas and the sky seemed full of burning aircraft and parachutes. We, meanwhile, flew on unconcerned - on auto-pilot. Joubie scampered back to his position and, with a fair measure of skill, coupled with his usual luck, got us home safely. It could only have happened to Joubie.' 63

Twenty-two year old Warrant Officer Mark Azouz DFC RAFVR of Chiswick, London, a Stirling III pilot on 196 Squadron made four supply flights over Arnhem in LK557. He had taken off from Keevil on the 17th at 1055 and returned at 1600; from Wethersfield on the 18th at 1150 towing a Horsa, returning at 1725; on the 19th at 1310, returning at 1820 having dropped 24 containers and four panniers but sustaining 27 holes from light and heavy flak at the TRV and LZ; and on the 21st in LJ810, leaving at 1200 dropping a similar load at Arnhem and hit by flak. His Stirling was then attacked by three to five FW 190s and shot down at 1415 and was killed. He kept the Stirling in the air whilst all but one of his crew (the rear gunner) escaped. It being Yom Kippor, Azouz could have taken leave that day but he refused as men at Arnhem were waiting for supplies.

A total of 23 Stirlings and Dakotas (20% of the force) were unaccounted for; a further seven were damaged by fighters and 31 by flak which was more intense than ever along the route and in the target area. [64] Only 7·4 per cent of the total number of tons of food and ammunition (including the wrong shells for the 75mm guns) dropped was collected by the beleaguered 1st Airborne Division at Oosterbeek (for, after the evening of the fifth day, that was what the airborne troops were). Just 41 out of 300 tons got through. 'It was bloody awful looking up', a

63 'Joubie should have returned to his beloved South Africa after the Victory in Europe but he became 217 Squadron commander. On VJ Day late on in the celebrations a stove pipe was produced and filled with Very cartridges and other combustible items. Someone was needed to ignite it. No one would take the chance. Joubie 'had a go'. The contraption blew up in his face. He died the next day, 16 August 1945.' Quoted in *Out of the Blue: The Role of Luck in Air Warfare 1917-1966,* edited by Laddie Lucas (Hutchinson & Co Publishers Ltd 1985).

64 A total of 52% of the force was lost or damaged. In the Arnhem area of operations alone 79 transport aircraft were lost - 68 of 38 and 46 Groups RAF and 11 of 52nd Troop Carrier Wing USAF; with the loss of 160 RAF, RCAF, RAAF and RNZAF aircrew killed and 80 taken prisoner and 27 USAAF aircrew killed and 3 captured. In addition 79 Army air dispatchers of the Royal Army Service Corps were killed and 44 taken prisoner.110 fighter aircraft of the USAAF and RAF (including Dominion Air Forces) were lost during Operation 'Market-Garden'.

soldier in the 3rd Battalion thought 'and seeing all that stuff dropping down. I thought to myself maybe there's a bottle of beer in that lot. God, I was thirsty!' Men risked their lives, crawling out into the open. Snipers were active, persistent and ubiquitous and all the roads were blocked by trunks and branches of trees, bricks and masonry strewn over their surface. Sometimes their brave attempts were for nothing. 'Bloody few rations there', Lieutenant Colonel Michael St. John Packe, in charge of the RASC elements in Oosterbeek, complained bitterly to Lieutenant Colonel Henry Preston, Brigadier Hicks' principal administrative officer, when he discovered that some that had got through was 'damn useless stuff' and that all the things the Division really needed had 'gone down the drain'. 'Do you know what these are full of?' he added, kicking viciously at some panniers against which Preston was leaning, 'Berets! Red, bloody berets! And that one. That's full of stationery!' And now when the men of the Division desperately needed food and ammunition and water - above all water - they got soap.

Henry Preston continued to watch the aircraft until only two Dakotas remained in sight. 'And from somewhere in both of them a slow flame started to curl, gradually enveloping each fuselage. Flying lower and lower they continued to drop their panniers whose parachutes showed for a moment, red and blue and yellow against the dark green of the trees. I could not get rid of the impression, which was strengthened by my being unable to hear their engines that this was no living scene I was watching but something out of a silent film. Soon they disappeared and for a short time there was a strange silence. Then the 88s, freed from the task of dealing with the aircraft, turned once again to us. The rain started again and the crowd in front of the hotel broke up. I exchanged a few words with Michael Packe, just setting out on his forlorn task of trying to locate the few panniers that had fallen within the perimeter. Then, carrying a useless Very pistol and an incongruously gay yellow handkerchief, I walked slowly back to the hotel, feeling more futile than I had done since the operation began.'

At 1715 came the encouraging news that the Poles were arriving on their dropping zone south of the river just east of Driel. From the southern part of the perimeter, the spire of Driel Church was a solitary and prominent landmark in the flat land beyond the river. By the time the aircraft carrying the Poles arrived in the Arnhem area the flak had become intense and when, at about a quarter past five General Sosabowski's long awaited Polish Brigade arrived, not on the polder south of Arnhem but south of the Heveadorp ferry near Driel, they were right in the middle of it. It was hoped that the Poles would be able to cross over into the Oosterbeek perimeter by the ferry, leaving a bridgehead on the southern bank into which could be driven the spearheads of XXX Corps and Sosabowski was soon organising his brigade for the river crossing. As he approached the ferry, however, a woman in the Dutch underground, Mejuffrouw Cora Baltussen told him that the British had been driven off the northern end of the Heveadorp ferry two hours before the Polish landings. The ferry itself was now destroyed and the crossings were dominated by German guns. Sosabowski moved into a deserted farmhouse to make fresh plans. He was, so one of his officers said, 'in a fearful temper'. Not only were all his glider-borne units and most of his heavy weapons on the other side of the river; but one of his three battalions had failed to arrive. The aircraft transporting it had been forced to return to base owing to bad weather and it was not to reach him for three days. As he was looking anxiously at his maps, the door was thrown open and a naked man, dripping with water and splashed with mud, a camouflaged net wrapped around his face, burst into the room. 'What the hell?' Sosabowski began, but then recognising Captain Zwolanski, his liaison officer at the British Headquarters, he stopped. 'I have just swum the Rhine', Zwolanski said, 'to bring you the latest news.'

'Yes, it looks as if you have', said Sosabowski with an abrupt gracelessness. 'Tell me about it.'

Zwolanski told the general that the British would bring rafts to the river bank during the night so that the Poles could cross over to the northern side. But for most of the night Sosabowski waited for the rafts in vain until, two hours before dawn, he felt he could wait no longer and he withdrew his men from the river line so as to be prepared to hold off the German infantry attacks which he knew would not be delayed much longer.' South of the now German-held ferry crossing, the Poles took up defensive positions around Driel and General Bittrich, so as to prevent their opening up the road from Nijmegen, sent Major Knaust's battalion with a Panther tank company south across Arnhem bridge to support those units of the 10th SS Division in the area of Elst. The disappearance of this tough battalion from the edge of the divisional perimeter made, however, only a slight and temporary improvement to Urquhart's position which by dusk was, in the words of one of his staff, 'extremely precarious'.

That same afternoon the Border Regiment was attacked in the west; Major Lonsdale's force having withdrawn from their isolated positions in the east to north of the lower Oosterbeek overnight to the Arnhem road was attacked in the south; and the KOSB, after a gallant attempt to halt the onslaught with bayonets, were driven from their positions in the north. They decided immediately to retake them. 'We were delighted to have a chance of having a crack at the Germans', Colonel Payton-Reid wrote proudly in his diary. 'We drenched them with fire first and then with bayonets. They wouldn't stand to the bayonet and made no attempt to fight us. They fired as we came up. We cleared them right out.' But by dusk the strength of the KOSB had been reduced to 150 men and it seemed as impossible for them as for any other battalion to continue much longer to hold their ground.

The Lonsdale Force was subjected throughout Thursday to violent mortar bombardments from the German positions behind the railway embankment. Towards evening, while he was standing beside Captain, Reverend Robert Talbot Watkins the 31-year old Chaplain to the 1st Parachute Battalion, Lonsdale was wounded again. 'Padre Watkins did great work in getting in the wounded', one of those he took to a dressing station remembers. 'He was always in the middle of it where the need was most great and didn't seem to care. The snipers didn't shoot at him or if they did they missed him. I don't think they did shoot, though. They were all right like that. There wasn't much firing round the dressing stations.'

Presently, Lonsdale received some good news. 'Luck hadn't been on our side, but suddenly it seemed about to change. I could have cheered when Lord Billy Buckhurst, our liaison officer with the 4th Brigade Headquarters, brought me the great news that armoured reconnaissance units of the 2nd Army had reached the far bank of the river.' XXX Corps would soon attempt a crossing of the river by the Heveadorp ferry, preceded by a barrage on the low-lying land between the river and the road.

Lonsdale Force, out on the open polder and in waterlogged trenches, were under direct observation and fire from the high ground to the north and from the railway embankment. Lonsdale therefore ordered their withdrawal to the little church of Oosterbeek Laag, but this had to be carried out in daylight and resulted in many casualties. The men, tired and soaked, were brought in to the church to dry out, clean their weapons and get more ammunition; they had been fighting continuously for four days and nights. 'It was a rugged, thick-walled, ancient church, recalled Padre Watkins 'and never in all the centuries of its quiet watch over the Neder Rijn had it sheltered such a congregation as now, came stumbling in. They sprawled in the pews, they 'brewed up' in the aisle and on the chancel floor, they smoked, they swore. Above all they rested. The crash of shells and the falling of plaster and roof-timbers was nothing to what was going on outside. This was peace.'

'A Padre who, noting that I was still in possession of the machine gun, which seemed to grow heavier with every step, stopped to offer words of encouragement' recalled Fred Moore, one of the men who sat down in the pews in the growing dark as it started to rain again. He was now one of the survivors of a mixed group, composed of remnants of the 1st, 3rd and 11th Para Battalions and some South Staffs. The noise of battle was evident, somewhere on our right flank, rifle fire, mortars and occasionally heavy artillery, but incredibly our progress was unimpeded. We reached the end of the track we were following, revealing a large expanse of grassy meadow. The leading elements of our group were part way across, completely exposed when a burst of machine gun fire from the woods on our right, cut them down. It was essential that we crossed this obstacle with the utmost speed, in order to join up with our main force at the far side. It was decided to cross individually, each man waiting until the guy in front was halfway across before commencing his run. Halfway across, running as fast as I could, hampered by the weight of the machine gun on my shoulder and under fire I stumbled and fell forward. The fellow behind me had fortunately commenced his run and I was able to get to my feet and reach the other side unharmed. We had now reached the outer defences of the designated defensive perimeter and I was ordered to surrender my machine gun in exchange for a rifle; not however, before discovering that no-one had thought to bring the ammunition!

'Major 'Dicky' Lonsdale of the 11th Battalion informed us that we were now under his command and designated the 'Lonsdale Force'. We also learned that the 2nd Battalion at the bridge were still holding out, though seriously depleted, surrounded and isolated; also that the Guards Armoured Division had reached the Nijmegen area.'

Cutting a striking figure, with a sling around his slightly injured arm, a blood-stained bandage covering the three head wounds he had sustained and a further bandage on his leg, Lonsdale proceeded to give his men, now numbering no more than 400 including the glider pilots, some words of advice and encouragement. 'The 3rd Battalion was down to 35 men' recalled Lieutenant James Cleminson. 'Dicky Lonsdale made his speech from the pulpit of the church. I have no doubt that he put heart into his command as a result of this short harangue, standing there with a bandage round his head and his arm in a sling; and saying, in effect, that we were going to stand where we were and hold Oosterbeek until 2nd Army arrived.'

'The scene as I spoke inside the shattered church lives vividly in my memory', Lonsdale wrote. 'I can still see the tired upturned faces of my congregation, the strangest ever gathered there... Yes, I thought, but they're still defiant though, still unbroken. 'You know as well as I do there are a lot of bloody Germans coming at us.' Lonsdale told them. 'Well, all we can do is to stay here and hang on in the hope that somebody catches us up. We must fight for our lives and stick together. We've fought the Germans before - in North Africa, Sicily, Italy. They weren't good enough for us then and they're bloody well not good enough for us now. They're up against the finest soldiers in the world. An hour from now you will take up defensive positions north of the road outside. Make certain you dig in well and that your weapons and ammo are in good order. We are getting short of ammo, so when you shoot, shoot to kill. My HQ will be in the area of the church. Good luck to you all.'[65]

The 'Lonsdale Force' would hold their new positions until the end of the battle. [66] 'No one, of course,' says Lonsdale, 'had any doubts now as to the seriousness of our position. All hope of breaking through to the bridge had been abandoned. 'I didn't care by then if I never saw the bloody bridge at all; and I don't think many of us did neither', Private George Wood thought. 'But we dug in and held on. That's how you get. Fed up but flipping stubborn. Those snipers, though. They were a bastard.'

Soon after seven on the morning of Thursday 21st, the Germans made a determined attempt to remove the remnants of the 10th Battalion from their positions on the most easterly position astride the main road through Oosterbeek with tanks and self-propelled guns firing phosphorus shells. The initial assaults were all repelled, but a self-propelled gun was later placed where it could not be attack and it proceeded to blow the occupied buildings apart, sometimes using phosphorus shells to set them alight. The parachutists had to withdraw from their houses which were soon burning fiercely. In the withdrawal Lieutenant Colonel Kenneth Smyth was severely wounded in the stomach and was half buried in one of the houses. Unconscious, he was brought down into the cellar of No.2 Annastraat with the other wounded. Upon waking it became clear that he was utterly disorientated and kept on asking 'Where am I?' As he drifted in and out of consciousness, the owner of the house Mrs Bertje Voskuil tried to explain that he was in Holland, at Oosterbeek, but he didn't understand. Soon after, German troops moved into the buildings and captured most of those inside. A German officer; a seemingly hideous man, with a centre parting and a monocle on a ribbon entered the cellar. Smyth regained consciousness and asked to see a commanding German officer. The man spoke

65 After the war, Lonsdale liked to give the impression that he used the Church as his headquarters; a romantic image but not factually correct, for his actual Headquarters was 300 yards to the north-west of it, from where orders were passed to the front line units by a field telephone, courtesy of the 3rd Battalion's signallers.

66 On Wednesday the Lonsdale Force was reorganised to include just the parachute battalions, whilst 'Sheriff' Thompson assumed command of the 2nd South Staffords and the Glider Pilots in the area, together with his artillery guns; collectively known as Thompson Force. On the following day, however, Thompson was wounded and so all the infantry in the sector were placed under Major Lonsdale.

no English and asked Mrs Voskuil what 'that man' wanted. She was quite outraged and abruptly said that 'The Colonel' needed a doctor. He left and returned several minutes later with a German doctor. He briefly examined Smyth's stomach wound and asked Mrs Voskuil to 'Tell the officer I am sorry I have to hurt him but I must look at his wound. Tell him to grit his teeth.' As the doctor began to pull back the clothing around the wound, Smyth fell unconscious once more. The wound was fatal and it left Smyth paralysed from the waist down. His suffering ended one month later on the 26th October in hospital.[67]

'It was getting 'a bit chaotic', a soldier records with characteristic understatement. 'Everybody was all over the shop and we just looked for Germans to knock out... Then the Tigers arrived and I heard a chap say, 'We can't do much against these bastards!' We still had PIATs but the ammunition was getting scarce and fresh supplies didn't arrive. We took three prisoners who had 'Players' and Woodbines on them, so we might have guessed that the supply drops had misfired.'

Frederick Hodges and the men of The King's Own Royal Border Regiment who were still holding out at Van Borselen Weg on the road outside Oosterbeek were mainly concerned about the lack of food. 'When we set out we only had enough food for two days and that soon ran out. We did get the odd container dropped by the RAF and managed to make a stew for dinner one night. The next day I broke into my emergency rations tin, which was a very rich chocolate. Maybe the Germans had this on them as well. I looked out into the field where four dead soldiers lay and my pal and I went out to check their pockets. We found a number of things including watches, but we only managed to find two black biscuits! Searching through one of the soldiers' pockets, I found something which changed my whole perspective on the war. This soldier carried a picture of his wife and two beautiful children and it was then I realised that the men on the other side of the line were exactly the same as us. They had families they had left behind and somewhere a mother and children were weeping for this lost man in battle. We left the bodies as we found them, taking nothing from them but the food they had.

'Another parachute landed shortly afterwards and many of us thought it was full of food. The Germans came out to retrieve it but we fired on them. They ran off before we could get a clear shot and so it was that the two sides started to fight over this basket. Eventually we pushed the Germans back and took the basket only to be let down as it was filled with 25 gallons of petrol but no food!'

Late on Thursday Lonsdale reorganized the defensive layout. The men of 1st and 3rd Parachute Battalions, under Major Alan Bush, took over the houses north of the road running east from this church, tasked to hold the road and to cover the high ground to the north, from where attacks were likely to come. The 11th Battalion were withdrawn into reserve close to the church; some had been sent to reinforce 'Breese force' on the western perimeter where Major Charles Frederick Osborne Breese commanding the 1st Battalion, The Borders in the absence of Colonel Haddon, had gathered the survivors of 'B' Company, numbering little

67 Of the 582 men of the 10th Battalion who landed on the 18 September, 92 were killed, 404 became PoWs and 96 were evacuated. The casualties sustained were never replaced and the battalion was disbanded after the battle.

more than a platoon and two depleted platoons of 'A' Company and 40 paratroopers (joined several days later by 35 Poles). Lonsdale Force's sector covered the southern end of the eastern perimeter and Major Robert Cain of the South Staffords was one of three Majors defending this sector of the line. 'B' Company of the 1st Border held a wide stretch of ground at the extreme south-west of the Perimeter when they came under heavy attack from German infantry and armour. Many casualties were inflicted upon the attackers but the Company was compelled to retreat, losing many of its number as it did so. Purely as a result of Breese's strong and fearless skills as a leader the area was made secure in only an hour and though German artillery singled out the area for a consistent and particularly heavy bombardment throughout the remainder of the battle, they did not feel confident enough to challenge this solid defence with another infantry assault.

Soon after their arrival and before occupying their new positions Major Robert Cain and his company found a laundry north of the Oosterbeek Church where the men 'had a wash and put on clean shirts which they found lying about.' Thus refreshed they took their stand on the high ground to the left of the church, a severe edifice with 'a funeral inscription on the wall with some Cherubs blowing trumpets round it.' In the houses around the laundry, which also covered open ground they were soon repeatedly attacked by tanks and self-propelled guns. A self-propelled gun which came into action every morning and afternoon was particularly troublesome. The whole area was under fire continually, mainly from mortars and it followed a regular pattern. It seldom let up for long and seemed to work round the area in a systematic manner. Snipers were a constant danger; several crept in during the night and had to be rooted out at daybreak. As the battle progressed Cain became determined to destroy as much enemy armour as possible and sited himself in a laundry's garden, much to the chagrin of the Dutch owner. Cain was everywhere, dealing with armour and snipers and encouraging his men. On that Thursday afternoon the South Staffords still held the laundry area; part of G Squadron of the Glider Pilot Regiment were in position around the road junction on Weverstraat to the north when two StuG III self-propelled guns approached the open flank to their left.

Major Cain, who was armed with a PIAT, prepared to lob bombs over the roof of a house behind which one of the SPGs lay concealed and an artillery sergeant, J. Daly got ready to take on the other with a Bren gun. Guided by an artillery officer, Lieutenant Ian Meikle from behind a chimney stack in a building above him, Cain waited in a trench until the first SPG was close enough to engage. Then as Meikle directed his fire, Cain loosed off about 50 bombs 'which blew my left ear drum in' said Cain. 'Meikle was shouting at me' Cain recalled, 'giving me instructions, when the chimney pot from his house fell into the trench I was in. Meikle was killed. The other man in my trench got out screaming and scrambling. I told him to come back but he wouldn't and I never saw him again. The explosion showered Cain with masonry but despite this, he kept his position. Staff Sergeant Richard Long of the Glider Pilot Regiment remembered that through the clouds of dust, Cain fired round after round from his PIAT until the SPG was disabled. Cain eventually entered a little shed with a PIAT and two bombs, put his head round a corner of the door and seeing the gun' fired at the thing and the bomb went off underneath it.' The last shot of the gun blew the shed to pieces just after. Cain had left it. 'Just after this' Cain said 'a tank came up the road. The chaps told me about it. I crept to the corner and there it was coming up the road. I put the bomb into the PIAT and fired at the tank. The range was about 100 yards. I think it must have struck the track. The tank fired back immediately in my direction and this raised a huge cloud of dust and smoke. As soon as I could see the outline of the tank again, I let it have another. This also raised a lot of dust again. The tank gun fired back straight down the road. Then I looked again and watched and through the dust I saw the crew of the tank baling out. They opened up with Schmeissers, but I got a couple of Brens onto the road and told my men to keep up continuous fire and the Germans were killed.'

Cain then fired at another tank, but the 'bomb went off in the PIAT', he said. 'I got bits of stuff in my face and two black eyes. It blew me over backwards and I was blind. I was shouting like a hooligan. I shouted to someone to get on to the PIAT because there was another tank behind. I blubbered and yelled and swore. They dragged me off to the Regimental Aid Post.' Within half an hour Cain's sight returned. He refused morphia and against all advice returned to the front lines, deciding that he 'wasn't wounded enough to stay where [he] was'. One of the 1st Light Battery's 75mm guns was man-handled by a detachment including the Officers' Mess Sergeant Roullier and an RASC clerk into a position and they blew the SPG apart.

No sooner had this danger been averted than a company of enemy infantry infiltrated between the lines of the Border Regiment and E troop of the 1st Airlanding Light Regiment, occupying a gas works from which snipers were able to fire into the heart of the divisional area. Captain C. A. Harrison, 'E' Troop's commander, led a hastily collected force of men from various regiments against the gas works and drove the Germans out of it. However, as soon as the Germans were driven back in one sector, they broke through again in another and Urquhart decided that he must constrict his perimeter still further. He pulled back the KOSB, sent the Independent Company with a squadron of Royal Engineers and the remains of the Reconnaissance Squadron to fill a growing gap in the north-east; and withdrew the forward units of the divisional RASC and sent them to fill another large gap in the south-east just north of 'Lonsdale Force'. Even so the defended area was still too large; it was rather less than a mile wide where it ran parallel with the river at the south and about three quarters of a mile wide at the north.

On the following day Cain's eardrums burst from the constant firing and barrage, but he was content to stuff his ears with bandages and continue fighting.

Private Walter 'Bol' Boldock who had withdrawn after the first supply drop had only got a few yards when searing pain snatched his arm. 'A bullet scorched through my side and tore out of my back. I looked at my arm, shattered, with blood pouring down, trickling from my fingers. My back, now numb, felt saturated in blood. (The bullet had just missed my main artery in my arm and just missed my spine but it had torn my back muscles apart). They came to me. Told me to rest. 'Be back with a stretcher Wally'. Death only comes to other soldiers. All soldiers know this. I felt the pain, the weakness flowing over me. This was it - This mustn't be it. My thoughts flooded back to my home - to my home. This mustn't be it - I don't want to die. A silent prayer. I forced myself to my feet, arm useless, in pain. Dead and dying lay all around, choking in filthy smoke. I caught the eyes of a comrade in desperate agony. 'I'm sorry mate, I can't help, sorry'. I stumbled drunkenly across a thousand miles of fields and ditches. My eyes unseeingly. My legs rebelled but I forced myself on. 'Whatsamatter Bol'? The voice of Ginger Pearce guided me to a large house being used as a dressing station.

'By Thursday the 21st' continues Major Guy Rigby-Jones 'the Tafelberg was in the front line and for the next 36 hours we were in and out of German hands, as the battle raged to and fro through the houses. We had expected to be relieved and move into proper hospitals in Arnhem. Conditions were far from ideal. It was difficult to decide whether to operate on patients or to defer them until better facilities were available. We hadn't a clue as to what was happening to XXX Corps. By the final night the Germans had evacuated most of the casualties and the remaining medical staff were concentrated at the Schoonoord. All through that night our shells passed overhead and I slept happily with the thought that morning would bring relief; but imagine our shock when the peace and quiet revealed nothing but Germans. I must pay tribute to the Dutch doctors and nurses, who risked their lives to give us so much help and I remember the terrible retribution that fell upon them during the following winter.'

'I was operated on in the billiard room, which was to the right of the main door' recalled Major John Waddy of 156 Parachute Battalion.' A day later he was moved to a house opposite as the number of casualties increased. Because the aid stations were in the front lines of the Oosterbeek perimeter, they came under constant fire and he was wounded twice more. A mortar round shell fragment lodged in his left foot and a later hit caused splinter injuries to his face and shoulder. On another occasion, as the battle seesawed around the aid post, Germans occupied his building. A British sniper shot a German rifleman, prompting a German sergeant to lecture the British about shooting at a Red Cross house.

'After a day, as the casualties poured in, I was taken across to the house opposite. The wounded lay close-packed in the rooms, some half-naked, having had clothes cut off by medics in the field: blankets were few and shared. We were soon in the midst of the fighting, with mortar bombs landing close and the occasional bullet smacking into the walls of the room. On one of the days our room received a direct hit from a mortar bomb, which killed several and wounded again others, including myself. This was followed by a rush of Germans through the house: an airborne counter-attack swept them out. This went on several times until we were finally in German hands. They set up a firing position in the wrecked bay window. A SS soldier started to push around a young Dutch nurse, shouting at her for helping the British; but one of the RAMC orderlies stepped up to him and rolled up his sleeves, said, 'Leave her alone or I'll knock your fucking head off!' One of their riflemen firing from the window was shot by a glider pilot across the road, whereupon a large SS sergeant berated the British for firing at a Red Cross house. He then stood over the wounded German shouting at him for whimpering, 'What would the Führer say if he saw you now?'

'Most nights we could hear the squeak and rattle of tanks and our hopes rose: 'That's 2nd Army, they've crossed', the optimists said, but it was the German armour edging closer through the streets in the darkness. Smells are the most evocative of memories and today I can smell that mixture of wet earth, burnt cordite, brick dust and rotting wounds. Food was almost non-existent and a little dirty water was got by buckets left in the rain. Medical supplies had more or less run out, but everyone bore it stoically and retained surprisingly good morale.

'The medics continued to work almost without rest for the full nine days in their task of caring for the wounded, despite the fact that they were not only in the front line, but between the two opposing forces. They were the unsung heroes of this battle, under the inspiring leadership of Colonel Graeme Warrack, 1st Airborne's senior medical officer, who took over direction of the area, with Lieutenant Colonel Arthur T. Marrable in command at the Schoonoord.'

On Sunday the 24th Waddy was wounded once more when a mortar struck the window sill of a large bay window and exploded, sending a fragment of shrapnel into his foot. Shortly after the room in which he lay was hit again and he received deep cuts to his face, chin and right shoulder from wood splinters were propelled in his direction and from bricks that fell on him. At this point Colonel Warrack rushed outside. As Waddy hauled himself up, he could see Warrack standing in the street and yelling at the Germans 'You bloody bastards! Can't anybody recognize a Red Cross?'

'On Tuesday 26th the whole of this area was hit, in error, by a heavy concentration of medium artillery fire from XXX Corps' continues Waddy. 'Many of the houses were hit; we received a direct hit which killed or wounded more men, including myself again; the house started to burn and after a while the survivors were dragged out of the rubble. For a time I lay in the back garden and close to a pile of some thirty bodies of those who had been killed here or had died of wounds.

'After a while I was rescued by a sergeant of my battalion and taken out on his jeep. I thought that we had been relieved and were driving to safety, but too soon he turned into a large building - the fire station. Other wounded were being collected here, including a small Dutch boy with one leg amputated and bandaged, carried in by an airborne medic. Soon the Germans drew up a convoy of ambulances and trucks on the main road and we were taken to Apeldoorn, but our journey was, at times, delayed by the attention of roving RAF Typhoons, which

68 Waddy spent the next six weeks in a German hospital in Apeldoorn. Once again the British patients were lectured about firing at the Red Cross after a Spitfire strafed the operating theatre, but overall Waddy was impressed by the kindness of the German staff and guards. He narrowly avoided having his foot amputated when a nurse removed the splinter embedded in it with a pair of forceps and once he had sufficiently recovered from his wounds he was taken to Stalag VIIA where he remained until the camp was liberated at the end of April 1945. John Waddy recovered from his wounds and saw active service after the war in Palestine, Malaya and Egypt. He then joined the Canadian Air Training Centre as an instructor during an exchange, attended Staff College in 1950 and was promoted to the rank of a full Colonel and given command of the Depot The Parachute Regiment and Airborne Forces. He was later to become Colonel of the SAS. Returning to Arnhem in 1954, he was presented with a blackened and severely battered silver cigarette case, bearing the inscription 'Waddy'. Upon returning home, he had the case repaired by a jeweller and it became clear that the case had belonged to Colonel Horatio Barlow, who had been killed at Arnhem. It had been presented in the mid-1930s by John Waddy's father (then Commander of the 2nd Somerset Light Infantry) to the then Captain Barlow as reward for winning a point-to-point race. The case was found 150 yards from where Barlow had been killed. Waddy later wrote *A Tour of the Arnhem Battlefields*. In 2000 he made a television appearance on the Channel 4 series, Great Military Blunders, of which the Battle of Arnhem formed a part.

had hardly been seen since we landed.' [68]

After Thursday, fire support from XXX Corps and later from 43rd (Wessex) Division artillery firing from south of the river broke up many of the German attacks against this vital neck of the perimeter, which was only 700 yards wide. On Saturday RAF Typhoons appeared for the first time and their rocket fire had a quietening effect on the enemy.

'We did get artillery support from the south side of the River Rhine' recalled Frederick Hodges of The King's Own Royal Border Regiment: 'Captain Hodson, our Company Commander, stood up directing it by radio (one of the few that worked). I believe some tanks were damaged. Once, while on lookout I spotted some tanks in the distance coming down the road from Utrechtweg. We knew that following the tanks would be infantry and so we got ready to attack. When they reached our position, the leading tank took one glimpse across and caught my eye, shooting me in the arm, knocking me flat onto my back in the trench. I felt my arm go dead and for a few moments I thought it had been shot off. Looking down though I saw it was still intact. The medic, Danny Fowler, arrived next to me to bandage the wound. I later found out that my arm was broken in three places. While this was going on, the fighting ensued between the British and the Germans. I saw the tank move forward to go around the corner next to the house we were in front of where I knew an anti tank gun was located. Out of the corner of my eye I spotted the corporal climb up to man it, as he did sadly he was shot. We were not defeated though and by the time I was finished being bandaged everyone in the French tank was dead. The leading tank had carried on around a bend and our anti-tank gun put four armour-piercing shells into it, killing the crew and setting it on fire. The other tank retreated. The tank behind retreated and no other attempted to attack our position again simply because the lane was too narrow!

'The wounded including myself were taken down to the cellar of the nearby house and I was one of the first to be led inside. The next four days heralded an assault on our position and every day it filled up more until bursting point where 30 to 40 soldiers lay injured inside. Next to me lay a badly wounded soldier Geordie Long from Newcastle, who sadly didn't make it back to see his family again. We had no food supplies left whilst we were down there but luckily we found some pickled apples and every so often some potatoes would be brought down dug up by those brave few who continued to fight on.'

'As night fell and the rain added to our discomfort' wrote Fred Moore 'we moved to a position near a mortar group, with houses in the vicinity. The night passed with very little activity on the part of the enemy and we were able to snatch brief periods of sleep.'

Urquhart called Hicks and Hackett to the Hartenstein Headquarters. Earlier in the day, after having a few words with Martin at the dressing station in the vicarage next to Oosterbeek Laag church, Hackett and his acting Brigade Major, D. J. 'Tiny' Madden were crossing the front lawn of the house when Hackett was struck in the face by the splinters of a bursting mortar bomb which killed Madden and badly wounded Colonel Thompson in the stomach. Returning from a party just before setting out for Arnhem, Madden had been involved in a bad car accident and was taken to hospital. It hadn't kept him away from Arnhem. Several other men were also wounded and had been carried into the crowded house for treatment. 'I want you to read this', Urquhart said to Hicks and Hackett, holding out a signal which he had drafted. 'They ought to know across the river that it's not too good here, but I don't really want to overdo it. Do you think this is going too far?'

'We read it slowly and quietly', Hackett says, 'sitting in wicker garden chairs and we reckoned that no, on the whole, that was fair enough... I said I thought it was about right. Pip said so too. Roy thanked us and handed it in for transmission.' It read: 'No knowledge of elements of Division in Arnhem for twenty-four hours. Balance of Division in very tight perimeter. Heavy mortaring and machine-gun fire. Our casualties heavy. Rations stretched to utmost. Relief within twenty-four hours vital.' This entry was made at 2144 in the Divisional diary.

The horseshoe was now roughly a thousand yards wide at the base, broadening to 1,200 at the top by two thousand deep and already Urquhart had lost many of the men that he originally moved into it. In this ceaselessly bombarded area of 450 acres, the 1st Airborne Division struggled to survive. The Germans were calling the tiny perimeter - 'Der Hexenkessel': 'the Witches Cauldron'.

'Market-Garden' Timeline

Thursday 21 September (D+4)

Dawn Fog and rain continues unabated. Generalfeldmarschall Model at Army Group B orders Corps 'Feldt' to hold its position. With Nijmegen bridge now in Allied hands Model places all troops as far south as Elst under II SS Panzer Corps, which is to wipe out the British at Arnhem while containing any drive north of Nijmegen. Student's 1st Parachute Army is to organize a coordinated pincer attack by LXXXVIII Corps and LXXXVI Corps against Hell's Highway for next day. In the Oosterbeek pocket, Urquhart reorganizes his defence.

0900 An attack by Kampfgruppe 'von Tettau' drives 1st Battalion of the Border Regiment back off the Westerbouwing hill, the crucial high ground that overlooks the Heveadorp ferry and away from the ferry itself, which is destroyed in the fighting. From the Westerbouwing, German fire can dominate any attempted river crossing.

Last fight begins at Arnhem Bridge as Gough and his men try to break out northwards against SS-Kampfgruppe 'Knaust'. There is no formal surrender or end to the fighting. In small groups, the British either run out of ammunition or are overwhelmed. Some refuse to give up or fight on with knives and the last shots are not fired at Arnhem Bridge for another two days.

1000 At Nijmegen, the way across the two bridges finally cleared of German snipers. Relieved of much of the responsibility for Nijmegen, 82nd Airborne begins a general attack late in the afternoon with 504th PIR and 508th PIR, which clears Corps 'Feldt' off the Groesbeek Heights before establishing a solid defence.

1200 SS-Kampfgruppe 'Knaust' at last cross the Arnhem Bridge. Frost's men have denied the use of the vital Bridge to the enemy for 88 hours without relief; the last twelve without food or water.

Plans laid on the 20th for airborne operations on D+4 calls for 117 RAF resupply sorties to a drop point near Hartenstein about 200 yards east of that used on D+3. To reduce the flak hazard the aircraft are to be sent in four waves, really separate missions, with the first arriving at 1315 and the last, not until 1615. The American troop carriers are to send 806 C-47s. Of these, 114 in the 52nd Wing carrying Polish paratroops will fly in the left lane of the northern route but not to DZ 'K'. As soon as it is realized that only its northern end the bridge at Arnhem is in British hands the zone is moved further to the west and on D+3 a radio message from 1st Airborne requests that the Poles should be dropped at Driel, south of the Heaveadorp Ferry, cross the river there and take up positions west of Oosterbeek. In the centre lane will fly 419 planes with gliders for the 82nd Division, 82 towing gliders to the 101st Division and a parachute resupply mission of 191 planes for the 101st Division. The glider and resupply serials for the 101st Division are sandwiched in between the first four and the last four serials going to the 82nd, probably to give the latter division time to clear its landing zone before the second batch of gliders arrive. At first the lead transport is scheduled to arrive at LZ 'O' at 1515 but the time is later changed to 1615. All missions, both RAF and US, are to fly the southern route and use Eindhoven as their IP. Protection of the first three waves of RAF resupply planes is the responsibility of six Spitfire squadrons of ADGB. One 8th Air Force Group will provide area cover. The last wave of RAF aircraft and the long American column are to be guarded from the Belgian coast to Eindhoven by 15 squadrons of fighters of ADGB; between Eindhoven and their destinations protection will be by 15 fighter groups of 8th Air Force.

The weather is almost identical with that on the preceding day. Thick fog is general over England during the morning but lifts in the south before the first resupply wave began taking off at 1100 hours. However, low stratus persists between 600 and 1,200 feet and haze restricts visibility to as little as a mile in some areas. Conditions are much better outside England and over Holland there is only 4/10 to 7/10 cloud at about 3,000 feet. Escort for the main troop carrier effort is also much curtailed because of weather. Five out of 15 RAF fighter squadrons fail to leave England because of the overcast and the 118 ADGB fighters which make sorties sight only a few German fighters, which make off as fast as they can. As for 8th Air Force, it cancels the missions of 13 of its 15 supporting groups, leaving one group of P-47s and one of P-51s to perform area patrol. Another group, the 359th, which is to escort the Polish paratroop mission manages to get 20 picked pilots into the air, but conditions are so bad that they have to be recalled. The P-51s run into low clouds over their base during assembly and are recalled. This leaves only 36 P-51s of the 353rd Fighter Group under MEW guidance to protect the troop carriers beyond Eindhoven. The 353rd patrols the Eindhoven-Arnhem area faithfully from 1610 to 1650. At 1630 about five miles southwest of Nijmegen it encounters approximately 30 German fighters, some attacking C-47s while others act as top cover. After a sharp clash in which the enemy displayed considerable skill the 353rd drive them off. One P-47 is lost and six Luftwaffe fighters reported shot down.

1600 SS-Kampfgruppe 'Knaust' reach Elst from Arnhem. Short of ammunition, artillery and air cover, the tanks of the Guards Armoured push up the exposed causeway road as far as Elst and halt in the face of German fire. 1st British Airborne establishes firm radio contact with XXX Corps through the Royal Artillery's 64th Medium Regiment. The distance from Nijmegen to Arnhem is only 11 miles and through this link Urquhart could call for fire support from the whole of XXX Corps' artillery, drastically reducing the German advantage north of the Lower Rhine. Without this fire support the Oosterbeek pocket would not have been held. Model orders specialist troops and equipment for street fighting to be flown into Deelen by Junkers Ju 52 transport aircraft and is promised 506th Heavy Tank Battalion, freshly equipped with 45 PzKpfw VIB King Tiger tanks from eastern Germany.

North of Eindhoven, 101st Airborne continue to push the Germans back on either side of Hell's Highway in a series of limited attacks supported by British armour. Lieutenant General Sir Miles 'Bimbo' Dempsey begins to move Second Army HQ to Sint-Oedenrode and Field Marshal Montgomery establishes 21st Army Group Tactical HQ just south of Eindhoven to be in closer touch with the battle.

All of the 64 Stirlings dispatched by 38 Group in the first three RAF resupply waves reach Holland and 61 are believed to have accomplished their mission but poor coordination by the RAF and persistent attacks by the Luftwaffe cause their supplies to be dropped 9.3 miles away on the opposite side of the Rhine. The weather keeps all but 19 of their Spitfire escorts from leaving England and they do not catch up with the mission until after it had reached the Arnhem area. Although the 56th Fighter Group sends 34 P-47s as area cover, they also arrive late. This inadequate fighter protection gives the Luftwaffe its first good chance to attack an Allied airborne mission and it makes the most of the occasion. Thirteen Stirlings fail to return and most of them have fallen prey to the enemy fighters. One squadron of FW 190s swooping down out of the clouds shoot down seven out of a sequence of ten Stirlings of 190 Squadron at Fairford within a few moments. The CO, Wing Commander Graeme Harrison is among those killed. The Spitfires do not appear to have engaged the enemy. Some of their pilots sight enemy fighters but mistake them for P-51s on area cover until it is too late to catch them. Near Lochem about 1505 the 56th Group does intercept 22 or more German fighters on their way back to Germany from the Arnhem area. The group claim to have destroyed 15 of them at a cost of two missing and one salvaged.

Fourth airborne lift. The RAF is ordered to drop on the Hartenstein. The 53 Dakotas of 46 Group which fly the last wave of the RAF resupply lift suffer ten aircraft lost to flak and fighters. In all, out of 117 aircraft dispatched by 38 and 46 Groups, 23 are missing and 38 damaged. Once again 1st Airborne Division have a 'Eureka' beacon functioning, at least some of the time, on the roof of its HQ, but only a couple of navigators are known to have signalled it and neither obtain responses. The lack of use may be attributed to the pilots' growing familiarity with the route and to the relatively good flying conditions over Holland. Again, panels, Very lights, smoke and an Aldis lamp are used to mark the drop point and once again the Very lights are by far the most effective with 30 pilots sighting them as compared to 14 seeing panels and one seeing smoke. Although 91 crews report successful drops and some others probably reach the drop point, the intense fire of the German forces surrounding 1st Airborne effectively disrupts the drop. Most of the supplies land outside the perimeter and German sniper fire and lack of jeeps makes it difficult to recover some of the containers that do land within the defences. Out of 271 tons of supplies parachuted, only about 11 tons or 4 percent is officially recovered. It is, however, likely that the starving and desperate troops pick up some food and ammunition which they did not declare or turn in.

1st Polish Parachute Brigade's three infantry battalions finally take off after two days of delay due to the weather. Layer upon layer of clouds from 150 feet above the ground to heights of 9,000 feet blanket the 52nd Wing bases in the Grantham area but these conditions are outweighed by the desperate need of 1st Airborne Division for immediate assistance, which only the Poles can provide. As one flier wrote, 'The weather was impossible. No one believed until actual take-off that the mission would actually run.' But it did. The mission is arranged in serials of 27, 27, 27 and 33 aircraft, the first two serials being flown from Spanhoe by the 315th Group and the other two from Saltby by the 314th Group. The lead serial of the 314th begins taking off at 1310 with instructions to assemble at the 1,500-foot level which is believed to be clear. The serial assembles successfully and starts out, but soon finds itself in a blind alley, completely blocked by cloud. The only thing to do is disperse and try to climb out of the overcast. In this attempt 25 pilots lose their bearings and return to base. The other two after long circling above the clouds sight a later serial and join it. By 1405 when the next take-offs are made tactics have been revised. The aircraft take off in single file, spiralling up to 10,000 feet and assemble there on top of the clouds. This works. Only six of the 87 aircraft in the last three serials become detached from their mates and have to return to base. However, at 1545 while crossing the Channel a flight leader in the 314th repeatedly receives a message on the flight control frequency which he is unable to decode. Deciding it must be a recall, he brings his ten C-47s back to Saltby.

Of 114 C-47s, 41 (including virtually the whole of 1st Battalion) turn back in the bad weather and three land at Brussels. Over the first part of its route the mission remains close to 10,000 feet, but near the coast the clouds thin and break, enabling formations to descend to the 1,500-foot level. One straggler, hit by flak near the mouth of the Scheldt has to drop its troops near Ghent and limp home on one engine. The rest swung up the west side of the salient to the drop zone, a large area of open, ditched land northeast of the town of Driel on the south side of the Rhine opposite Heveadorp. No pathfinders have been sent to mark the zone, but the leaders find their way to it by good visual navigation, checked occasionally by 'Gee', which is functioning well and without much jamming.

Three fighter groups of 8th Fighter Command fly support but the bad weather forces recall of one group near the Dutch coast. Other groups encounter about 50 fighters, claiming 20 destroyed against four aerial combat losses. The mission has neither anti-flak patrols nor fighter cover to protect it over Holland. The one fighter group on patrol beyond Eindhoven leaves the area just before the troop carriers arrive. Fortunately no hostile fighters spot the serials, but there is some ground fire along the way and much light flak and small arms fire near the zone. Several C-47s are hit and at least one very hard hit during the approach, but all manage to make their drops. The three serials pass over the zone at 1708, 1712 and 1715 at altitudes between 700 and 850 feet. The Poles, who are overloaded with equipment and are making their first drop into combat, are a little slow in getting out. This causes many of them to jump several hundred yards beyond the zone. It also prevents the troop carrier formations from turning homeward as soon as they had intended. As a result, several flights after turning south pass over Elst, a German stronghold bristling with anti-aircraft guns. So many were the guns and so incessant their firing that the little town reminded one flier of 'a pinball machine gone mad.' The formations exposed to this barrage disintegrate instantaneously. Most of the pilots dive onto the deck and fly across Holland at minimum altitude and maximum speed. Very few aircraft return to base that night. However, next day it is found that only five, all from the 315th Group, have been destroyed. The other missing aircraft have had to land in Belgium or southern England because of damage, darkness and thickening fog. Some pilots landing at Bradwell had to have the aid of a fog dispersal unit. German fire has damaged 33 aircraft, 14 of them so severely that they have to be turned over to service groups for repair. Casualties are 11 men dead or missing and at least 10 wounded or injured.

At about **1715** two of the Polish Parachute Brigade's three battalions are dropped amidst heavy German fire, opposite the 1st Airborne Division's position on a new drop zone south of the Rhine near the village of Driel. Over 100 Luftwaffe fighters are waiting; 25 of which break through and together with anti-aircraft fire claim 13 more C-47s. Of the 1,511 Polish troops and around 100 tons of supplies and equipment carried, 998 troops and 69 tons of supplies are dropped in the vicinity of the prescribed zone. About 750 paratroops, three-quarters of those who had been dropped, are able to assemble that evening. Statistically speaking, the mission is only about 50 percent effective. In terms of difficulties and hazards overcome it is a brilliant performance. General Sosabowski, the Polish Brigade commander wrote: 'I cannot praise too much the perfect dropping, which in difficult weather conditions and in spite of strong enemy anti-aircraft fire over the DZ was equal to the best dropping during any exercise this Brigade Group has ever had.'

At **1700** Major-General Stanislaw Sosabowski lands at Driel with 750 men and no heavy equipment, which had been lost in the gliders two days before. The Poles are unable to cross the river because the Heaveadorp Ferry has been scuttled by the Dutch ferrymen the night previously. Contact is made with 1st Airborne by sending some staff officers swimming across the river. Great efforts are then made to take them across the river. Altogether 250 Poles crossed the river and formed a valuable reinforcement to the north-eastern corner of the defence. Here they fought with their proverbial gallantry.

2144 Urquhart signals: 'Relief within twenty-four hours vital'.

Chapter 6
Nijmegen

'The First Platoon was held in reserve in our original position to support the Company 'E' attack, led now by the Second Platoon. We opened fire as the attack began, but Lieutenant Colonel Vandervoort came into our front room position to observe the action and told me to cease fire for fear we might hit our own men. The Second Platoon charged into the park with the tanks and quickly overran the German defences and the bridge was taken. The German artillery had the area well zeroed in however and immediately began shelling the park. This continued even after dark and Company 'E' had several casualties from the artillery fire.'

James Coyle, referring to the German attack on the road bridge at Nijmegen which resumed on 21st September.

The following day (22nd), Company 'E' crossed the bridge and went as far north as the village of Lent. Here we were ordered to establish a position in reserve as the British tanks attempted to drive north to relieve the British Airborne troops at Arnhem. The 30 Corps were unable to reach Arnhem and later the British Airborne had to be pulled back across the northern branch of the River Rhine. In the following weeks Company 'E' was assigned to defend several areas along the narrow corridor from Belgium that had been secured in Operation 'Market-Garden'. I cannot remember the order in which we occupied them but they included areas near Mook, Beek and Wyler, amongst others. In the operation at Mook, Company 'E' relieved a company of the 325th Glider Infantry. We took over ready-made foxholes but the first thing I noticed in moving into the position were the one hundred and sixteen bodies of German soldiers laying in the area (I made an actual count). The position was in a heavily wooded area and the enemy appeared to have been killed by artillery tree bursts. I had the First Platoon cover the tops of the two man foxholes with logs and pile dirt over them. A foxhole under a tree is no defence against an artillery burst directly overhead. On the second day in this position, I had just completed my round of checking the men and returned to my foxhole when a sudden barrage of flat trajectory artillery fire burst all over the area. I could hear the guns going off only a second or two before the shells exploded, so I knew it was high velocity direct fire. When the shelling ceased I called out to the men to see if any were wounded but got no reply. I was very concerned because when I was making my rounds many of the men were out of their foxholes and cleaning their weapons. I went to check and I was glad to find that they were all down in their foxholes and no one was wounded. I was only half way back to my foxhole when I heard the guns fire again. I was caught in the open. I hit the ground as the shells burst all around me. I wasn't hit and as soon as the shelling stopped I got up and started to run for my hole. I heard the guns fire again and knew that I would not make it to safety in time. One of the shells exploded in a tree right over me. I saw a large piece of shrapnel tear up the ground just inches in front of my eyes. At the same time I felt a sharp pain in my leg, I had been hit. Fortunately it was not a large piece, but I couldn't tell that at the time. I knew that I was somewhere near the Platoon Aid man, Pfc Tony Jazrowski and I called out his name to locate his foxhole. When he answered I hobbled over to him, jumped in and he patched up my wound which wasn't too bad but it hurt a great deal.

When it seemed that the artillery fire was over for the time being, he helped me to the Company CP to check with the Company Commander. He put another officer, Lieutenant John Walas, in command of my Platoon. Pfc Cullen Clark helped me back to the Battalion Aid Station. There Captain Lyle Putnam, a good friend, examined the wound and said the piece of shrapnel was still in my leg, but it was best to leave it there. He told me it would be all right to return to my Company. I was limping for a week, but it finally healed. My friend, John Walas, was delighted at my speedy return to Company 'E'. He was an Assistant Platoon Leader and he told me frankly that his ambitions did not include leading a platoon; his main ambition was to get through the war alive. It didn't work out that way in the end. John later led a platoon in the Ardennes and was killed in action.

In the area near Wyler, the First Platoon had a very rough detail. In a last minute change of assignment, I drew a platoon outpost position instead of a regular front line section which I had reconnoitred in daylight. As a result, I had to take the Platoon into a position I had not seen, except on a map, in the dark.

It was about three quarters of a mile ahead of our main front line and was under enemy observation from high ground. I was very concerned about making a mistake and missing the position in the dark and walking into the German lines. I was very relieved when finally challenged by the troops we were looking for. They had let me reach the front line of their outpost before challenging me. Another one hundred and fifty yards and it would have been the Germans doing the challenging. This was a nerve-wracking position to occupy. We were there for two weeks and were not able to move out of our foxholes in the daytime. We could not even remove our clothes or boots to wash. Washing consisted of brushing our teeth.

The enemy knew exactly where we were. They sent combat patrols into the position every night. In addition they moved a tank up close to us after dark like clockwork and withdrew it just before dawn. At one point when a couple of men went into a house in daylight to heat their K rations (against orders) they immediately attracted an artillery barrage which blew in the thatched roof and wounded both men, one of whom ran to my foxhole in front of the house. It was Jazrowski, the Medic who had patched me up the week before. He was hit in the shoulder by shrapnel. I patched him up, but we had to wait until dark before he could walk back to the Aid Station. The other man was hit in the elbow but ran out of the back of the building so I could not see him. I found out later that he had been given first aid by the mortar squad.

Two days later, a Sergeant from Battalion Headquarters was shot in the head by a German sniper. He was an observer for the 81mm mortars and was in a foxhole with one of our men. Our replacement Medic, Pfc Calvin Kaufman told me over the sound-powered telephone lines, that were rigged to each squad position, that the chances were he would not survive. I called back through Company 'E' Headquarters and spoke to Captain Robert Franco, the Battalion's Surgeon at the time. I described the wounded man's condition and told Franco that I thought I could get him out under a white flag and back to the Aid Station. We had allowed the Germans to come out under a Red Cross Flag to evacuate some of their wounded the day before. The Doc said, however, that it would not be worth the risk and that there was no hope for the man. He was right - the man died in a few hours and a detail carried his body back to our lines after dark.' [69]

When Bill Tucker and his squad had reached Nijmegen German bodies were lying all along the banks of the Waal River. 'These were good German troops too. The 504 finished up on the nice flat land to the north of Nijmegen towards Germany and were in constant engagement with the enemy. Fire from 88s was coming down on the bridge and it could not be crossed in safety. All anyone could do was to crouch down on each truck and go like hell across the bridge, one truck at a time. This Company 'I' did while shells came right over them and exploded. On the other side we started marching in the rain; this time towards the railroad bridge which is about a half a mile to the west. No one knew what was happening and all the troopers seemed to do was to get soaked to the skin, stopping and starting, the old Army way. We stopped at the north

69 Our mission on the outpost was to alert the main line of resistance in the event of a large scale attack. It really should have been manned by a squad and changed every three nights. When we were relieved by a British unit after two weeks, they took one look at the position, mined it and abandoned it. While in another defensive position in the Wyler area, I saw two V-2 rockets launched in the distance. I had no idea what I was seeing and did not even report the first one to Battalion HQ. I thought I was hallucinating. No one around me saw it. When the second one went up a night later the British searchlights nearby futilely tried to track it so I knew I was not 'cracking up'. About this time, I saw my first jet airplane. We had been hearing the sound of jet engines for days, but had no idea what might be making that sound. Eventually I saw the German jet flying very low and streaking home across the German border a few miles away. I had occasion to take a patrol into the Reichswald on the Dutch border and so set foot in Germany for the first time in October 1944. About the middle of November, the 82nd Airborne Division was finally relieved by a Canadian unit. We moved back to a French army barracks at Suippes, near Rheims.' Within a week of arriving at Suippes after the Division was relieved in Holland, James Coyle was given some unbelievable news. Based on time overseas, in combat, wounds, etc., he had been chosen to take the first group of men home for rotation leave. Within two days he was on his way home to spend thirty days leave, after which, he would return with the men to the 505th PIR to wherever they might be at the time. When he rejoined my Company Coyle received a shock. 'The boys had been in very heavy combat in the Battle of the Bulge and there were many missing faces. Lieutenant John Walas had been killed. Bill Meddaugh was in hospital with pneumonia. Lieutenant Colonel Vandervoort had been wounded and lost an eye. Half the men in Company 'E' were replacements from the 551st Parachute Battalion which had been disbanded.' *Put On Your Boots and Parachutes!: The United States 82nd Airborne Division* written and edited by Deryk Wills (self published, March 1992).

end of the railroad bridge and found that we were to be an inner defence core. The mortar squads again joined together and got their machine guns back. A good house was found to stay in, right beside the bridge and for a day or two we had a good set-up there. It was a lot of fun with Boone Crusenberry; he was always finding some kind of old clothes to wear and he was an expert with a little Coleman burner. Boone was always eating like a horse and if you didn't watch your food, he would have it.

'There was a two hour guard schedule and in their spare moments they played pinochle in the house. Once in a while German bombers came over and there was a great deal of British ack-ack around the bridge. The Germans couldn't seem to get too close as the nearest bomb fell about a mile away. In the evening I had a chance to walk around to look things over. I was surprised by the number of Germans being buried. It was a rather mysterious place on this north side of the bridge. While we were there the remnants of the First British Airborne Division and some of the Polish Brigade marched back through the lines from Arnhem. That is, what was left of them. The GIs' feelings went out to those men as they marched down the road, mostly bandaged and in rags, many of them badly wounded. I got a pretty good idea of what had happened. The SS Division hit them hard in Arnhem and they were badly torn up. It was guessed that they must have left Tommy in Arnhem, because I never saw him again. Company 'I' had actually seen the Polish Brigade go in by parachute to help support the British but they were murderously hit by ack-ack and even German fighter planes, so that a lot of them didn't even reach the ground alive. It was a bad feeling to know that the overall mission had failed, but at least the 82nd knew that its part of the operation was accomplished on time and with the least men lost.

'The next thing that happened was an order to move the Second Platoon onto the railroad bridge to guard it. The orders were to shoot at anything that moved in the air or below the bridge. Everyone was told, from Corporal to General, that they would be broken if anything happened to the bridge. My squad and Larry Leonard's squad were at the southern end of the half mile long bridge. They were over the water and there was a gun tower there. There were altogether three gun towers on the bridge. Right beside the Squad's tower there was a swivel pom-pom gun which 'Old Man' Jones and I took over. We had a pretty good time on the bridge shooting at everything that moved. The men were anxious to fire every time the planes came over. They argued to see who would get in the seat which controlled the German gun and they may have been the culprits who shot down an American B-26 when it flew over. Leo's squad was down underneath the bridge, guarding from below. Leo was drunk all the time; evidently he had found some wine. My Squad were on the bridge for two days, during which time he managed to scout around for food and sneak into the city of Nijmegen now and then. It was a beautiful city and still is. For the greater part of it has, like most European cities, clean narrow streets. On the whole the stay in Nijmegen was rather pleasant. Orders came to move back to Groesbeek as heavy fighting was taking place.

'The first night they had to wait in the woods before going to the old positions. It was just a miserable night. The rain came down through the trees, the wind blew and everyone got wetter than hell. No fires could be lit so they were glad when the morning came and the sun shone again. Back into the old positions they went. For the next exciting seven days the mortar squads were tied up between the observation post and the Company Command Post. Throughout that time, day and night, they fired continuously as the attacks got heavier. The attacking German troops were not the best they had seen. Wally, Jim Downing and Tucker spent their time shuttling back and forth between the windmill and the Command Post. The windmill, which had a cluster of houses around it, was fifty yards behind the First and Third Platoon lines. During most of the time it was a lot easier to stay back at the windmill than at the CP, because there it was under constant shelling, although there was no doubt that the Germans had spotted the windmill being used as an observation post. The mortars were in such a position that they could fire and hit almost anything that moved beyond the combat lines both night and day. Telephone lines connected the firing positions with the windmill and the Command Post. Various target points were all zeroed in, but at night it wasn't necessary to stay in the windmill because the Command Post called back to the Company and let them know where the targets were.

'There were two or three attacks almost every day. After a day or two, numerous German bodies started to pile up in front of the position. The shelling was terrible back at the Command Post. Mike Terella had it good and it was kind of fun for Tucker to be with him and Scotty Hough again. Tucker recalls several funny incidents. The back yard of the house, where the mortars were, had an old dug-out 'cold cellar' with kind of a narrow door to it. The shells that the Germans were throwing were pretty big stuff and they could be heard coming most of the time. Once, when a shell came in and they heard it coming, Tucker saw Stald and Terella both making a flying dive for the door. They both got there at the same time and with the same velocity that they got wedged side by side in the doorway. Luckily neither of them was hit. There were several people hit, however, one was Rudy Tepsick and that was quite a loss. Tucker was promoted during this time, as was Jim Downing. The ammunition kept coming up for the 60mm mortars as there was a road that was well secluded behind the position. Some of the best gun crews were there. Intrieri was a good gunner and Logan too, he knew no fear, he would stand right out in the open where the shelling was coming in. There seemed to be enough to eat and there were always plenty of apples. Tucker recalled that it was good to work with Jim Downing and Wally Wallace because they were both nonchalant guys. The trouble was they made him risk his ass too many times. After the first few days the shelling around the windmill began to get tough, there were a few hits and some very near misses. By this time the German's artillery observers realised, only too well, that the only way to drive them out of the windmill was to hit the driveway or doors just beneath it. It was tough for them to do that but they were beginning to get a few pretty close.

'The observers were up in the windmill most of the time and on the whole Jim Downing seemed to enjoy himself and so did Wally. Wally fired a few times himself and once when he hit one of the Germans spot on with a mortar shell, he really let out a yell. Just as he was yelling to everybody that he had hit someone, a bullet splattered about a quarter of an inch away from the window on the side of the wall. From that time on it was dangerous to get too near the windows, because the rifle fire was directed towards them. Jim Downing used to sit up on a table, about in the centre of the windmill, take off all his clothes except for a pair of coveralls, cross his legs, rest his elbows on his knees and peer out with his binoculars and direct the firing. He even took off his boots.

'For the first three or four days they did have some other observers. There was the 81mm mortar observer, one for the 75mm guns and some from the British artillery. After things began to get too hot they began to clear out. Before they all left there was one day when they looked out and saw hundreds of German soldiers in the distance coming through the woods towards the front positions. The British heavy artillery observers called for priority from their control centre. Then, of course, the 82nd 81mm mortar observers stepped up along with the 75mm observers but they could not get priority orders either. Tucker yelled to them to 'step aside' and started firing the little 60s and they did a better job of disbursing, killing and wounding the attacking Germans, possibly better than all the others could have done even if they had put all the big guns on them. The Mortar Squad really had the road from the Reichswald zeroed in.

'Jim Downing was usually there during the daytime and lots of times it was impossible for him to get back until after dark because he had to travel across an open field. One cloudy morning, it was the fourth day of this seven day period, there were so many German dead and wounded, a German officer came with a Medic carrying a white flag. Speaking English he asked for a truce to bring in his casualties. He was blindfolded and led to the Command Post. He was rather young looking and even though he was covered in quite a bit of mud, he really looked a soldier. He stood with his hands tied behind his back and a blindfold over his eyes with 'Old Man' Jones guarding him. Tucker passed the German officer and yelled 'Heil Hitler!' The German snapped his heels together and in the perfect example of discipline and soldierly conduct, replied 'Heil Hitler!' Whereupon he was immediately hit with the butt of 'Old Man' Jones's rifle.

'About the fifth day a squad of Germans broke through the lines in the night and holed up in the cellars around the windmill. Jim Downing and several others were trapped. It was impossible for them to get out of the windmill at all. One 81mm observer stuck his head and shoulders out of the door and took a bullet through his shoulder. At the same time Albert 'Frenchy' Dusseault was leading a squad along the hedge and a bullet went into his lower back, passed through his body and came out of his shoulder. After that Dusseault was hauled into the windmill and lay beside the 81mm observer. It seemed that the 81mm observer was feeling pretty good because he only had a shoulder wound. Dusseault was coughing up blood. The observer died about twenty minutes later, but surprisingly, Dusseault lived. It became increasing apparent during the afternoon that something would have to be done to clean those Germans out. Lieutenant James Howall led the attack from the Company CP down the road and tried to out flank them. There was some skirmishing during which time Downing managed to get away from the windmill and across one of the streets. Several men were hit during this fight. After Howall had led his men into the attack, Tucker started out with Ed Morrissey and a couple of others. On the way they met Lieutenant Degenhardt with some men carrying the wounded. Me, together with Morrissey, Downing and the other two men started to cross the open field. The German mortar observer spotted them and started firing mortar shells. Tucker was only a third of the way across, lying alone in the field with the German mortars shells kicking up dust all around. Somehow or other they all made it.

'Towards the end of the day the windmill suffered from some very heavy shelling. The doors had been finally blown off and the inside hit by phosphorus shells and was on fire. It was a sort of funeral pyre for one of the most successful defence operations that had ever been attempted. This windmill observation post for the mortars had held off two or three large German attacks, preventing them from penetrating the 505 positions to any depth for a period of a week, night and day. Tucker couldn't resist taking a last look, so after it got dark he sneaked back. The excuse was to get a map case, a couple of German pistols and some other equipment that he had left behind.

It was very quiet when he arrived. The windmill was filled with smoke, even though there were no flames and it was deathly silent. He picked up the few things and took that last look. To get out he had to climb over the sandbags covering the doorway which a shell had hit. At this point he heard more shells coming in again and Tucker took a big dive over the sandbags and landed on something warm and wet. Reaching out he found he had landed on several German bodies.[70]

'The next day a new observation post had to be found and they still couldn't leave the windmill without a note of regret. For seven days it had been their home. For a week before they went to Nijmegen, it had been even more so. They did find a new post in a house which was about 300 yards in front of the Company Command Post. This had no combat line in front of it, just bare fields stretching for five to six hundred yards before it reached the woods where the Germans were dug in. The observers made a little hole in the roof and started taking turns looking out but it wasn't anything like the windmill. They couldn't do much moving around because if the Germans thought they were in there, they would have blown that house off the face of the earth. For that reason I didn't spend all his time there and there was a chance to get around a little bit and see some of his friends in other platoons. Tucker had a good chance to talk to his buddies, particularly Sergeant Matash. He also went over to Company 'G' and took a look at the Germans from a room which was on the Second Platoon's left flank. While he was up on the roof the Germans attacked Company 'G' and he got a few pot-luck shots at them by firing his rifle. Also there was Richard Cutler with a Browning Automatic Rifle banging away.

'On the seventh day we were relieved and went back into the woods and hills overlooking Nijmegen. This became our home on and off during their stay

70 The windmill was destroyed and never rebuilt, but its site is clearly marked today by an elevated square of land. The same family, the Hoof's, still own the site today and they used the old bricks from the mill to build the barn next to the house.

in Holland, perhaps a day and a half at a time and it wasn't so bad. It was an opportunity to practice with the mortars when we weren't actually fighting. Everybody shared the food and all used Boone Crusenberry's Coleman stove to cook it. Crusenberry was the only man who ever had a stove that continually worked, or perhaps he was the only man who knew how to work it. When he was around there was always a chance of hot food. Finally, the order came through that the Second Platoon had been picked to attack and clear out the church area in a small town beyond the Third Platoon's lines. The Second Platoon was directed to make the attack because it had suffered the fewest amount of casualties. It didn't turn out to be much of an attack because as they started down the main road leading to the church area things got confused. Eventually they turned around and came back and never found out why this action was stopped.

'During one halt we found it interesting to look round at the houses. These were the same houses we saw where they first arrived in Holland and where the people were trying to dig in to save their homes and families. Now every house was just about in a shambles. Not too much on the outside but on the inside there was broken glass, pottery and dirt everywhere. The civilians had all gone. Tucker couldn't help but remember and admire them for their attempts to hold on to their homes. When he saw those men digging in with their families and little children around them, digging into the ground behind their homes, he knew they could not stay. During the course of their wanderings they ran across a couple of bicycles and practised riding them. They stayed another two days or so under the trees on the hill overlooking Nijmegen. There were quite a few equipment shelters around in the area and it was interesting to see they contained a large amount of German supplies. Orders came to move into Nijmegen again. This time the guys were worried because there had been a lot of talk about the 504. It was rumoured that they had been taking quite a beating up there on the east flank, out on the flats and dykes and the 505 were going to relieve them. Nobody was too happy about that. On the road to Nijmegen it was interesting to see what changes had taken place. Mostly it could be described in one word - destruction. It was after dark when the trucks arrived in the city. It seems like they sat around forever because it was one of those nights when everybody was very tired and nobody had much idea what was going on. The equipment was heavy and every time they stopped they went to sleep. So off they went into the flats to relieve the 504. It was a weird area; anything that was built there or grew there seemed to be completely destroyed. There was an overpowering smell of dead animals and dead men everywhere. There had been some very tough fighting between the 504 and the Germans. I spent three hours marching. Somehow or other, in his travels, he got hold of a small cart to carry the mortar and some other equipment. As his Platoon got near the 504 positions the pace quickened and they got lost from the rest of the group.

'By chance we did finally get into the spot held by the mortar squad of the Second Battalion of the 504. This was right out on the edge of the battle line and it consisted of a large house enclosed by rectangular woods. It was like an oasis, as all around the house there were shell holes of all sizes. One look was enough to tell them that this place had been thoroughly combed by enemy shells. Tucker talked to the 504 just enough to find out how glad they were to leave and long enough for them to point out that anything which moved in daylight was dead. Then they spent the rest of the night going back to look for some equipment which got lost on the journey. It certainly was a relief when it was found.

'When the orders came down that there was to be no firing of mortars, Downing, Wally and Tucker thought it was going to be pretty dull. The three grabbed the cellar and decided that they would stay there; the others would have to find foxholes in the back of the house. It wasn't much of a deal but the cellar felt pretty comfortable. They didn't fire a shot and didn't even stir around the back of the house during daylight. At night they would go out to the Command Post. To do that the route was along a road which was behind the combat lines and this was the most ghostly road they ever travelled on. There would always be swirling mists and fog seeping across the road and every once in a while tracer bullets would fly from nowhere. Here and there would be a broken cart wheel, a dead cow or a German body, pieces of helmets and equipment. Nobody was really anxious to travel that road alone at night.

'During the daytime they would go up into the attic of their house along with another observer, who popped up from somewhere, to look around for targets. Of course, firing the guns was out, because if they had they would have been dead men inside half an hour. This artillery observer organised a few shots here and there. About 300 yards away in the German lines there was a little black spot which was actually a very deep foxhole occupied by one German soldier with red hair. About 1500 it became very urgent for this German to relieve himself. About that time the observer was in the attic ready to go with his big guns to get this lone redheaded German. Everybody watched with great anxiety and curiosity every afternoon and the same picture unfolded. The German would make a jump and run about ten yards from his foxhole and there would be a scurry of dirt as a little hole was dug. He would then unfasten his belt and put himself in a rather vulnerable position.

'About one minute later he would be back in his hole again and about two seconds later the artillery shells would be landing. While they were there they never got the redheaded German and Tucker just wondered how much he cost the United States in artillery shells. On the fifth day the Third Battalion went back to a reserve area where they could take it easy for a few days. The system was going to be that they would stay in the front line for five days and then the Second Battalion of the 505 would relieve them and this would keep going on a semi-permanent basis. Meanwhile the First Battalion was about a mile across an open space to the right at a place called Beek. It was quite a long walk back to the reserve area but it was well worthwhile. Company 'I' was billeted in a little hamlet of about ten or twelve houses and each unit had a house of their own. The mortar squads had possibly the best house. Tucker's crew had a bureau to themselves, some blankets and even sheets. On the first morning the owner of the house, who happened to be in the Dutch Resistance Movement, came to pick up something. He certainly wanted them to be comfortable and showed a pretty good spirit about the whole thing.

'Lutz and Boone Crusenberry were the cooks and they did a darn good job. I was able to go into Nijmegen in the afternoon and take a shower. The shower rooms weren't bad. This was about all I could do other than take a good look round. It was difficult in keeping Moe Green and a couple of the other boys from taking off for better things. The day before they were due to go back into the line, Downing, Wally and me got together and decided that if they were going to be of any use to the Company then they must prevail on the Company Commander to accept their plan to get an outpost. Mortars were no good unless the gunners could fire with some assurance of cover. Downing was commissioned to go up with an advance party and scout a new position. It was a long walk on the return journey and it wasn't as easy as the walk a few days ago. This time the Company had a new position to occupy. In front of them was a dyke about a hundred yards out, but the line was to be dug along a sort of a hedgerow. About 200 yards behind were two houses. The house on the left was to be the Company CP and the other earmarked for the mortar squad. This was a beautiful setup for them again as it meant they could live in the house, dig in and fire the mortars in the back and still eat steak. The Command Post and the observation post for Jim Downing, Wally Wall ace and Tucker was an old house which was just behind the Third Platoon's line. When they first got there it was a great problem stringing the telephone wires out because they had to criss-cross several small dykes. Lieutenant Charles Christian had a CP about 75 yards to the rear in an old house. That CP was shared with the Third Platoon. [71] Harry Buffone and some of the others were over to the left. About 150 yards beyond Tucker's line, by the end of a dyke, was a cluster of woods that had been ripped to pieces by shells. Here a group of Germans had dug themselves in.

'In a short time I didn't like it at all. I fired a few rounds and right away the 88s started coming in. Richard Cutler came upstairs into the attic and said that this was the Third Platoon's property and to get out. Tucker wasn't very anxious to argue about it, so he left. Again there was trouble with the telephone wires and he had to fix them on the way. I also ran into another live cow and decided to bring it back. That was not as easy as it sounds as he had to run behind hedges and throw things at the cow to keep her from wandering out towards the German lines. When he got her back to the house, she got away into an apple orchard which was facing the enemy. If she had got out into the open beyond the orchard no one would have a chance to get her as the Germans would surely cut her down. Only a fool would go out there after a carcass. Three or four of the Squad got at each end of the orchard and started throwing apples which were lying everywhere. Finally Moe Green hit her on the neck and they grabbed and pushed the cow behind the house and out of sight. Anything in front of the house was too dangerous to try.

'Those five days weren't too bad. There was no real heavy shelling coming in and there seemed to be a mutual agreement for a time where nobody seemed to try. At any rate the orders were that the Third Battalion was not to start it. They did however, set up a system of targets so that the mortars could be fired

71 Lieutenant Charles Christian had been transferred from Company 'B' to Company 'I'. He was one of the original members of the 505th and a veteran of the four combat jumps.

by the map. I couldn't see very well from the top of the house but he could see the woods and the German dyke. Most of the firing was by remote control whereby the people in Platoon headquarters and in the outposts would call back and tell them how they were doing on the targets. The basic fire points set up were one in the woods and a couple of points along the dyke. There was a system of target codes which were used for each point. One target off to the right, Tucker designated as 'Cicero'. From that day on, Boone Crusenberry and the others used that as Tucker's nickname and for the rest of their relationship in the Army he was known as 'Cicero' by the mortar squads. For some relaxation they played cards and always managed to scrape up something new to eat. They had steak most of the time and Dikey did most of the cooking. Dikey was Boone's gunner. On about the third day as Boone Crusenberry finished skinning the cow, the Executive Officer showed up and demanded a hindquarter. The officer and Downing got into a heated argument and Tucker was amazed by the fact that Downing made no bones about telling the Lieutenant that if he was to get any of the cow, it would not be a hindquarter. During this time it was rumoured that the Captain played rummy with Sergeant Howard Melvin and lost about a hundred bucks a day. After the five days were over they returned to the reserve area. Again it was showers and a comfortable bed to sleep in, except for two things. Now there was not enough food around to eat and on two nights they had to man outposts near the hamlet because the Germans were sending patrols down the river behind the lines.

'The Commander of the outpost, a Lieutenant, was the new Assistant Officer of the Second Platoon. During the night Leonard and Maglothin, his machine-gunner, picked up a German riding his bicycle down the road and brought him in. He did quite a bit of talking about some buzz-bomb sites behind the German dykes and that the Germans were going to open the dykes and flood the Allies out. After a while they did begin to see the buzz-bombs being launched, but the Germans didn't flood the dykes as yet. The five days on the line and five in reserve continued. It began to get pretty rough on the line at night and it rained most of the time. The rest area was still the same good deal. Tucker and his friends used to get together at night where Robbie was, talk things over and play cards.

'Robbie got a letter from Degenhardt who had been sent back for special duties in England and they never enjoyed listening to a letter so much. Degenhardt told Robbie he had a heck of a deal there and there were all the girls that he wanted, available to have a good time. Lieutenant Richard Degenhardt to all of them was always a good guy. At night the English bombers used to fly over the position and bomb somewhere in the vicinity of thirty to forty miles away. They could hear the bombs from where they were and it would go on practically all night, every night. Tucker guessed it was a sort of shuttle bombing, like the Wellingtons used to do in Africa. The last time Tucker was up on the line, Doug Roth and Bill True of the 506 came to visit him from the 101st Division. The 506 had been sent north across the bridge and they were on the combat line, probably five or six miles to the left and temporarily attached to the 82nd. They all sat down underneath an apple tree to talk and there was some shelling nearby, but not in their area. Tucker noticed that both of his visitors were pretty jumpy sitting down in the open. [72]

'It wasn't uncommon for the Mortar Squad to have guests for dinner. We had a long table in the dining room and Crusenberry used to cook and serve the food. On this day we invited Doug and True to dinner and the two guests were amazed to see that we were eating steak and French fries with silver cutlery and on porcelain plates. Underneath the house was a cellar full of potatoes. Sergeant Melvin showed up and had dinner too. They were really two very surprised guys when they left after having the best meal since they got overseas.

'There was quite a bit of activity along the line at night and during this last period they used to have to do some work. The Company was hollering for more men to go out on Command Post duty. That was really tough because every night it was raining and blacker than hell. It got so bad for a while along the line that even mortar Sergeants volunteered to go out and do duty. They would go out and watch for a while and if they should see a German lighting a match to a cigarette, the guns would get on him pretty quick. Even though they hated to walk along that weird road at night, they did it just to get that feeling. Ritchie was continually running back and forth from the Second Platoon to the Command Post. From him they got word that the 505 were going to be relieved from Holland in a couple of days by the Canadians. Tucker had on hand quite a bit of mortar ammunition, so he started firing it. The firing had not been going for long when it became increasingly apparent that there were quite a number of short rounds, but that didn't seem to bother Tucker.

'While we had been on this line and back in the reserve area we had been receiving whisky and beer rations as per the British Army regulations. The men got rum and the non-coms got brandy and whisky and there was also a lot of Dutch beer. [73] The first night after the Mortar Squad got the rum, some of the boys didn't dilute it. A half a canteen cup would just about knock a cow out. After they had been drinking the rum, Fisher and McNary were running up and down the dyke making a lot of noise and firing their 45s. The Germans were very quick at night and the minute there was some movement or light on the American side, they would open up with machine-guns and put some slugs on the spot in no time at all. It wasn't a very sane thing to move around at night. By that time the opposing forces had got to know each other pretty well and they knew that the German chow truck used to come in about 14:30. For that reason, every night when someone had a little rum inside them, they would go out on the dyke and tie some tin cans together and put some pebbles in them. The tin cans would be tied to the back of a bazooka shell; then fired out of a

72 Tucker, Roth and True trained as paratroopers together in Company 'F', 506th Parachute Infantry Regiment at the start of their service.

73 To Gavin's embarrassment when Horrocks asked the troopers what they wanted they said they wanted more to eat. They were missing their American 'C' Rations. Horrocks immediately doubled the rations. As Gavin recalled later, 'When the days grew shorter and colder in the fall of 1944 and the dampness of Holland seemed to penetrate everywhere, Horrocks' staff enquired about a rum ration - I declined. Finally on our last evening with XXX Corps he sent me a message. 'You will issue a rum ration this evening' - a nice Horrocks touch. We enjoyed it.' *Put On Your Boots and Parachutes!: The United States 82nd Airborne Division* written and edited by Deryk Wills (self published, March 1992).

cardboard cylinder. It made a weird shrieking noise and no doubt upset the Germans during their meals. Anyway, if the GIs had nothing else better to do they would all start firing or doing something else to upset the Germans when anyone heard their chow truck coming in.

'The second last day before being relieved from the combat line, I did quite a bit of firing with the mortars. A couple of shells landed near Lieutenant Christian's CP, so he liked him all the less. Christian had continually warned about firing too much, but there were 150 rounds left on the last day and Tucker was determined to give the woods on the left, beyond the Second Platoon lines, a thorough going over. On top of that, the mortar section captured one full barrel of Dutch beer and everyone drank to their hearts content. Moe Green was really feeling aces on the last day and decided to top all things off with a little experiment. The first thing the Squad tried to do was fire a mortar at a record distance. So two or three of them got down in the big hole and set the mortar at 45 degrees, which was lower than safe. Two extra charges were added and the shell dropped down the tube. The result was a sharp compression in the hole, following which my ears rang for about a year. The shell went harmlessly in the air and exploded about fifty yards from the house. They checked the mortar and found the base plate was cracked and broken. This was about the seventh base plate they had destroyed. In the afternoon of the last day it was decided to fire the greatest 'barrage' of the war. Each gun was to fire twenty-five rounds in succession into a patch of woods on the left. It was hoped that none of the rounds would be short. Of course one (Tucker) would be in trouble if there was because Lieutenant Christian's CP was nearest to where the firing was to take place. Not only that, when they were firing the night before, one of the shells had a hit near the CP and set part of it on fire. Well anyway, they started firing the rounds and there were deafening roars from everywhere. After the guns had been firing for several minutes, calls started coming in that rounds were falling about both lines, particularly near Christian's Command Post. There was no way to stop it and they finished firing all rounds in the record time of less than three minutes. The woods had probably caught about fifty shells but of the other 25, some had landed near Company 'G' and near the Second Platoon line with about three of them directly on Christian's CP. They were simply bad rounds, but Christian's CP was burning merrily and his gunners had to leave in a hurry in broad daylight and scurry across the fields.

'The last night there was spent with some regret, waiting for the Canadians to relieve them. 'With regret' because, again, they found it was a sort of a home, at least in the mortar section and there hadn't been any real danger to the men. Downing, Wally and me never worried too much about our own skins because we were always too busy to worry. The toughest job we had to do was to get out and fix those wires. There was always just that little bit of regret leaving a place that you had got used to. It was raining as hard as hell that night as they sat in the barn at the rear of their house with the guns packed and equipment ready, waiting for the Canadians.

'Finally, we were ready to leave Holland. Other than the bridges over the lower Rhine not much had been accomplished. It was near Thanksgiving, it was cold and raining very hard. The Canadians were due to relieve us shortly after midnight. They had raised holy hell for the last day or two, firing all their guns constantly. I was kind of tired of Holland, but in a way I felt a little melancholy as I waited for the relief. The GIs were very much concerned about the number of miles they would have to walk back to board the trucks. The Canadians did not arrive until 1400 or 1430 in the morning. When they got to me I had a chance to talk with them and found out they were pretty damned disgusted with everything. They had been attacking at Walcheren, outside of Antwerp for two or three months and had finally reduced the fortresses held by the Germans on the approaches to the port. When they came in, their ranks were really depleted from this fighting. Even where the 505 were short on men, they only had three or four to put in the place of about ten or so of the Americans. I felt sorry for them. They said they hadn't had any replacements from Canada for months. The GIs did the best they could to line them up in their positions, wished them well and then started on the long march back towards Nijmegen.

'I stopped and took a last look at the city. The British Army traffic was flowing in and the 82nd were going out, leaving Nijmegen for the last time. Again, there could be said that there was some sort of a melancholy note remembering the hours of comradeship, without too much loss, that had been experienced in this area. Most men were not in any shape for a long march and it was understood that there was 35 to fifty miles to go that day. Not only that, it was cold, damp and raining. All along the road we heard rumours of what Montgomery was going to do by Christmas, but we didn't take much to heart in that because Montgomery hadn't seen much of the German soldiers and the 82nd had. Sometime after dark we arrived in a wooded assembly area where we immediately tried to catch up on some sleep under a downpour of rain. A lot of time was spent trying to start a fire but it wasn't successful. By morning it really was wonderful to feel heat from the fire and get hold of 10 and 1 rations, some hot rum and just sit around and take it easy. We counted their casualties, talked to the Dutch people and had some fun. These areas where we would stop like this and spend a couple of days were very educational in the sense that we could put aside our operations and look around and see the difference in a man's face from just a few months ago. It was a long rough day and I can't remember much except that my feet were killing me. All this after a gruelling two months campaign without sleep and proper clothing.'

'The two American airborne divisions... succeeded entirely' wrote Martha Gellhorn 'and having succeeded they stayed in Holland to hold the land they conquered. This was regarded by the troopers of the 82nd as fairly easy work, all things considered. 'Easy' is only a word: in twenty-two days the division hospital handled 2,974 wounded and over 400 major surgical operations were performed. But if the troopers were not engaged in fighting far their lives, they always found ways to amuse themselves. A dinner party in a half shelled house less than a mile from the German lines, with a sheet for table cloth and marigolds in a broken battle as ornament and an electrifying assortment of drink; it seemed a good idea to have a dinner party for a change and everyone shaved. Or dated the girls in Nijmegen which was shelled off and on all day and night; or amused themselves helping put out fires started by German artillery, rode bicycles, played baseball, made interior improvements on their beat-up billets; read comic strip magazines or played cards, tinkered with liberated cars and motor bikes and were constantly happily occupied trying to find something to drink, something interesting.ro eat or a comfortable place to sit and tell each other stories' about women and fighting. They had learned that war is long and life is short and the trick is to be as merry as possible. They were being whittled dawn every day and every day they killed more Germans, but the main drive of the war was elsewhere and they hated sitting in one place, with nothing much to show for it. And every day the little city of Nijmegen which they liked and the people of Nijmegen whom they liked and admired, were being pounded by enemy artillery, until the town grew uglier and uglier and the hospitals overflowed with wounded women and children. When they finally left Holland after nine weeks of this dismal war, they left behind a neat cemetery with more than 800 graves marked by white crosses: the school children of Nijmegen tend those graves. The division had done its part of the job; it was their sorrow that the main plan had failed and that the war could not be finished that winter.'

US Airborne Divisions' and XXX Corps' Timeline

22 September (D+5)

The 214th Brigade of 43rd Division pushes forward. Two troops of the Household Cavalry, under cover of the early morning mist and working their way along side roads to the West, link up with the Polish Parachute Brigade in Driel. 214 Infantry Brigade, having crossed the Waal at dawn, make a flanking attack to the west, but meet opposition at Oosterhout, where the lead battalion is held for most of the day. German pressure against the 82nd Division in the Groesbeek area slackens and their main effort is made against the 101st Division to the south. Model has ordered that the XXX Corps axis be cut at Veghel. Major General Maxwell Taylor has anticipated this and had starts to move his troops north from Son and Best, which are now more secure as VIII and XII Corps has now moved up to the flanks. The 506th PIR is on its way to Uden and a battalion of 501st PIR held Veghel. In heavy fighting all day the American paratroopers hold these two villages, but German tanks cut the road south of Uden and drive down towards Veghel, destroying British transport on the road. Kampfgruppe Huber's attack from the west is delayed by American counter-action around Schijndel, but comes in later in the afternoon against Veghel and captures the Zuid Willems canal bridge. They are then driven off by a company of the 501st PIR and a squadron of 44th Royal Tank Regiment. Attempts to cut the road south

74 Martha Gellhorn settled in London after the war, re-married and covered the war in Vietnam, the Arab-Israeli conflict and wars in El Salvador and Nicaragua and the US invasion of Panama. All her life she was both fascinated and repelled by war. *The Women Who Wrote the War* by Nancy Caldwell Sorel (Arcade Publishing, New York 1999).

of Veghel are repulsed by the two battalions of 327 Glider Infantry Regiment marching up from the south. The two battalions from the 501st and 502nd Regiments fall back from the west towards Veghel and Sint-Oedenrode. Fighting continues all day around Veghel.

1700 Oosterhout is cleared and at once the 5th Battalion Duke of Cornwall's Light Infantry, with a squadron of tanks of the 4/7th Dragoon Guards and 130th Brigade, burst through and, in a spirited half-hour drive, join up with the Poles at Driel. 129 Infantry Brigade cross the Waal but make no further progress towards Elst.

By nightfall Veghel is still firmly in American hands and defended by six battalions and two squadrons of British tanks. Uden is still held, but the road between Veghel and Uden remains in German control, preventing further reinforcements from moving forward and blocking supplies for the three Allied divisions to the north. As German pressure from the Reichswald decreases Horrocks orders both the Grenadier and Coldstream Guards Groups to turn back and reopen the road to Veghel.

Saturday 23 September

2/501 are sent southwest on an attack to reinforce 3rd Battalion at Eerde. The attack across open ground turns out to be for naught. Soon after arriving on the outskirts of Eerde, most of the battalion is recalled to Veghel where 6 Parachute Regiment (which had fought against the 101st in Normandy) from the west and a battered Walter Group from the east sever the British convoys on Hell's Highway between Vechel and Uden. Cadets sent from the Hermann Goring Panzer Division's training school at Amersfoort are also identified in the fighting. With the highway cut, long caravans of trucks are halted along the narrow road leading from Eindhoven to Arnhem. All available division elements are rushed to the vicinity of Vechel where they are formed into a task force under General McAuliffe. Enemy penetrations are deep. German tanks and infantry move within 500 yards of the vital bridges. Vicious fighting follows, but the 101st hold firm. The enemy is forced to withdraw toward Erp and the highway is reopened.

Simultaneously, the Germans renew their strong but unsuccessful attacks to recapture Veghel. The two battalions of the 501st PIR beat off the German parachutists in hard fighting with heavy casualties on both sides. The Walter Group does not press home its attack and breaks off when VIII British Corps starts to cross the Willems Canal to their south. After heavy fighting the Coldstream Guards take Volkel. The Grenadier Guards start to advance down the road from Uden, as two battalions of the 506th PIR move north and in the mid-afternoon the two forces link up. The road is open and traffic starts to flow again after a serious 24 hour hold-up.

Improved weather finally allows the remainder of the American gliders to land, with the long-delayed 325 Glider Infantry Regiment of 82nd Division and the balance of 101st Division artillery and glider infantry. Plans called for all missions to the airborne to fly the revised southern route, via Bourg Leopold and Eindhoven. The postponed glider missions to the American airborne were to fly the centre lane to LZ's 'O' and 'W' with the lead glider reaching LZ 'O' at 1400. Again the two glider serials for the 101st Division were to go from England to Eindhoven in the middle of the glider column slated for: the 82nd Division. One plane had been added and 14 of the 442nd Group withdrawn from the 82nd Division's mission, giving it a total of 406. The gliders going to the 101st had been increased from 82 to 84 and the 442nd Group, formerly scheduled to tow a serial, had been replaced by the 434th, which was more experienced in glider work.

The Polish troops who had been returned to base on D+4 were to be dropped on DZ '0' at 1447 by a 42-plane serial, flying the left lane. The ground situation no longer required a drop at Driel and a drop at DZ '0' was safer for the troop carriers. A resupply drop to 1 Airborne would be made at 1400 by 123 aircraft of 38 and 46 Groups, flying at 2,500 feet. After reconnaissance by weather planes on the morning of the 23rd, all arrival times were postponed two hours to give the weather on the continent more time to clear after the cold front passed.

From England to Eindhoven and back the troop carrier columns were to be given cover by 14 Spitfire squadrons of ADGB and four more squadrons would fly area patrol between Bourg Leopold and Eindhoven. Between Eindhoven and Volkel (west of Uden) three Mustang squadrons of ADGB would be on area patrol. 8th Air Force was to provide 13 groups and one squadron of fighters. Three P-51 Groups were to fly area patrol and escort between Bourg Leopold and Arnhem at height of 2,500 to 5,000 feet. One group of P-51s and one of P-47s would fly high cover in those areas. A perimeter connecting Maastricht, Cleve and Zwolle was to be guarded by 5 groups of P-51s and one of P-38s, under MEW direction. Two groups of P-47s and the rocket squadron were to neutralize flak between Nijmegen and Arnhem. All 8th Air Force units were to be in position by 1530. The RAF fighters flew 193 sorties without meeting air opposition but lost one or two planes. The 8th Air Force units made 580 sorties and suffered 16 losses, largely from ground fire.. The pilots reported sighting at least 185 enemy fighters, generally in groups of about 35 and claimed to have shot down 27 at a cost of 6 of their own. Out on the perimeter in the Geldern-Wesel area the 339th Fighter Group had three clashes with enemy fighter formations and the pilots claimed to have destroyed six enemy planes while losing three. These interceptions occurred when the troop carriers were over Holland and may have been important in protecting them from Luftwaffe forays. In another big battle the 353rd Group, flying high cover southeast of Arnhem, met some 50 enemy fighters. Its pilots reported shooting down 19 aircraft and losing three. This fight came at 1745, by which time the last troop carriers had passed Eindhoven on their way home.

Anti-flak sorties were made by 88 aircraft, which fired 23 rockets, dropped 85 bombs, mainly 260lb fragmentation bombs and did much strafing. Although still restricted by the rule that they should not attack until fired upon, the flak-busters had a good day. They reported 18 gun positions destroyed and 17 damaged. One of the planes was shot down and 22 damaged. The 78th Fighter Group, which neutralized many German positions in the drop area of the British resupply mission, probably saved that mission from disastrous losses.

The great array of gliders which had stood marshalled on the airfields of the 50th and 52nd Wings in the eastern midlands since 19 September finally began taking off at 1210 on the 23rd. In the 406 Wacos were 3,385 troops, 104 jeeps, 59 loaded trailers and 25 pieces of artillery. The units involved were the 325th Glider Infantry. four batteries of the 80th Airborne Anti-aircraft Battalion, two companies of engineers, the divisional reconnaissance platoon and an MP platoon.

As usual when large numbers of gliders involved, assembly was a tedious business taking from 40 to 60 minutes. However, it was handled and only three gliders aborted - one breaking loose over England and two turning back with mechanical difficulties. Inevitably there was a certain amount of jostling and trouble with prop wash. The tugs and gliders in the rear were particularly affected. As formations tightened or loosened they had to vary their speed, from 110 to as much as 160 mph. To avoid prop wash rear elements flew above those preceding and some got well over 2,000 feet up. It is not surprising that a few of them were jolted by wash from the RAF Stirlings at 2,500 feet. The intercom sets worked better than in the past, but over 20 per-cent of them failed or worked poorly. Although for most of the way visibility was over five miles and cloud bases over 2,500 feet, the column did pass through slight rain at some points. When all these difficulties have been noted, the fact remains that for most pilots the trip across the Channel and over Belgium went quite smoothly. Only one glider, which ditched successfully, went down in the Channel; and none did so in Belgium.

The mission apparently turned north at Gheel rather than Bourg Leopold, flew outside of the Allied salient and as a result was subjected to some small-arms fire in an area west of Eindhoven. Five gliders were released in that area, one because of flak damage and one because it was out of control, the others for unspecified reasons. Real trouble came when the column reached the Veghel area. The Germans, beaten back from the highway, were still massed in strength along its flanks. The earlier serials flew over them for a distance of about five miles and while doing so received a barrage of accurate and intense light flak and automatic weapons fire. Nine planes were shot down on the mission and 96 were damaged, about 20 percent of the damage being serious enough to require repair by service groups. Casualties aboard the planes were 13 dead or missing and about 17 wounded or injured. Nearly all of this toll was inflicted in the general vicinity of Veghel and Uden.

The first serial was especially hard hit, three of its planes going down and several gliders being shot loose or forced to release because of damage. The two lead gliders of the 29th Squadron had to cut loose and this set off a succession of premature releases from its half of the formation. In some instances the tug flashed the green light; in some the glider pilot released of his own accord or at the request of the airborne. The upshot was that 21 gliders in that serial came down prematurely between Veghel and Grave. None were demolished and only a couple made rough landings. Except for three or four which landed on an airstrip near Volkel, they were strung out close to the highway in friendly territory or so near it that with Dutch assistance and some rescue work by Allied troops it proved possible to bring in all occupants and cargoes.

A similar situation occurred in the fourth serial when a squadron leader, whose plane was about to crash, released his glider near Veghel. His men faithfully followed his example with the result that 18 gliders in that formation came down within about six miles of Veghel, Six of these landed in hostile territory and all aboard were lost. The last three serials while still over Belgium received radio reports from returning formations on the danger spots ahead and adjusted their course accordingly with such beneficial results that they had only one plane shot down and two gliders released in the Veghel sector.

Some 348 gliders were brought as far as Grave. The 'Eureka' on the zone was not functioning, probably because the batteries were worn out, but none of the pilots appear to have had trouble finding their way there. In the northwest part of the LZ near Overasselt, the pathfinders had laid out panels and sent up smoke signals which were sighted by most of the formations.

The first serial reached LZ 'O' at 1603 and during the next seven minutes released its gliders there at altitudes of 900 to 2,500 feet. The second serial had already reached the zone and made its release between 1602 and 1607 from heights of 600 to 1300 feet. This overlapping would probably have caused confusion had not half the first serial released before reaching the zone and the remainder been much dispersed. Both timing and formation left something to be desired. Two more serials arrived out of sequence and only the last two, which arrived at 1710 and 1717, were exactly on schedule. However, there seems to have been no serious interference between serials and approximately three-quarters of the gliders descended in formation after release somewhere between 800 and 1,200 feet and took a 90° or 180° turn to the left (depending on their angle of approach) so as to land into the wind. A minority of stragglers and non-conformists followed widely divergent patterns, making turns of 3600 or more after high releases, turning right when the rest went left, or pulling away from their mates to avoid crowded fields. Nevertheless, the results compared very favourably with those in previous glider operations.

The main focus of the landings was in an oval a mile across and 1½ miles long lying northwest of Overasselt and centred on the pathfinders. Within that area were some 210 gliders. A looser concentration of about 100' gliders gathered in an open area of similar size and shape along the riverbank opposite Grave. Of the rest, all but one were on or close to the zone and all but about six were within half a mile of one of the main concentrations.

Although LZ 'O' had the great advantage of being out of range of the enemy, landing OD it was no easy matter. The zone had originally been regarded as unsuitable for gliders because so much of it consisted of very small or narrow fields bordered by fences, hedges and drainage ditches. Large numbers of livestock grazing in the fields created an additional hazard. Most of the glider pilots came in at speeds of 55 to 75 mph, frequently using arrestor chutes to great advantage. They had to do a great deal of dodging and hedgehopping, but found that they could smash through the hedges and light fences almost unscathed. Only about eight of the gliders landing on the zone were destroyed, almost all by running into ditches. At least 102 received damage. Noses and wings were battered, wheels and undercarriages smashed, but the contents of the gliders came through almost intact. Out of 24 guns, 82 jeeps and 47 trailers put down on the LZ, only one jeep was unusable. Of over 2,900 troops landed there all but 10 were fit for duty.

The last gliders carrying the 325th Glider Regiment had landed at 1703. By 1800 the Regiment was assembled at 75 percent of strength and was moved immediately to the Groesbeek area to take up positions on the east flank of the 82nd Division. Most of the missing personnel reported in during the next two days. It was a most welcome reinforcement, but the time when it could have any significant effect on the outcome of 'Market' was already past.

For much of the way the little 53rd Wing glider mission to LZ 'W' was flown in conjunction with that just described. Its 84 tug-glider combinations took off from the bases of the 436th and 438th Groups with 395 troops and 100 tons of supplies and equipment, including 15 guns, 13 trailers and 23 jeeps. Four gliders aborted over England, one because a nervous soldier pulled the release handle. The rest flew to Bradwell Bay and there fell into position between the 5th and 6th serials of the mission to the 82nd Division. One more glider was released over Belgium. The other 79 went almost unopposed to LZ 'W' and were released there from a height of about 600 feet at 1632 and 1636 with excellent results. On the zone, fit for action, landed 338 troops, 14 guns, 12 trailers and 22 jeeps. Two gliders had crash-landed killing three soldiers and injuring nine.

The one and a half battalions of the Polish Brigade drop near Grave and start to march up to Driel. An airstrip at Oud Keent near Grave is available and HQ 2nd Army sanction its use for the landing of supplies and reinforcements. North of the Waal 43rd Division makes slow progress. 129 Brigade is still held at Elst by strong German artillery and tank defence. 130 Brigade is sent forward to Driel to relieve 214 Brigade, which later in the afternoon attacks Elst from the west and fighting continues into the night. Lieutenant Colonels Mackenzie and Myers of HQ Airborne Division had reached HQ Airborne Corps and HQ XXX Corps and tried to emphasize the serious plight of their division, but to them there seemed to be a lack of urgency. Doubts about the feasibility of getting up to the Rhine in force and crossing the river to relieve the

British airborne troops are being discussed at various levels of command. Later in the evening HQ 2nd Army gives permission to withdraw the 1st Airborne Division if the situation warrants.

Sunday 24 September

0930 Lieutenant General Sir Brian Horrocks, with Major-General Ivo 'Butcher' Thomas and Major General Stanislaw Sosabowski view the 1st Airborne Division position from the church tower at Driel. Horrocks had hoped to be able to send across the river a brigade of 43rd Division and to carry out a left hook with another brigade. He left with this intention in mind, but stopping shortly on his way back at HQ 43rd Division at Valburg, he may have been convinced that it might not be feasible and that the Airborne Division might have to be withdrawn. HQ 43rd Division were told to prepare contingency plans for the withdrawal, should it be necessary. Horrocks, still optimistic, orders that another crossing should be made that night to strengthen and widen the perimeter. A Polish Parachute Battalion and the 4th Dorsets are ordered to make the crossing. 129 Brigade remain stuck in the southern part of Elst, while 214 Brigade is still fighting house-to-house in the village. The Guards Division have not taken Bemmel only 2 miles NE of Nijmegen. Boats and bridging material to affect a river crossing of the Rhine in strength are not yet available in the forward area. Horrocks then drives south to Sint-Oedenrode to meet Dempsey for the first time since the start of the operation and brief him on the situation, especially the serious situation of the Airborne Division that he had seen at Driel. Depending on the outcome of the river crossing by the two battalions, he suggests that there are two options: pass a brigade of 43rd Division across the Rhine west of Arnhem and establish a bridgehead or withdraw the 1st Airborne Division. Horrocks said that he and Browning made the decision the next Monday after he had returned to his HQ in Nijmegen, having had to bypass the German block on the main axis and heard that the Dorsets' crossing during the night had been an utter failure. Early in the morning, in another attempt to cut the road, the Germans attack Eerde, south of Veghel, but after heavy, close fighting all day they are held off by American paratroopers and British tanks. Towards dusk a fresh enemy battalion comes in from the east and establishes a strong block astride the road at Koevering.

About 0900 the Germans attack at Eerde in a new attempt to cut the road. The attack is repelled, although it takes all three battalions of the 501st PIR to handle it. The front appears to have been stabilized and truck convoys are pouring up the road. Encouraged by this turn of events, Dempsey and Horrocks, meeting early in the afternoon at St. Oedenrode, decide to make one more bid for victory. That night the balance of the Polish Brigade and two companies of 43 Division would cross the Rhine in assault boats to buttress the lines of 1 Airborne. On the next night there would be a crossing in strength to make the foothold secure. There was no expectation of taking the Arnhem Bridge, which by that time was strongly held. Hardly had the plan been made when at 0430 a fresh German thrust cuts the supply line three miles south of Veghel and the enemy brings up guns and tanks and digs in for a long stay. It takes 101st troopers combined with British tanks 40 hours to reopen the road. Thereafter the thunderous roar of armour and supply trucks rolling up the highway continues uninterrupted.

Meanwhile, General Taylor shuttles troops up and down both sides of the British Second Army's supply route to repulse German forces determined to sever General Dempsey's lifeline. Airborne troops, glidermen and paratroopers plug gaps in the line with courage and M-1 rifles. During the campaign in the canal-divided lowlands, hard-hitting 101st paratroopers and glidermen again meet a reorganized Normandy foe, the German 6th Parachute Regiment, which sustains heavy casualties and is driven from the 101st sector. The 101st moves to a strip of land between the Neder Rijn and Waal Rivers with Arnhem to the north, Nijmegen to the south, which soon becomes known as the 'Island.' This marks the beginning of the end for the 383rd Volksgrenadier Division.

Taking over a quiet sector of the Island, the 101st prepares defensive positions. Within 24 hours the 957th Regiment, who, told that it is opposing a handful of isolated Allied parachutists, hungry and without adequate weapons, attacks from the west, only to be driven to destruction. The Germans reorganize battered elements and are joined the next day by the 958th Regiment. German artillery and armour supports a fresh attack. By nightfall, the battalion occupying Opheusden, focal point of the German effort for three days of fanatical fighting, withdraws to a defensive line east of the town. Opheusden changes hands several times. Either attacking or withdrawing, the 101st inflicts tremendous losses on the 363rd Division, now completely assembled with the 959th Infantry Regiment, 363rd Artillery Regiment and its engineer and fusilier battalions in the fold. Airborne soldiers eventually capture the town. In its reorganized Volksgrenadier status, the once-proud 363rd Infantry Division has lasted exactly 10 days in the battle with the Screaming Eagles. From then on, activity in Holland is limited to patrols. Highlighting the action was the work of an intelligence section patrol of the 501st PIR led by Captain Hugo S. Sims, Orangeburg, NC, Regimental S-2. The patrol crossed the Rhine in a rubber boat at night and following a number of narrow escapes, reached an observation point on the Arnhem-Utrecht highway, eight miles behind enemy lines. After relaying information back to the division by radio, the patrol captured a number of German prisoners who gave additional data on units, emplacements and movement in the area. Moving out next day, the six-man team nabbed a German truckload of SS troops, including a battalion commander. When the truck bogged down, patrol and PWs, now numbering 31, walked to the river, then crossed over to the American-held bank. Early in November, the division was relieved in Holland and once again returned to a base camp, this time in France.

Monday 25 September

The operations of the troop carrier units on 25 September are restricted, mainly because of the weather. Ceilings over the Channel and the Low Countries are between 1,000 and 1,500 feet and although England has satisfactory weather in the morning, rain and low clouds with bases between 600 and 1,000 feet spread over the island from the west during the afternoon. One composite resupply serial of 34 aircraft of the 434th, 435th and 436th Groups is loaded at Ramsbury with 49 tons of howitzer ammunition for the 101st Division. It flies unopposed over the southern route to Hechtel and from there up the road to DZ 'W', the only damage being caused by a rough landing on the return. The formation shifts at the IP from the V of V's to a column of three-plane V's and at 1641 makes a very good drop. Each plane has carried 6 parapacks and three door bundles. Practically all of the former land in a small area and are recovered. None of the latter are found, probably because of the time it takes to shove them out.

Another strong German attack comes in against the axis, from the direction of Hertogenbosch, but it is held after hard fighting by the Grenadier Guards. Further south, the battle to remove the German force at Koevering continues. The 506th PIR, having just reached Uden, turn round and march south again to deal with the German block, with the support of 44th Royal Tank Regiment, but they are stopped on the road by well-directed artillery fire and from dug-in tanks. Horrocks sends in stronger forces to eliminate this block and to get the road open again. A brigade of 7th Armoured Division of XII Corps moves up from Eindhoven in two columns, one along the main route and the other directed towards Schijndel. Under threat of this pressure the Germans start to pull out, but leave the main road heavily mined, which is not cleared until late on Tuesday the 26th. The crossing by the 4th Dorsets is a disaster. Myers and a Dorset major, each with a copy of the 43rd Division plan for the withdrawal, reach HQ Airborne Division at the Hartenstein. Urquhart signals that he agrees with the plan and that it must take place that night. 43rd Division spend most of the day in preparation for the night's withdrawal. 214 Brigade would hold firm the east flank around Elst; 129 Brigade, now in reserve south of Driel, would make a noisy feint to the west to simulate a major river crossing downstream of the perimeter and 130 Brigade would be responsible for the actual evacuation operation and reception of the airborne troops. A large-scale and complicated fire plan by the Division artillery, mortars and the Corps medium artillery regiments was drawn up in conjunction with HQ Royal Artillery, 1st Airborne Division.

Tuesday 26 September

On the east flank 11th Armoured Division of VIII Corps has reached the Maas at Boxmeer and linked up with XXX Corps. To the west 7th Armoured Division of XII Corps links up with the Guards Division on the Maas north of Oss. By late September Hell's Highway south of Uden is mostly secured. The 101st Airborne moves north, to be used as supporting infantry in Montgomery's army for the next two months. During this time, the 101st would subsist on British rations, along with whatever food they could scrounge from local Dutch houses, farms and liberated jam factories. Moving unit by unit in truck convoys, the 101st Airborne Division would leapfrog past the 82nd Airborne, which had been fighting hard since 17 September in the area surrounding Nijmegen.

Chapter 7

The Angel Of Arnhem

'We were to dip as low as possible to try to establish by visual observation who controlled the bridge, the Germans or the British. I thought that this regularity was crazy and mentioned it to Edwin R. Cerrutti, 654th navigator. His only comment was that the German Command wouldn't believe that we were that stupid.'
Lieutenant Roy C. Conyers, a USAAF Mosquito navigator in the 25th Bomb Group, 22 September.

B weather grounded all except three essential Bluestocking reconnaissance missions by American crewed Mosquitoes over the Arnhem Bridge, one of which was flown by Lieutenant 'Paddy' Walker and his navigator, Roy Conyers. As they flew over the north end of the bridge just below the fog, at less than 500 feet, 'Paddy' Walker and Roy Conyers could see Germans running for their anti-aircraft guns. 'Ground fire began almost immediately' Walker remembers. 'This continued as we flew over and past the other end, on towards the coast. Tracer fire could be seen coming up around us and the plane was hit. I saw the left wing drop tank disintegrate and jettisoned both. The right engine was shut down and the propeller feathered. The fire went out, but the engine was inoperative. I was flying as low and as fast as possible to get out of range. As we crossed the coast additional fire was received; spurts of water coming up near the plane from the barrage; however, we were not hit. After we got out of range, I climbed up into the weather to gain enough altitude to make an emergency Mayday radio call, to get a 'steer' to the nearest base where the weather was suitable to land. We steered to Bournemouth. My Mayday call was answered by the sweetest girl's British accent - 'Tommy' Settle, a beautiful blonde WAAF at Tangmere. During the days that it took to repair the plane she and I became better acquainted.' [75]

In Holland the beleaguered men in the perimeter at Oosterbeek already knew that the Germans had overrun the defences at the Arnhem Bridge and could concentrate all their available forces against them. At dawn Urquhart had received a reply from XXX Corps' Headquarters: 43 Division ordered to

75 On 25 September another Bluestocking mission was launched as evacuation of the surviving paratroops from Arnhem began. 1st Lieutenant Clayborne O. Vinyard and his navigator, 1st Lieutenant John J. O'Mara, took off at 0126 hours in fog so thick they could only see 300 yards in front. They flew too deep into Germany, reaching the Frankfurt area before turning back. They descended to 18,000 feet, but a night fighter got on their tail and shot them down. Both men bailed out and later joined Dean Sanner at Stalag Luft I.

take all risks to affect relief to-day and are directed on ferry. If situation warrants you should withdraw on or across ferry.' Despite the tone of this signal Urquhart did not feel that XXX Corps were fully aware of his predicament or that 'all risks' were being taken to relieve him and so, by noon Urquhart considered it essential to send two officers across the Neder Rjin to acquaint Browning with his situation. He chose Lieutenant Colonel Charles B. Mackenzie, his GSOI for the dangerous crossing of the Rhine. Urquhart told him that he wanted him to make their situation unmistakably known and also to find out all he could about the efforts and whereabouts of the relief force. 'It's absolutely vital that Browning and Horrocks should know that the Division no longer exists as such' he told Mackenzie 'and that we are now merely a collection of individuals holding on. Make clear to them that we're terribly short of men, ammunition, food and medical supplies and that we need some DUKWs to ferry the Poles across. If supplies don't arrive tonight it may be too late.' Urquhart knew that the ferrying arrangements would soon need priority and their specialist nature suggested that it would be useful also for MacKenzie to take Lieutenant Colonel 'Eddie' Myers who was commanding the Royal Engineers, a most able engineer. Myers had already studied the problem of ferrying the Poles across the river and could give XXX Corps an accurate estimate of what craft and equipment were required. Urquhart asked them also to try and have a look at the river banks in order to give the advancing elements of the 43rd Division some reliable picture of crossing possibilities. He wished them luck and called: 'Above all, do try and made them realize over there what a fix we're in.' [76]

The enemy renewed its attacks at 0900 on the morning of Friday the 22nd. At about that time the 1st Battalion The Border Regiment ammunition dump received a direct hit, which caused considerable damage in the area and destroyed all but two of the remaining serviceable battalion vehicles. The explosion caused a fire, which set ammunition exploding in all directions, yet 34-year old RSM Albert 'Bish' Pope who had served with the Regiment since 1927 and CSM Les Fielding and a party of men managed to salvage mortar bombs and .303 inch ammunition before the fire reached the plastic high explosive. Everyone reached cover before this went up with a deafening roar, the loudest, said Les Fielding that he had ever heard. Trees within a radius of hundreds of yards were stripped of leaves and small branches. The fire caused by the explosion became the registration point for the enemy mortars, so any movement from the slit trenches would result in casualties and RSM Pope was fatally wounded. He was taken to the Regimental Aid Post, where, even as he lay dying, he joked with a Medical Orderly about getting his hair cut. He died shortly after, a much respected and well-loved father-figure. [77]

Staff Sergeant Bert Harget and others were all standing in the small courtyard at the rear of the house in a forward area, discussing the move back to Division HQ, when a mortar bomb came over the roof and exploded right among them. 'Of the eight men who were there I was the only one not hit by shrapnel' says Harget. 'I managed to get stretcher bearers to the others and

76 Urquhart.

77 He was initially buried in front of the Tafelberg Hotel, Oosterbeek, but he now rests in the Cemetery at Oosterbeek 22.B.13.

helped carry one of my glider pilot colleagues to a dressing station. For the next few days it was back to the perimeter defence, moving back continuously and digging in. I had no food of my own, only what I could scrounge from the houses.'

Inside the perimeter the enemy shelling and mortaring was causing more casualties. 'The perimeter was now subject to intense mortar fire and snipers were inflicting heavy casualties' recalled Fred Moore. 'We remained in a defensive position during the morning, but with a lull in the intensity during the early afternoon, a small detachment of us were sent out on a scouting mission. We searched a group of houses and noted the total devastation around us, with bodies and debris from previous battles lying everywhere. There were still a number of Dutch civilians occupying buildings, mostly living in the cellars. Without warning we were subjected to a barrage of shellfire. A soldier near to me dropped and although he was dead, there was no sign of an injury, so we presumed that he had been killed by the blast. Having established that the area at that time was clear of enemy, we returned to our lines to report. The Germans seems to have a strange reluctance to fight during the hours of darkness, so as the light began to fade our hopes of surviving to another day and maybe rescue by the British Army, were rekindled.'

Sapper Philip Andrew Hyatt of No.3 Troop, 4th Parachute Squadron broke up a strong attack on the 4th Parachute Squadron RE defensive position. The enemy advanced to within 50 yards of the position under heavy small arms fire. Hyatt jumped out of his slit trench and ran towards the enemy throwing hand grenades, killing three or four Germans. The enemy attack was checked. Hyatt continued to throw grenades until they withdrew. He was recommended for an immediate award of the Military Medal.

Major Alan Bush second in command of the 3rd Parachute Battalion, who had been wounded during the fighting in the outskirts of Arnhem, had now rejoined the remnants of his battalion in their new positions. Bush broke out of captivity to rejoin and then command a section of the perimeter. This, though again wounded, he held till the order to withdraw came. 'I took command of the remnants of the 1st and 3rd Battalions' recalls Bush. 'We were in what seemed to be a bare market garden surrounded by houses on three sides. We knew that this had to be the last stand; there was nowhere else to go. Enemy attempts to penetrate this area were frequent, but fortunately predictable - every 4 hours from dawn to dusk; no serious night attacks were tried. Tanks and infantry following a mortar strike was the pattern. During these five days I worked closely with Robert Cain of the South Staffords. We had no communication with Division HQ until word reached us by runner in the early evening of Monday 25th that we were to withdraw at midnight; and not before time as we had little ammunition left.'

At the Mill Hill Fathers' House there were two English soldiers hiding behind the Rhododendrons in front of the villa. 'They were calling out to Wenceslaus who was milking the cows' wrote Father Bruggeman. 'They asked for food and we gave them milk and tins from the sisters basement. The two boys who had been here since Monday left to try to get back to Oosterbeek where they lived. That leaves us with ten refugees. The whole Albers family is with us as well. Father van Laar went walking in the woods behind the garden and was stopped by a German soldier with two English prisoners. His collar saved him; without that he would have been taken too. The two prisoners were badly wounded and could hardly walk. At the Sisters' they were allowed to rest and eat something. Mother Immaculata [an English nun], with tears in her eyes, saw her countrymen but wasn't allowed to help. After 15 minutes they went on all the way to Arnhem.

'On Friday Father Claver and Odulph had to bury bodies. They came back as sad as they went because there weren't any food baskets anymore. The supplies from the sky always came after 1600. This time a heavy German car came with an anti-aircraft gun and parked it next to the chapel. The Friday service had just started and we tried to sing louder than the gun, but that didn't work, so Father Gijsman was wise enough to stop the service. As soon as we came out of the chapel we had to run for shelter. Above Oosterbeek I saw burning planes going down. One of them came very low over the house. A drunken 'Mof' [akin to 'Boche' or 'Kraut'] fired a couple of bullets in the sky. Several parachutes with supplies came down, but all in the hands of the Germans. We didn't try to get any this time because there were too many Germans and nobody wanted, just like Father Thijssen yesterday, to get smacked in the face. Around supper some Germans came and stole our best blankets from the beds. It didn't help to protest. Later they came back for more, but by that time we had hidden the best that remained. Nobody knows what the situation is, but now, even the optimists, are convinced that the airlanding wasn't as successful as we hoped.

'Next morning after breakfast a couple of Germans came and demanded meat. Talking didn't work and they went outside and shot two calves. They dragged the calves to the car and drove off. All we could do was watch and be quiet, or we could have had a bullet too. Throughout the whole morning the Amsterdamsestraatweg was full of people running in the direction of Ede. The village of Huissen was evacuated. Later in the afternoon the elderly came, about 20 to the Lichtenbeek. They were accompanied by several nurses. They came from Oosterbeek and had to run when shells hit their homes several days ago. They had been running ever since and their last days were spent in 'La Cabine' of the water company on the Amsterdamsestraatweg. Although Father Wieschermann looked to taking more people in, we made the best of it and made the bicycle shed into a place to sleep. We covered the floor with straw and blankets and made some toilets. This was the first day of the air landing without supplies from above.'

There were still some Dutch civilians sheltering in their houses. One of these families, Evert and Bertha Breman and their two daughters, stayed in their house, 117 Benedendorpsweg, just east of the church. Corporal Danny Morgans and his section of 1st Battalion were dug-in in their garden.

'After leaving the church we moved out to our new positions. Our 'platoon' was in the gardens of houses on the Benedendorpsweg, facing north with the ground rising to our front. We literally had to wreck a beautiful house. First the windows had to be smashed, so the glass couldn't be blown in on us. Then the furniture was piled into barricades inside the room. Everything that was watertight, from the bath to buckets, vases and jugs, had to be filled with water, as the Germans were using incendiary ammunition to burn us out. Very soon the place was an organised shambles. Suddenly the old gentleman who owned the place appeared in his wrecked lounge. He was carrying a tray with glasses and a bottle of Advocaat. He solemnly filled up the glasses and handed them round to the men who'd just wrecked his home. I apologised for what we had done and he replied, 'It is not you, my son, it is the war.' And he returned to his cellar.

'We had a Polish anti-tank gun with us and it knocked out a tank as it topped the rise. There was much probing by tanks, but the infantry became shy; they just stood off and plastered us with mortar and shell fire, but the line held to the end. Food had long run out and the only water was from a pump in the yard of the Breman family. We shared what little food they had and despite the heavy shelling and constant attacks they looked after our wounded and helped us. The family will never be forgotten by our motley crew, who shared their house during this battle. In addition, they had already put their lives at risk by hiding a Jewish refugee. He withdrew across the river with our battalion survivors.'

What remained of the Division still held approximately to the perimeter that had been established. The water scarcity was a severe handicap and the younger soldiers especially were feeling the effects of hunger. One ration distribution on Thursday night had been 'one sardine and some biscuits per man'. Even the war correspondents did all they could to help. From the bottom of a slit trench writing was not easy. Later, Stanley Maxted, a Canadian working for the BBC and Alan Wood, who covered Arnhem for the *Daily Express* and had also worked in New Guinea and China, produced excellent reports on the battle. [78] Wood was among those trapped in the shrinking perimeter: 'It has been a nasty morning - cold and misty - and the Germans are plastering us plentifully with mortars, big guns and 88s. The 88s are worst because you do not hear them coming. Machine guns have just opened up on the right. In this patch of hell our men are holding a few houses that still stand. An old lady in black stumbled out of one of them a few minutes ago and a British soldier ran out and put his arm round her. She collapsed and he carried her down to safety in a cellar. It is now just five days and five nights since we flew out from England. God knows from what secret source of strength these fighting men have drawn the guts which have kept them going.'

Despite the mortaring and the sickening stench that pervaded the area it was the wounded who were suffering most. 'Shan' Hackett, on the way back to his command post after arranging for the arrival of the Poles, was caught by a mortar burst and hit in the thigh and stomach. A Recce Squadron man

78 Major Roy W. R. Oliver commanded the Public Relations Team during the Battle of Arnhem. This unit consisted of himself, as a Public Relations Officer, two BBC civilian broadcasters (Stanley Maxted and Guy Byam), two newspaper journalists (Alan Wood of the *Daily Express* and Jack Smyth of *Reuters*), two censors (Captains Brett and Williams), three men of the Army Film and Photographic Unit (Sergeants Mike Lewis, Dennis Smith and Gordon Walker) and four signallers (Butcher, Cull, Hardcastle and Noon). For his conduct during the Battle, Oliver was awarded the Silver Star.

accompanying him was also hit. When Hackett found that the man's leg was broken and that his own was only bleeding he made his way to the Hartenstein and collected two stretcher-bearers. He led them to the place where the man lay and then sought attention for himself. Graeme Warrack, who was at Divisional HQ to give Urquhart the medical picture and twice had to take cover, went off to see Hackett who was always trying to persuade Warrack to open the brandy which he knew doctors carried; yet even on such occasions as St. Andrew's night and on the ship coming home from Italy Warrack had made unsatisfactory excuses. Now Hackett said to Warrack: 'You can now produce those medical comforts.'

Warrack was apologetic. 'The brandy has run out,' he said.

'And this,' retorted Hackett, 'is the moment we've waited eighteen months for!'

Warrack gave him a short of morphia.

Hackett was carried with four other wounded, two of them stretcher cases lying across the bonnet, in a jeep through some shelling to the St. Elizabeth Hospital. Hackett was heartened by the evidence he saw all around of the work of the 2nd Army medium guns. He was feeling very sick by the time he was delivered on to the stone floor of the hospital. Nearby lay his sergeant clerk, Dudley Pearson. Presently a British medical officer, Theo Redman, paused on his rounds and when he asked Hackett what was wrong with him the Brigadier replied that he had 'a hole through the leg and felt sick.' Redman checked him over and observed the serious stomach wound that Hackett thought was caused when a shell cap hit his equipment over the solar plexus. Redman asked him where it came out. 'Blimey!' said Hackett. 'Don't ask me!' Redman made a further inspection and said, 'There's no exit.' His face, recalled Hackett, 'fell a yard'. Hackett was given an anaesthetic and was out when an SS doctor accompanied by Captain Alexander Lipmann-Kessel, a South African and one of the divisional surgeons reached him. The German had already seen several extreme cases and he was pronouncing a verdict on each. Of Hackett he remarked: 'We always say a head wound or a stomach wound, euthanasia's best'.' As casually as he could, Lipmann-Kessel said, 'Oh, I don't know. I think I'll have a go at this one.' Hackett was wearing no badges of rank. 'You're wasting your time,' the German said. Lipmann-Kessel operated; splitting his patient from breastbone to navel, removing the splinter and for three hours repaired the dozen holes in his lower intestine. His superb surgery managed to save the brigadier's life. Hackett did not doubt for one minute that he would get well, he later wrote. 'I took it completely for granted that I would get out as soon as it was possible.' Hackett's place was taken by Lieutenant Colonel Iain A. Murray DSO, the Commander of No. 1 Wing of the Glider Pilot Regiment.

'Captain Lipmann-Kessel must have saved many lives by his skill as a surgeon working under most difficult conditions' said Brigadier Gerald Lathbury commanding the 1st Para Brigade when he wrote up his recommendation most strongly for the immediate award of the Military Cross. 'On several occasions the hospital came under both German and British fire. The windows of the operating theatre were blown in and apart from these difficulties, the Germans often interfered and attempted to remove the personnel from the surgical teams. Later when most of the wounded had been evacuated, Captain Lipmann-Kessel was left behind with 30 seriously wounded cases. He continued to perform his duties as a surgeon with the greatest skill and, at the same time, forestalled the Germans in any attempt they made to interfere with the working of the hospital. Finally, Captain Lipmann-Kessel showed great initiative in escaping from captivity. This officer has a great reputation for his gallantry, skill and devotion to duty while carrying out his work under the most difficult and dangerous conditions on many occasions...'[79]

Captain Lipmann-Kessel was taken prisoner when the Queen Elizabeth Hospital was occupied by the Germans on 18 September. Following the evacuation of the lightly wounded, he was one of a small rear detachment who, whilst they were unguarded were not asked to give their parole. In addition to his medical duties, he found time to organise a 'transit camp' for evaders in the area. It was due to his efforts that a wireless and a quantity of machine guns and detonators stored in the hospital reached members of the Underground. On 13 October the remainder of the patients and staff were removed to Apeldoorn. As the majority of the wounded had already been sent to Germany, Captain Lipmann-Kessel received permission to escape and two nights later he left the building unchallenged, with three other members of the RAMC. After marching North for two nights the four escapers came into the hands of friends and were hidden for a month until an evacuation of a large number of Allied personnel had been arranged. Lipmann-Kessel acted as interpreter to the expedition, which unfortunately was not entirely successful. When he and two officers found themselves alone after an encounter with Germans, they returned to the Otterloo - Barneveld area. Captain Lipmann-Kessel made two more efforts to reach safety before he finally met a British Unit near Lage-Ewaluwe on 10 February 1945 after a very hazardous journey. [80]

On the fourth day 20-year old Robert Bollington was blown up and taken to the Regimental aid post at the Old Vicarage. He was eighteen and a half years old when he was called up and served in North Africa until he was nineteen. He then spent from September 1943 until February 1944 in Italy. He was then pulled out of line and returned to England. 'Due to such severe injuries, I remained unaware of my surroundings for the next two days, but I do remember my wakening thoughts. I overheard someone say: 'Don't give him any! He'll be gone before morning.' I knew then, that people lay dying around me. I was a mess. I had received injuries to my arm, leg and face.'[81]

At night, when German tanks rumbled past or shells and mortar bombs shook the walls, Kate ter Horst would console her children in the cellar with a fairy story, then climb the stairs to visit the wounded by candlelight, quietly

79 As well as being awarded the Military Cross he was later made a Member of the British Empire.

80 During the 1950s, Lipmann-Kessel wrote a book of his experiences, 'Surgeon at Arms', under the pseudonym of Daniel Paul. This was reprinted in the 1970s under his real name. He died in 1986 and, at his request, was buried near Arnhem to be near his airborne friends.

81 After the surrender Bollington was taken by train, to Stalag XIB Fallingbostel near Hanover. He remained there from the end of September, until the end of April and Liberation.

reading an appropriate verse or two from the Bible. 'I was evacuated to the Rectory' recalled Captain Frank King 'and after some preliminary treatment by a clearly overworked young doctor I was consigned to the Garden room... I noticed how the whole room brightened up at her arrival; and how the soldiers hung on her every word. She talked to me of her children and her hopes for her family in a free Holland...; thus while Kate radiated hope and happiness for the future I was filled with remorse, for I knew that the battle was not going well. The soldiers, not knowing her name, referred to her simply and with reverence as 'the Lady'. No day was complete without a smile or a word from her and she invariably ended it by reading a psalm from the bible of the Light Regiment's padre. One evening she read the beautiful words of Psalm 91.'

Moving from room to room, her bible in her hand and in the light of a torch read aloud the words of King David her soft voice speaking most carefully for,' said she, 'it has comforted my children and may' comfort you.' *'Thou shall not be afraid, for the terror by night, nor for the arrow that flieth by day. Nor for the pestilence that walketh in darkness; nor for nor for the destruction that wasteth at noonday... A thousand shall fall beside thee and ten thousand on thy right hand; but death shall not come nigh thee, for Thou, Lord, are my hope and Thou hath set Thy house of defence very high.* Above all, by her calm and brave manner she did much to comfort those men. Conditions in the Old Vicarage were very bad, for it was soon housing upwards of 200 wounded and little beyond first aid could be given to them. Kate ter Horst worked without rest or food, helped by a boy of seventeen who did likewise. What water there was had to be brought from a pump close by, till it ran 'red with blood.'

Around Oosterbeek Laag church the attacks on Friday were particularly sharp and wearingly persistent. Held off by Lonsdale's still gallantly fighting but rapidly dwindling force, the Germans would withdraw for a time and then come back again, sometimes supported by Focke-Wulf 190s which, although the weather was 'too bad for any flying from England', were in action intermittently throughout the day. One of the men of Lonsdale Force was the gallant Sergeant Walker of the South Staffords, who knocked out two tanks and was then wounded but, disregarding this mishap, seized a Bren gun and with it halted dead a German counter-attack, only to fall a victim shortly afterwards to the fire of a German tank. One group of parachutists commanded by Major Alan Bush and Jimmy Cleminson (now the only surviving officers in the 3rd Battalion) and encouraged by a lean and astonishing colour-sergeant called Callaghan in an absurdly tall and dusty Dutch top hat ('it doesn't matter at all. Nothin' could hit me under this') destroyed a self-propelled gun. Another self-propelled gun was put out of action by the Polish crew of an anti-tank gun who ran down the road as fast as they could, straight at any German vehicles which came into view, pushing their gun in front of them. These Poles, indeed, attacked anything which looked as if it might be German and an English officer told them only to fire at tanks as 'it drew down all sorts of things'. But the Poles took no notice and their officer said, 'Sometimes I fire. Sometimes I do not fire.' 'Eventually they fired once too often,' according to the English officer, 'and were all killed. We weren't sorry as a matter of fact, though the gun was smashed.'

Urquhart recorded that Friday was 'a terrible, desperate day. In places there was some enemy penetration but the Germans were winkled out by gallant counter-attacks and daring stalks. As evening approached the perimeter was substantially unchanged, but the Germans appeared to be everywhere.' At all times communication between Major General Urquhart and Lieutenant General Browning, was difficult and often impossible. A large number of the wireless sets carried into action were damaged either on landing or subsequently by enemy action; a large number were unserviceable almost from the beginning. 82

Throughout the time he spent at the Headquarters of the 1st Parachute Brigade on the outskirts of Arnhem, Urquhart was out of touch for many hours with the 2nd Battalion at the bridge and his own headquarters at Hartenstein, though the distance between was not large and was well within the range of the standard equipment carried.

A Staff Sergeant Armament Artificer Telegraphist in the REME recalled: 'On the whole we had plenty of work. On the wireless side, we had to do a good deal of improvisation. One thing of which we were called On to do pretty frequently was the repair of battery leads. Perhaps the most unusual job we did was to improvise a choke for a No, 76 set by scraping down a piece of wire until we got the 'resistance right. Altogether the wireless artificers did 37 repair jobs while we were there. The armourers were even busier. Their QMS went out with a jeep round the units in their various positions collecting damaged equipment and taking out the repaired stuff. This repair work was very important, for there were no replacements and there was a lot of damage done to the small arms and automatics by the kind of fighting that was going on.

'Div HQ was in a large hotel and we were in the grounds, or in the cellars. It had been an attractive place, a holiday resort, I should think, with tennis courts and a running track in the grounds at the back and plenty of trees. There was an orchard, too and an ornamental garden alongside it and in front plenty

82 Some loss of communication between the bridge and Divisional Headquarters in one of the drop zones was expected, because 8.1 miles separated them and the main radio used throughout the Division was the Type 22 set designed to have an effective range of 3.1 miles. The British radios did not function at any range; some had difficulty receiving signals from just a few hundred metres and others received nothing at all. It was found after landing that the radios had been set to different frequencies, two of which coincided with those of German and British public broadcasting stations. Other theories have been advanced to explain the greatly reduced range of the 1st Airborne Division's radio sets. Thus communication between 1st Airborne units was poor while German defences were being coordinated and reinforced. Radio communications failures were experienced by the Division before, were warned about prior to the operation and provisioned for by bringing extra field telephone wire. The more powerful WS19HP set was used by 1st Brigade on D+1. The only means of calling for close air support was through two special American units dropped with the 1st Airborne Division. These units were equipped with 'Veeps': jeeps having VHF SCR-193 crystal sets. It was found impossible to communicate with aircraft on the higher of two frequencies for this and the sets could not be tuned to the lower frequency. Despite efforts to re-tune them, one set was soon destroyed by mortar fire and the other abandoned the next day, cutting the 1st Airborne's only possible link with RAF fighter-bombers. The pilots were under orders not to attack on their own initiative since from the air there was no easy way to distinguish friend from foe; together with poor weather, this led to a critical lack of air support.

of flower beds. The building itself was of two storeys, with a lot of verandas and big windows. It was gradually blown to pieces by the shellfire and mortaring.

'We had not much food. The sgt-major at Div HQ got some potatoes from a cottage just outside the grounds and kept things going and there was a well there from which we drew water.

'The mortaring became more intense as the week progressed. There was a morning hate which at first lasted for half an hour. On the last morning it started at 7 am and went on until 11am. But you could tell if they were coming close. Some of the men were a little nervous as it was the first time they had been in action, but I found that if you kept them busy they were quite cheerful.' One man went to a blazing jeep loaded with ammunition and jacked it up to take off the front wheel before it burnt as he knew we wanted a spare wheel for another job. Snipers were a nuisance towards the end. I' had to go out for them myself. I got one, too, when he broke away to try and get back to his own lines.'

The Brigade Major, Royal Artillery recalled: 'Practically the whole of the Div artillery landed intact. It consisted of two anti-tank batteries, with both 6-pounder and 17-pounder guns and a Light Regiment with 75 mm field guns. This was later augmented by the anti-tank guns of the Polish Para Brigade which came in by glider. The batteries suffered various fates. About one and a half troops of one anti-tank battery went with 'A' Para Brigade into Arnhem and some of them later extracted themselves back into the perimeter. The anti-tank battery with the other Para Brigade lost half of its equipment when the Brigade was overrun moving into the Div area on the Tuesday. The close country was a big help to the enemy's armour. The remainder of these came into the perimeter with the Polish guns and were positioned around the sectors by CRA. We finished up inside the perimeter with about twelve anti-tank guns. 'The gunners fought magnificently. Often a tank or an SP gun could get within 100 yards of their position under cover and with the infantry support and the gunners would have to fight off the infantry with small arms while engaging the armour with the piece itself. They were mortared continuously and although they dug in they had to leave their pits big enough to give them a wide arc of fire and were so much more vulnerable in consequence.

'When their guns were knocked out they fought on as infantry and some of the sectors and units finished up with gunner officers and NCOs in command of the remaining infantry. The field guns stayed together as a whole throughout the operation, in the area of Oosterbeek Church. There they held part of the line as well as giving supporting fire all round the perimeter. Their guns were more use to other parts of the sector than they were immediately to their own front. They were handicapped by ammunition shortage and by the Thursday were down to 40 yards a gun, so fire had to be husbanded. Until the Thursday they were the only field artillery we had. From the Thursday onwards we had the support of 30 Corps artillery and without it I don't think we could have held out as long as we did. They were magnificent. The mediums were in range first and finally the 25 pounders were pushed far enough forward to reach our side of the river. We got on to the Corps Artillery net and directed their fire. It was amazing how accurate they were, even at extreme range, when firing solely from the map. They broke up concentrations of armour and infantry before an attack, put down fire when the attack was coming in 'and harried it when we had beaten it back. It made all the difference and helped the morale of everyone a lot.

'As an instance of what they could and did do, our CRA directed a shoot of mediums, firing at extreme range, on a wood inside our lines only 200 yards square and only 200 yards away from the dugout on the steps of which he was standing. Another shoot came down just on an attack which was formmg up without, apparently, anyone having ordered it. The shoots were directed to the man on the spot, gunner or anyone else, using Infantry channels to Div HQ Command Post and W/T from there. One thing did stand out. Everyone should be able to take a shoot. They may have to.'

On Wednesday the 21st Independent Parachute Company had taken up a defensive position in the grounds of a big house called the 'Ommershof' with 1 Platoon on the west side, 2 Platoon on the north overlooking the wooded grounds of 'White House' on other side of Graf Van Rechtenweg and 3 Platoon forming the east flank with the outpost LMG (Bren gun) in a hut overlooking open ground. The 9th SS Panzer made sustained attacks uphill against the 2 Platoon position from the 'White House' area across Graf van Riecher Weg, which were repulsed with casualties. Then the enemy, moving to east, regrouped on open ground and returned through the woods to resume attacks on 2 Platoon's position. Lieutenant Hugh Ashmore commanding 3 Platoon and his platoon sergeant, Sergeant Joe Smith, noticed this and quickly told Lance Corporal Bill Barclay to get some men to reinforce the LMG in the hut overlooking open ground. Barclay did so accompanied by one of the Jewish members of the unit. Finding the gunner dead, Barclay manned the Bren gun and put fire onto German troops. He relinquished the LMG on his return after the attacks died down. On Thursday night the Company moved from the Omershof to join the Divisional perimeter in Oosterbeek, taking up positions in houses in the Paasberg and Piersberg Roads and in Station Weg north of the main Utrechtweg.

On Saturday at around 0300 the members No.3 Platoon, regarded as 'the young ones' by the Company's more seasoned personnel, were ordered to relieve the remnant of 10 Parachute Battalion occupying a salient position 400 to 500 yards in front of the perimeter along the Utrechtweg. The 10th Battalion had been overrun in their positions in front of the Main Dressing Station on the Utrechtseweg-Stationsweg junction and the Independent Company was ordered to fill in the gap that this had created. No.3 platoon was told to occupy the hotel along the main road, which was an isolated and vulnerable position. 'Boy' Wilson strongly recommended against this action but he was overruled by Brigadier Hackett as a force had to be put between the Germans and the Dressing Station and 3 Platoon duly took up positions in three houses. A Mark IV tank and two self-propelled guns soon demolished these positions and dislodged the platoon and Wilson took the opportunity to remove the survivors and bring them back across the road, much to Hackett's annoyance.

1 Section commanded by Sergeant Jerry Thompson was on the left of road, 2 Section under Sergeant 'Paddy' Cockings was in front of Platoon HQ with the remnant of 3 Section on the right of the road. At barely first light, the Germans attacked with a hundred or more Panzergrenadiers supported by a Mk IV tank and two 88mm SP guns. Bill Barclay was dozing in a slit trench on ground floor of house occupied by Platoon HQ, woke as shells ripped through house. Joe Smith, sitting a few yards away, suddenly realised that their only Bren was upstairs with no-one there. He called out to Barclay 'Slip upstairs, old chap and bring down the Bren and box of magazines' which Barclay duly did. Hugh Ashmore having been in radio contact with 'Boy' Wilson was ordered to withdraw from this exposed position but it was too late for 'Paddy' Cockings' section which was overrun. Despite casualties Jerry Thompson withdrew to the 1 Platoon area where he was finally killed. Ashmore got Platoon HQ and 3 Section to move back with the withdrawal covered by Sergeant Joe Smith and Barclay with his Bren and eventually returned to the perimeter.

3 Platoon occupied a position in a house and small school along the Paasbergweg area where a hospital had been established in a large house. Fighting was fierce and continuous, the enemy being in some of the houses and the airborne in others including one next door to the hospital. The Independent Company were presented with an ultimatum: withdraw from their positions, or a self-propelled gun, which had been moved up to within sight of them, would blast them out. There was little in the way of anti-tank weaponry available and so Major 'Boy' Wilson decided to bluff his way out of this, telling the German who had contacted him on the wireless, 'We have a lot of PIATs here; if you don't clear off we'll blast you out'. The vehicle withdrew. When a truce was arranged to evacuate the wounded from Oosterbeek on the afternoon of Sunday 24th, this sombre procession passed the positions of the Independent Company on the Utrechtseweg. Despite the truce, two Mk.IV tanks were reported to be in front of No.3 Platoon and the German commander sent a message by the regimental doctor to the effect that, if they did not evacuate the house, he would blow them to pieces with his tanks, of which he had three. Wilson sent a message back saying that he would comply, but only if they withdrew from the vicinity and put their tanks back at least a mile. He was prepared to move if the German promised not to enter the hospital. At the same time Wilson told Private Frank Dixon, the Platoon cook, who was now the PIAT gunner No 1 to slip out by the back door and fire on the leading German tank with a PIAT. Sergeant Joe Smith went on the 'scrounge' and returned with a couple of PIAT bombs. Bill Barclay helped Dixon to reassemble the PIAT which had been stripped and hidden under pile of coal as all bombs had been expended. As assembly was being completed, Joe Smith came along and told Barclay and Dixon to hurry up as two Mk IV tanks were approaching through gardens on the left flank. Smith and Barclay accompanied Dixon and crept through bushes up to about 50 yards from tanks. Dixon prepared the PIAT to fire while Smith and Barclay took up covering position. Dixon's first shot hit the tank at the rear. At first it appeared as if nothing happened and then the ammunition exploded, fire broke out and the crew tried to leave. They were shot down by Barclay and Smith. The second tank rapidly withdrew before

Dixon could fire again. This incident resulted in Dixon being awarded the Military Medal. For his conduct in the Oosterbeek Perimeter Bill Barclay was awarded the Military Medal also.

Platoon HQ moved from the school to further south and occupied two houses which they held until they were relieved by 1 Platoon who handed over the original house in Stationweg to the Poles. There were some probing attacks and on Monday the Company beat off number of probing attacks during the morning. The afternoon was quiet and at 2230 the Company acted as rearguard on withdrawal across the river. 'Boy' Wilson was wounded and Lieutenant John Horsley was killed during withdrawal.

Though he had started the Battle of Arnhem as a Private, Bill Barclay ended it as a Lance Corporal and rapidly progressed through the ranks. Eighteen months later he was a Lieutenant serving in India with the 1st Battalion The South Staffordshire Regiment.

The dawn of Saturday 23 September was grey and damp and a clammy mist hung over the battlefield. It was drizzling with rain from a heavy, forbidding sky as the Germans renewed their attacks, starting as soon as it was light. And then, the prodding attacks began again. At seven o'clock, Lieutenant Stevenson remembers, 'we came under a terrific mortar barrage - first it came down directly on us, then it lifted three hundred yards back, smack on Squadron HQ The SP guns came up again and began systematically destroying every house which might give shelter. All this time in the cellars of almost every house were Dutch civilians, women and children who had been caught by the battle. By now we were rather losing count of time. More SP guns and some shell fire.'

The 9th SS Panzer fought in four Kampfgruppen (battle groups) - Sturmbannführer Ludwig Spindler's, north of the main Arnhem-Utrecht road; Hauptsturmführer Hans Moeller's engineer battalion was already on that road fighting near the Schoonoord Hotel; Hauptsturmführer Klaus Von Allwörden's to clear the houses south to the river road and Obersturmbannführer Harzer's along the river directed at Oosterbeek Church. The main objective was the Hartenstein Hotel, although its significance as the Airborne Division HQ was not then known. They were all ordered to mount ceaseless attacks by day, while heavy weapons were to pound the pocket at night. The British 'were to be battered into submission'. Despite the relentless pressure from the east, the 9th SS Panzer achieved 'only small gains'. Spindler was ordered to shift his Schwerpunkt towards the lower Rhine with the aim to cut the British off from the river. The Germans were, however, suffering equally high casualties as the British defenders, but, unlike the dwindling British airborne strength, they were being constantly reinforced with men and resupplied with ammunition and rations, some of it dropped by the RAF on to enemy-held DZs. Despite the almost continual artillery, mortar and sniper fire and against repeated attacks by infantry, tanks and SP guns, the British held their positions for the next four days. There was a steady drain of casualties, many of whom had to stay in the houses, but most were evacuated to the Regimental Aid Post of the Light Regiment in the Old Rectory.

'We, a small detachment, under the command of a Sergeant, were, before first light' recalled Fred Moore, 'instructed to relieve a similar group, who were defending a house on a road overlooking a T junction. The garden at the back of the house was separated from a similar house and garden by a hedge, which by now had been flattened. The other house was one of a cluster of houses, on a road running parallel to the road which we controlled. The force which we were relieving had been involved in a number of desperate enemy assaults by tanks, supported by infantry. Once we had taken up strategic positions in the various rooms of the house, the Sergeant instructed me to liaise with the forward Airborne units and then the group of pilots of the Glider Pilot Regiment, somewhere along the junction road facing the front of the house. Having accomplished this mission, I was then told to make our presence known to a group of South Staffs, located on our left flank, along the parallel road. I traversed the two gardens, noting with alarm the carnage and destruction, which signified the significance to both sides of the position we were holding. Emerging from the left side of the house, I found an Airborne soldier, the solitary occupant of the small front garden.

'Vaulting over the low wire fence, I proceeded down the road, which was long and straight. A few yards further on was a stationary Tiger tank, obviously no longer serviceable. Stopping to look inside, I saw the driver slumped forward with his head shattered. I had gone about 200 yards, but no sign of defence forces, so I shouted, 'Any South Staffs around?' No reply! Another 50 yards or so, then I heard the sound of digging on the opposite side of the road. Crossing the road I located the source of the sound behind a low brick wall at the front of a house. Jumping over the wall I said; 'Are you the...? 'Shit, the enemy'! I kicked his machine gun into his trench, jumped back over the wall and starting running back, not straight but zigzagging. A hail of bullets escorted me down the road and reaching the wire fence, I literally dived over it. Running down the garden, I was passed by a figure; the guy from the other garden!

'Describing my experience to the Sergeant, he instructed the two of us to return to the forward garden and watch for any movement from the German position, while he called for a salvo from our Light Artillery Battery to shell the position they occupied. We saw a German standing in the road shouting. He sounded very angry. Then a few minutes' later shells started exploding around the area.

'Returning to my original position, I took up a position in the roof, taking advantage of one of the numerous tile-less areas, behind a chimney, as cover, from where I had a vantage point, with a clear view in all directions.

'The sound of caterpillar tracks approaching down the road, presaged a determined attack by a Tiger tank, supported by infantry. The troops dug in forward of our position opened fire, supported by limited covering fire from us. After a skirmish with casualties on both sides, the opposing force withdrew. In the afternoon a line of Germans, presumably the unit I had found earlier were observed approaching down the rear garden. We opened fire and they quickly withdrew, occupying the house in the rear. One of them had obviously been hit because we could hear him moaning.

'As the light deteriorated, it was obvious that we could not leave them occupying their present position, yet we also could not abandon our post without notifying headquarters. The sergeant left to report the situation and shortly after returned with an officer. We were to storm the position and eliminate the threat to our rear. As instructed I left my rifle behind, replacing it with a hand gun. In the fading light, we moved in single file through the gardens adjacent to our position and having reached the rear of our objective, without detection, I was left in the rear to guard the closed back door, while the rest moved to the side of the house. When in position, the officer shouted, in German, a command to surrender. There was no reply or sign of movement, so I fired my revolver through the panels of the back door. This brought an immediate response and the occupants came out and surrendered with no sign of opposition. We started to march them down the garden, when the officer turned to me and said, 'Go back and make sure there are no enemy still in the house!' Not me again! I thought and reluctantly proceeded to obey his instruction. Moving through the various rooms, with the speed of light, I was happy to report that the house was now unoccupied.

'We marched our captives to the enclosed tennis court, reserved specifically for enemy prisoners and proceeded to search them, prior to locking them away. I was about to search one of them when suddenly there was an explosion. I found myself on the floor and my immediate reaction was, 'Is this it? Am I about to die?' There was no pain and I found that I was the only one hit and yet in three places, my hand, arm and leg. My luck had run out. Bleeding profusely, I was taken to a temporary refuge in the cellar of a nearby house, where my wounds were bandaged with shell dressings. Later in the evening I was moved to the house of Mrs Kate ter Horst, a few yards removed from Oosterbeek church.'

While his platoon was in a defensive position at Oosterbeek Church, 28-year old Private Ernest Holt of the 2nd Battalion The South Staffords was given the job of observer on the extreme right flank of the position. During his watches he kept constant vigilance and on many occasions, while the rest of the platoon was forced under cover by enemy mortaring and shelling, Holt kept watch and observed enemy moving into position under the cover of this mortaring and likely attacks forming up. In spite of heaviest shelling and mortaring, Holt brought the information to Platoon HQ on the left flank and the likely attacks were broken up by machine gun and 2" mortar fire from the platoon. During one of his stand down periods, Holt observed a sniper attempting to infiltrate along a ditch on our right flank. In spite of heavy enemy sniping and machine gun fire, he left his trench, crawled over difficult and open ground and killed the sniper with his rifle. Ernest Holt, who had three sisters and six brothers, all of whom fought in and survived the Second World War, was awarded the Military Medal. His reports from his OP were most valuable in the successful defence of the Oosterbeek Church area. [83]

Further to the south, Lonsdale's men were heavily attacked by a German force which was making yet another attempt to cut the Division off completely from the river. And in the west the Border Regiment, which had been heavily

83 Ernest Holt died in February 1975 aged 59. His Military Medal can be seen on display at the Staffordshire Regimental Museum, at Lichfield Barracks.

shelled during the night and by nine o'clock had lost all its vehicles except two jeeps and a motor-cycle, was also strongly attacked again. One of its companies was overrun and surrounded and another, 'B' Company, was driven back to the outskirts of Oosterbeek.

'A counter-attack failed' Major Charles Breese recorded 'and so reinforcements in the shape of two Platoons of HQ Company under Major Morrissey were sent to assist 'B' Company. This composite force succeeded in regaining some of the lost ground, but in the course of these operations Major Tom Armstrong was severely wounded and captured. The enemy made repeated attempts to break through in this area but the indomitable courage of the soldiers, led by Major Morrissey and later by Major Stewart, despite considerable odds and heavy casualties beat them back time and again. There were strong attacks in the north and the north-east too and all day long the mortaring and shelling continued, dying down into a temporary lull only to open again with stronger force than ever. Flame-throwers came rattling down the streets through Oosterbeek to burn the men out from their forward strongholds and numerous snipers slipped through into 'the Cauldron' to shoot them down as they withdrew. The smell of the battlefield hung about in the damp air, constant and inescapable. Ammunition was running dangerously low and many men had had nothing to eat for 24 hours and only the rain to drink.' 84

Major Geoffrey Powell, 156 Parachute Battalion recalled: 'It was as morning stand-to ended that we heard the distant thuds and the familiar whistle of the Nebelwerfers; the Boche morning 'hate' had started, but this was worse than before, for other mortars and guns had joined in. They must be softening us up for an attack. Then it ended abruptly. I heard our Brens and rifles open up and in the orchard opposite figures could be seen running towards us and then more of them. The attack came in all along our front, but they didn't stand a chance - we just shot them down. 'In the midst of this attack a tall, fair-haired young German officer stood in the open some 50 yards off, waving his men to follow him. My finger tightened on the trigger, but someone else fired and he fell dead. His death marked the end of the attack. Then, as we waited for the next attack, German stretcher-bearers came forward: first one pair, then several more: no Red Cross flag. Deliberately they lowered their stretchers and picked up the wounded - a dozen in all - and then went back. I prayed that none of my soldiers would fire at them, but they did not; instead they watched in amazement at this display of courage. But why hadn't the Boche attacked with tanks at the same time? If they had, then we would not have stood a chance.'

Similar attacks were made against the Reconnaissance positions to the west, but these were also repulsed. Then, about noon, German SP guns edged forward all along the line through the narrow streets, firing at close range into the houses. A significant part in keeping the German infantry at bay was played by the close fire support provided by the XXX Corps medium artillery, but it

84 Major Breese was wounded, but refused to be evacuated to a dressing station until the Division withdrew across the Rhine and he was amongst the last to depart for the other side of the river Breese was promoted to Lieutenant Colonel and given command of the 1st Border on 24 November and he led them in Norway, immediately after the war had ended in May 1945.

had less effect on the SP guns, which were able to blast away at the houses until they became untenable. The whole group here - 156 Battalion, Reconnaissance and Glider Pilots - were forced to leave the houses and dig-in in the gardens behind. 'D' Reconnaissance Troop was also forced back. A local counter-attack by a 156 Battalion platoon led by Captain Stevens, Royal Artillery, failed to drive back the enemy. For the next two days the Germans continued to mortar and snipe at the airborne defenders and their infantry in small groups tried constantly to infiltrate between and around the houses where there were gaps in the defences. German and British were often intermingled in the houses and gardens fighting at close range with grenades and small arms. For some reason this infiltration by their infantry was not supported by their tanks and if it had been, then the defence line would have collapsed and the way opened to the Hartenstein. Airborne casualties mounted in these continued skirmishes: 156 Battalion was down to 37 men, but the Germans were also suffering heavily, although they were being reinforced by fresh troops, whereas the airborne soldiers, without food or sleep and almost out of ammunition, were nearing the end of their tether, but they still fought on.

When a Tiger tank approached the building in which Lieutenant The Honourable Oliver Piers St. Aubyn's platoon in the 156th Parachute Battalion were located and opened fire upon it. A PIAT was brought forward and scored a hit on the tank. It was still mobile but this resistance worried the crew sufficiently for them to withdraw. St. Aubyn's men were not content, however and under cover of smoke from phosphorus bombs, two men ran out of the house and into a building alongside the tank. Several minutes later a hand was seen hanging out of a hole in the roof and a Gammon bomb was dropped on top of the Tiger, prompting a loud explosion. The two men successfully made their way back to the platoon's positions and the Tiger tank did not move again. Either the blast had killed the crew or left them concussed.

Sergeant James Pyper of 'D' Troop, 1st Airborne Reconnaissance Squadron was defending a house with four men on the north side of the Divisional defensive perimeter. His house was attacked by a Self-Propelled Gun firing 88mm shells. The house was demolished by this gun, two of his men being badly wounded. Under intense small arms and mortar fire Pyper got back to his Troop Headquarters to ask for stretcher bearers. He then returned to the house himself and started to get the wounded out. Still under heavy fire he carried the two wounded men to safety when he was met by stretcher bearers. Next day Sergeant Pyper's troop, finding it impossible to remain in houses owing to fire from Self-Propelled Guns, dug-in in front of their house in the garden. In the evening a direct hit from a heavy mortar killed his Troop Commander and the other remaining officer and one other rank. Before Sergeant Pyper had time to recover from the explosion, his rifle having been blown 30 yards away with the blast, a German section descended upon the remaining men of his troop from the garden next door. They were taken prisoner and escorted back to a German occupied house. That night with Captain J. G. Costeloe and six men Sergeant Pyper escaped to a neighbouring house where they laid up until the following evening. They had had no food and water for 48 hours. By this time they were completely surrounded and had little idea where their own troop were situated. However Sergeant Pyper after consulting his men, decided to make an effort to rejoin his own troop, by splitting up into pairs and moving off at intervals. Pyper and Costeloe broke through the German defences under very heavy fire and sniping and crawled to the area of Divisional Headquarters. Here they laid up for 20 minutes before they were certain that the house occupied by Divisional Headquarters was still in British hands. They were then told that the Division was withdrawing and they made their way down to the river. Sergeant Pyper was subsequently awarded the Military Medal.

There were some soldiers, of course, who were by now unable to control themselves. After six days of continuous fighting their nerves had completely broken. Two young privates in the 3rd Battalion were seen on Friday at about noon to run away screaming towards the enemy lines, their hands in the air, tears streaming down their cheeks. And Alexander Johnson said that 'a whole company' of another regiment ran away shouting, 'Tanks! Tiger tanks! Dozens of them!' 'We were mortared steadily', Johnson went on. 'Our numbers decreased. One officer's nerve cracked nearby. The situation grew tense. We were very dirty and hungry now. I took over a platoon belonging to the Airlanding Brigade. Temporarily. I think I was viewed with hostility, as an intruder.' But one man found the spirit to march up to him, salute smartly and say, 'Sir. It's my 21st birthday today. May I have the day off?' Encouraged by demonstrations of cheerfulness such as this, General Urquhart felt able to report to Corps Headquarters that morale was high. He reported also that the perimeter was unchanged, but unless reinforcements could be got across the river soon, the chances of holding on would be negligible.

'In company with Lance Corporal Chillingsworth' recalled Jack Bird of the South Staffords 'I was manning a Bren gun which was covering a crossroad at about midnight on Saturday evening and it was 'all quiet on the western front' for a change. Jerry must have thought it was too quiet as he started slinging mortars over. Anyway we didn't take much notice until one dropped about fifteen yards away and the next one landed right in our positions. 'Willy' was badly hurt, receiving a bad wound to his right side. I was dazed for a bit, but after pulling myself together I looked around for Chillingsworth and he was staggering about shouting 'Oh Jack I've been hit'. So I went to him and quietened him down. Corporal Pegg went across to the RAP for a stretcher and putting him down on it we carried him to the RAP. This place was absolutely crammed out with casualties; many dead and many more dying. There was not an inch of room on the floor so you can guess what a job we had with a stretcher. However we accomplished the journey and carried him into the MO's room. I waited outside and after a while one of the orderlies came out and I asked him if there was any chance of Chillingsworth getting better and he said that he was in a bad way but they were operating right away and he didn't give much hope for him. I asked him if he had seen Corporal Pegg and he said 'Yes he's over there' and pointed to a body which was covered with a sheet. Well this shook me as he seemed OK when we carried the stretcher across. As I went and had a look and saw he had been hit above his left eye. He was very quiet and seemed to be asleep so I left him. I was told afterwards that

Chillingsworth died next day but I think Pegg recovered and was taken prisoner.

'I shall never forget the cries of the blokes for water (while I was in the RAP) and the trouble was, unfortunately, that there wasn't any water. I know that because I asked the MO for a drink as he was making his round and whether he thought I was 'bomb happy' or not but he gave me a very queer look and told me there was no water.

'Next morning I joined up with No.1 MMG Platoon who were out in front of the church in defensive positions. It was there that I met Ernie Young out of our platoon, also Jimmy Renwick, a Geordie boy and one of the best. He had a remarkable escape from injury, a mortar dropping right in the trench, but luckily for him it was a dud. All day Sunday we didn't have much respite from Jerry, what with his mortars, SP guns, tanks and aircraft, he gave us hell and still there was no news or any sign of us getting relieved, so it looked as if we had 'had it'.'

By about midday most of 43rd Wessex Division were across the River Waal and making their way forward to the Rhine. The 214th Infantry Brigade was held up by enemy around Elst. The 130th Infantry Brigade arrived in the Driel area during the afternoon and evening of Saturday and took up positions on the river, with two battalions forward opposite Oosterbeek church and the railway bridge. Throughout the day the attacks on the British perimeter continued and at a quarter past eight General Urquhart sent off the following signal: Many attacks during day by small parties, infantry, SP guns and tanks including flame-throwers. Each attack accompanied by very heavy mortaring and shelling within Division Perimeter. After many alarms and excursions the latter remains substantially unchanged, although very thinly held. Physical contact not yet made with those on south bank of river. Re-supply a flop, small quantities of ammunition only gathered in. Still no food and all ranks extremely dirty owing to shortage of water. Morale still adequate, but continued heavy mortaring and shelling are having obvious effects. We shall hold on. But at the same time hope for a brighter 24 hours ahead.' Their hopes were not to be realised.

Outside the aid station dead lay against the walls when 'Bol' Boldock arrived. 'Inside there was hope' he wrote. 'Get out'. 'Only wounded in here' because I wasn't carried in, I wasn't wounded. God let me in. I fell in. They dressed my wounds, injected morphine and helped me to an upstairs room. A room where wounded lay all round the walls. No beds, no stretchers left for me. They lay me, belly down, on a narrow table. A seven-day clock ticked in a corner. To sleep. The morphine helped. How it helped. I don't remember waking but I must have awakened. The mists were slow in dispersing and the pain came back. As consciousness returned I listened and heard and saw. At least I think I saw. I must have seen. Yes I saw. The clock ticked on, uncaring. The wounded lay suffering below my eyes. The lesser wounded could move around a little. The stench of blood prevailed. I had no shirt, just a thin blanket. They gave me soup and water. Sometimes twice a day. A thumb joint depth of soup in a cup and the same of water. Water was precious now - paid for in blood. It came from a pump in the garden of the house. Around the pump lay many dead, sacrificial bodies of men, fallen in the run to the pump. For water for us. I was lucky; sometimes Corporal Stan Lunt came to see me, from the battle outside. He gave me a 'swig' of water and a cigarette. This we shared, a 'drag' a time with the others. [85] Beyond the window, away from the blur of pain, so they told me, was a fruit laden apple tree. This tree became the conversation and the hopes of the wounded. Fine red apples. One of our wounded, unbelieving, strained to the window, to believe. He fell - shot. Death the reward for the curious. Fine red apples. Outside the battle raged. Tanks grinding and wheeling. Machine guns' gibberish chatter resounded through the house. The building shook. Indiscriminate tank fire penetrated the lower rooms. Armour piercing shells added death to the already wounded. One shell tore through the walls above my back. Plaster and debris falling everywhere, clouted my injured back. What's a little more pain? The apple tree remained unshaken. They told me after this a fearless Airborne Padre went out with a Red Cross flag, confronted the tanks and demanded that the Germans ceased fire and to recognise the house as a hospital. The tank commander agreed. We were left alone for the little time remaining. All these days we had been aware of a Dutch lady passing among us, helping, heartening.

In the seven days of hell that she and her family lived through her house, now in ruins, Kate Ter Horst given shelter to over 300 wounded British and Polish soldiers and some Germans. This very gallant lady would always be remembered by the soldiers of 1st Airborne. Nor would they forget the hundreds of other people of Arnhem, Oosterbeek and the surrounding villages who helped them in the battle at the risk of their own lives, both during the fighting and from subsequent German reprisals. As a punishment for helping the airborne soldiers the German authorities ordered all the Dutch people of Arnhem and Oosterbeek to leave their houses within a few hours. They also intended to turn the area along the north bank of the Rhine into a heavily defended line against an expected renewed British offensive.

Kate and her family, with a few belongings piled on a handcart, set out walk through shattered Oosterbeek to Arnhem and then on to Apeldoorn. Her warm and courageous character had been an inspiration and 'the Angel of Arnhem' - a title that she was too modest to accept, saying that there were many other women, indeed some young girls, who also helped 'the airborne' - became a legend to all the airborne soldiers who fought at Oosterbeek.' [86]

85 Stan Lunt ultimately made it across the river in 'Berlin' on 25/26 September.

86 In November 1947 her oldest son, Pieter Albert, was killed by a left over anti-tank mine in a meadow along the Rhine. She starred in Theirs is the Glory in which survivors were asked to re-enact the parts they played in the battle. (The film was directed by Brian Desmond Hurst, who was born in East Belfast and worked in a linen factory before joining the 6th Royal Irish Rifles in 1914. He later survived the slaughter of Gallipoli and in the 1930s became a film director). In 1980, the British ambassador to the Netherlands decorated Kate and her husband as Honorary Members of the Most Excellent Order of the British Empire. Kate died on 21 February 1992 after she was struck by a police car outside her home. In 1994, during the 50th anniversary commemoration of the battle, a memorial was unveiled to record the admiration of the veterans for the gallant part played by the Dutch men and women who nursed the wounded during the battle and who afterwards hid them in their houses and guided them to safety over the river during the long, cold winter months that followed. Jan ter Horst died at the age of 98 in 2003

The renewed activity of the Allied air forces was a bright feature of D+6. Weather at last was favourable. In England the day was fair, the clouds high and broken and only a few patches of light rain marred the prospect. Fog and overcast lingered over the Low Countries during the morning but were swept away early in the afternoon by a cold front, which left behind it clearing skies and brisk westerly winds. At 1421 hours Colonel Fred Gray led his P-47s off from Duxford to Holland to carry out flak suppression in the RAF resupply drop-zone although unbeknown to the Allied Commander the British troops had withdrawn some time previously. Circling Arnhem, the Thunderbolts approached from the south and turned 90 degrees west to Kasteel where they were enveloped by 20-40mm light flak from along nearby hedgerows and woods north of the town. Colonel Gray took a squadron and temporarily silenced these guns while enemy guns in a church south of the woods were put out of action by other P-47s. Just west of Heteren, 2nd Lieutenant Dunstan D. Hartley, Gray's wingman, received a direct hit and he went straight into the ground. Another formation of C-47s approached the drop zone from the south at extremely low altitude to drop their supplies. Three were shot down by some of the guns, which were soon silenced again by the Thunderbolts. The enemy flak emplacements were very well hidden and the Germans held their fire until the P-47s had passed and were banking away. It was only when they began firing again that the Thunderbolt pilots knew where they were and could attack them again. More and more C-47s and Stirlings appeared at very low level and in areas which had been flak suppressed they were able to drop their supplies without drawing fire but in an area where there was no flak suppression, four Stirlings were shot down in flames. Thirteen of the Thunderbolts returned to Duxford showing signs of battle damage.[87]

The Polish troops who had been returned to base on D+4 were to be dropped on DZ 'O' at 1447 by a 42-plane serial. Major General Sosabowski received information that the Heaveadorp ferry had been destroyed and the site was in German hands. He had no radio link with HQ 1st Airborne Division but later, during the night, Captain Zwolanski, the Polish liaison officer with that HQ swam the river and arrived at the Polish HQ at Driel , bringing news that rafts would be brought to the river to ferry the Brigade over that night. At 0300 the next morning no boats had come over, so, to avoid the battalions being under direct fire from the German-held high ground in daylight, they were ordered to withdraw and take up positions around Driel. Here during Friday, harassed by mortar fire, they held off attacks from the east and south, some

87 The 78th Fighter Group flew no missions on the 25th because of the weather. Next day Major Leonard Marshall, the new 84th Squadron CO vice Ben Mayo, who having finished his tour returned to the States, led the Group on their final Arnhem support mission. The P-47s patrolling the area at 2,500 feet for almost an hour but the only activity they saw was a few bursts of flak at Arnhem and Hertogenbosch and some C-47s landing and taking off from a strip in the area. The 237 sorties the Group flew in support of the operations at Arnhem and Nijmegen earned the Duxford outfit its first AAF Distinguished Unit Citation. Altogether, the Group claimed 13 aerial victories, 47 ground victories and 80 locomotives during twenty momentous missions in September but 18 P-47s were lost. Losses were high mainly because of the strafing missions on 10 September and six flak-suppression and air support missions the Group flew during Operation Market-Garden, 17-26 September

supported by tanks against which they could only use their short range PIATs, as Lieutenant Stanislaw Zankowski of the 6th Company, 2nd Polish Parachute Battalion, recalled: 'At about 1430 the position of our Company situated right in the centre of Driel came under attack by German infantry and we shortly noticed a German armoured car slipping out of the orchard and moving towards us. Actually we weren't at first quite sure whether it was a German car or one of ours, but when one of my men started waving to them it opened fire. A moment later there appeared from behind the armoured car also a tank and stopping at a distance of about 300 metres turned its turret in our direction. As we only had PIATs with an effective range of 100 metres we were at a loss as to what to do, but the commander of the nearest platoon ordered his PIAT to open fire and after the third projectile exploded at a short distance from the tank it withdrew.' [88]

When volunteers were called for to start an attack to Driel, Obergefreiter Heinz Ackermann attached to 10 SS Panzer Division 'Frundsberg' was one who volunteered.

'We gathered near Driel and there they put together the storm troopers of the Waffen SS. Our position was about 300 metres from the village. There I met a Dutch family, who had been looking for shelter in one of the trenches and now had got right in the middle of the battle area. The man's arm was hurt seriously. A comrade and I quickly bandaged his arm and we helped them to get through the fences to reach the area behind the battle line. At this moment Oberfeldwebel Spieß gave us the order to attack. He shouted: 'Vorwärts Jungens; run...!' ('Go ahead comrades...'). Then he was hit in the head by a bullet. After we broke into the village, the close quarter battle started. We spread out on the right and the left side of the road. The men on the right side were shooting left into the windows; the men on the left side were shooting right. Inside the houses there were several close combats. In one I saw a Polish soldier, his radio still on, but he obviously had been killed in action during our assault. The battles went on during the whole afternoon and the Polish defended with desperation. But after some time we lost our zest and many comrades fell in action. Suddenly we were attacked by heavy rifle-fire and there was no going further. One of the best positions to survey the street had been taken by an enemy observer. From one side of the house, I tried to get near this soldier, but I didn't know where exactly he was, because nobody had seen him yet. When I carefully looked around the edge of the house, I suddenly felt a hard strike on my carbine, which had been directly hit on the butt and it just missed my hand grenade. At the same moment, I saw a red beret disappearing into a hole. Now I only had my two hand grenades. After a quick look around the edge, I aimed and threw the first of my hand grenades, but it missed by about 1-2 metres. Now I only had the second hand grenade. It landed straight in the hole. So, the way was free. This action had been watched by a Leutnant, who had been lying in a house near me so now, I got a machine-gun (MG15) and ammunition. Because of him, I became a Feldwebel on 1 October for courage in the face of the enemy.

88 Quoted in *A Tour of the Arnhem Battlefields* by John Waddy (Pen & Sword 199, 2001).

'The attack still went on. After some time I was alone. Near Driel, I met a British lieutenant, who had been lying with an injured comrade in the trench. We dressed his wounds and sent him back about 100 metres and he safely reached the other side. Paratroopers like him fought very fair, so, we didn't shoot at him, because he clearly was injured. Now, it was our turn to get over the battlefield. When we started to run, we were shot from aside by machine guns. The shots were all well aimed and missed me only by only 20-30 cm. While I took cover, some shots close behind me, hit my flask, which I kept in my belt. Now we were also shot by trench mortars. Finally I managed to cross the battlefield and get shelter. The lieutenant behind me tried to jump over the trench, when a shell detonated behind him and he was mortally wounded. Next, I threw some machine gun magazines into the brook, to be lighter. All the time, I'd had five magazines with me, but now, I only let one in the machine gun and took another one with me. After some time, I reached the RV, but most of my comrades had been wounded and many of them had been killed in action. I was the only one of my troop who got through this day without any injuries.' [89]

At around noon a Troop of the Household Cavalry, led by Lieutenant The Honourable Richard Wrottesley, slipping past German positions and using side lanes, drove in from the direction of Heteren to the west. This was the first contact by ground troops with the airborne force in the Arnhem area, albeit with the Polish Brigade and still south of the river. Sosabowski was able to use the Troop Commander's radio to contact HQ XXX Corps and to send his first report that he held the south bank of the river opposite Oosterbeek church.

At 1600 the RAF mounted its usual gallant attempts by the re-supply crews to get supplies into the perimeter as the flak took a further heavy toll. The 73 Stirlings and 50 Dakotas dispatched to bring supplies to 1 Airborne had a most difficult mission. The area still held by British troops had shrunk to 1,000 yards in diameter and was ringed with enemy guns. The drop point was even harder to locate than before. The 'Eureka' was not working because the batteries were dead and the Germans had captured the pathfinders' reserve stock. Parties attempting to use visual signals were harassed by snipers, by mortars and twice by strafing. Moreover; the Germans seem to have used bogus signals to mislead the pilots. Very lights were seen by 22 crews and other signals by 13, but only a handful dropped their loads within the British lines. Even well-placed bundles were hard to retrieve, since much of the terrain still held by the British was under observed fire and hardly any vehicles were left for supply details to use. No doubt some were recovered by individuals and small units and used on the spot without any accounting. Even if we assume arbitrarily that four times as much was picked up as was ever reported, the amount reaching the troops was still less than 10 percent of what was sent. There was no alternative. Landing gliders in such a situation was out of the question.

Two aircraft aborted. Six were shot down, all apparently in or near the drop

89 On 2 November 1944 Canadian soldiers landed on the Isle of Walcheren and Heinz Ackermann was taken prisoner. His captivity was spent in England, near Nottingham. In June 1946 he was returned to Germany.

area and 63 were damaged. Had not the 78th Fighter Group been on hand to keep down the fire the toll would have been much larger. Air Vice-Marshal Leslie Hollinghurst, who was controlling these operations from Eastcote had naturally been concerned about the high cost to his squadrons. Earlier in the week, the extent of the losses and the uncertainty about the usefulness of the dropping points had prompted Air Commodore L. Darvall, commanding 46 Group, to inspect at first hand the tactical situation as it affected re-supply. The upshot of this visit was that one of the supply squadrons was moved from England to an airfield near Brussels on this Saturday. [90] On this Saturday afternoon only a minute proportion of the panniers came our way and the food contents were taken to the wounded.

'Rations as such', Major H. S. Cousens wrote afterwards, 'were non-existent and men were living on potatoes and any other food they could find.' They looked at each other with red-rimmed, bloodshot eyes asking 'what the hell had happened to the 2nd bloody Army and what the devil the RAF thought they were at'. No one blamed the transport crews whose bravery was evident to all. 'The cold-blooded pluck of the pilots was quite incredible', a soldier who watched them thought. They came on, in their lumbering four-engine machines, at 1,500 feet, searching for our position. The ack-ack was such as I have only heard during the worst raids on London but concentrated on one small area. The German gunners were firing at point-blank range and the supply planes were more or less sitting targets... It made you feel terribly small, frightened and insignificant... One could do nothing but stare awe-inspired at the inferno above... The Americans were included in our boundless admiration, for they came along in their unarmed, slow, twin-engined Dakotas as regularly as clock-work... Hardly any of their supplies reached us.' Less than one-seventh of the total tonnage dropped during the operation was collected by the Division and the sight of the Stirlings and Dakotas flying unhesitatingly into the German barrage where sometimes, although hit and on fire, they continued to circle above the German lines while the Royal Army Service Corps despatchers threw out the supplies before the aircraft crashed into the earth, was so moving that for many of those who witnessed it no more poignant memory of Arnhem remains.

Louis Hagen recalled: 'That afternoon, another fleet of supply planes came over to drop urgently needed ammo and food. The cold-blooded pluck and heroism of the pilots was quite incredible. They came in in their lumbering four-engined machines at 1,500 feet, searching for our position. The ack-ack was such as I have only heard during the worst raids on London, but concentrated on one small area. The German gunners were firing at point blank range and the supply planes were more or less sitting targets. The rattle of machine guns from the scores of planes, the heavy ack-ack batteries all round us, the sky filled with flashes and puffs of exploding shells, burning planes diving towards the ground and hundreds and hundreds of red, white, yellow

90 Darvall also suggested to Horrocks, Browning and Air Vice-Marshal Broadhurst, commanding 83 Group of the 2nd Tactical Air Force, that fighters might be used for supply dropping in place of the more vulnerable Dakotas and Stirlings. It appears that there was some measure of unanimity about the advisability of such a move, but no fighters joined in re-supply missions over Arnhem.

and blue supply parachutes dropping all in this very small area, looked more like an overcrowded and crazy illustration to a child's book. This was war on such a concentrated scale that it made you feel terribly small, frightened and insignificant: something like an ant menaced by a steam roller. All activity on the ground seemed to be suspended and forgotten on both sides. One could do nothing but stare awe-inspired at the inferno above.

'How those pilots could have gone into it with their eyes open is beyond my imagination. Later on, when I got back to the 'drome, I heard something of what they had felt. And. I was told of their tremendous losses.

'When we saw the supply planes coming in over our position, we knew nothing of the hell they had been through already; many of them had failed to get this far. They had first had to deal with great packs of Focke Wulfs and in one of the trips; they crossed into Holland without any fighter support as the weather did not permit it. When they met the Fokker Wulfs, they had very little chance to defend themselves. The Americans were included in our boundless admiration, for they came along in their unarmed, slow, twin-engined Dakotas as regularly as clock-work. The greatest tragedy of all, I think, is that hardly any of these supplies reached us. It makes the heroism of the crews of the planes even more incredible when one realises that they must have known that there was very little chance of their sacrifice being of any use to us.'

Despite mounting casualties and an almost impossible task, the supply aircraft continued their gallant if fruitless efforts. Altogether eight supply lifts were flown in circumstances which became worse and worse. 'On D Plus 6 we guessed that things were desperate' reports the rear gunner of a Stirling, 'for we had been given a new dropping zone very much smaller in size and ringed by the enemy. All was plain sailing until we reached the Neder Rijn where we encountered very heavy fire. The Stirling bounced about all over the place... We decided we should drop immediately, then turn to port and go down low. This we did, descending to 300 feet and I could see everything very clearly. There were men shooting at us with rifles and light machine-guns and Bofors on lorries. I fired one long burst into a lorry in which I could see German soldiers, their heads tilted back looking at us. At that moment my turret jammed and... I got a bullet through the shoulder'. The Stirling was riddled but could still fly and it landed safely at Harwell, two of its engines seizing as it touched down. 92

Lieutenant Mike Dauncey of the Glider Pilot Regiment was elated that he was still alive. On the Thursday when a German took a pot shot at him the bullet went through his beret and cut his skin slightly. On a patrol with two paratroopers he succeeded in returning with eight prisoners, a machine gun and several Luger pistols. The capturing of German soldiers, given the nature of the fighting around Oosterbeek, was a rare event. Those who witnessed the Lieutenant returning with these prizes took great heart from it. Dauncey's luck

91 *Arnhem Lift* by Louis Hagen.

92 'Market-Garden' cost 38 and 46 Groups 55 aircraft lost with a further 320 damaged by flak and 7 by fighters. The Second Tactical Air Force, though fully conversant with the situation in Holland, was unaware of the immediate changes of plan necessitated by the exigencies of the situation. It could not and did not therefore, provide the full air cover of which it was capable.

continued to hold on Saturday.

'Lieutenant Max Downing had been killed in action going forward to engage the enemy and 2nd Lieutenant Frank Derbyshire was missing from a patrol, [93] so we reformed and with some reinforcements (who had had a rest in the church, or the school hall) took up new positions on the Arnhem side of the Weversstraat road. Mike Corrie's group and mine were next to each other. We occupied the upper floors of adjacent houses, the one I was in having a distinctive brick design. During the day enemy mortars and SP guns engaged our lines. When they were too close to us we went downstairs and behind the houses. However, the German infantry did not follow up their advantage. By the early evening a group of the enemy had been pin-pointed in a house about 30-40 yards in front of our lines. So, supported by a little Bren-gun fire, two paratroopers and I went out to get them. After throwing a grenade into their house and threatening them as to what would happen if they did not come out at once, eight sheepish Germans appeared, three of them wounded; We were so pleased with ourselves that the whole party marched straight across the open ground to our lines. This was too much for the enemy mortars. One bomb brought down the branches of a leafy tree five yards from us and we were all covered in leaves. Miraculously no one was seriously hurt except one German, but most of us had scratches. We also brought back a German machine gun and some Luger pistols. We were delighted with our unexpected success at this stage; it certainly boosted morale. The prisoners were handed over to Major Croot; sadly we never met again as, after Arnhem, he was killed in an aircraft accident en route to the war in the Far East. He was a wonderful commander, a fine shot and an able pilot.'

A river crossing by a small party of the Polish Brigade to be made opposite Oosterbeek church was set for 2100 during the night of the 22/23rd. When it was almost dark and after a brief exchange of fire with the Polish paratroops, a column of tanks and infantry carriers drove up from the south. It was the leading two companies of the 5th Battalion, Duke of Cornwall's Light Infantry and a squadron of the 4/7th Dragoon Guards, under the command of Lieutenant Colonel George Taylor. They had battled through to link up with the Poles at Driel. Taylor recalled: 'I had been told that as soon as the Somersets had cleared Oosterhout my battalion was to break through and move with all speed up to the Rhine The Airborne Division was in a desperate situation and we must link up with them that night, taking supplies loaded on DUKWs. It was already late in the afternoon. The battalion formed up in two columns - an armoured Column in front with two companies mounted on tanks and carriers and then behind the second column with the other two companies mainly on foot. It was near dusk when we roared off, tracks clanking, dashing headlong and ignoring the danger of enemy tanks on our right flank. We crashed through the streets of Valburg to the delight of the cheering Dutch people. 'Light was fading as we reached Driel, where the leading tank was blown up on a mine laid by the Poles. We had completed the ten miles in under thirty minutes. We

93 Lieutenant Francis Alexander Derbyshire (25) was KIA.

felt that George Patton would have approved. Contact was made with the Household Cavalry and the Polish Parachute Brigade HQ. As the companies took up defensive positions north of Driel we heard the sounds of battle behind us and soon a despatch rider rode up to report that enemy tanks were attacking the rear of the armoured column. With Major Parker of 'A' Company, I decided that in the dark these tanks could be held off and it also gave us a chance to ambush them as they returned to Elst and this 'A' Company did very successfully, knocking out the first four tanks with PIATs and 75 grenades. Two more panicked and slipped off the road into a deep ditch. Sergeant Major Philip made sure that each one was well and truly out of action by dropping grenades down the turrets. This was a very gallant action and showed that infantry imbued with fighting spirit can deal effectively with tanks at close quarters.' [94]

The 3rd Polish Parachute Battalion meanwhile, had moved up to the River Dyke road and at 2100 the crossing began. The crossing was an extremely improvised affair. Engineers of 4 Parachute Squadron sent down from the perimeter to assist had gathered six two-man reconnaissance boats and an RAF dinghy which were linked together with signals wire and pulled back and forth across the river. With the few rubber dinghies available it was a very slow operation and only about fifteen Polish soldiers could be taken across at a time. It was hoped that by dawn, 200 of them would be north of the River. In the event, however, only 52 made it across.

The night, which quickly fell, was so dark that it was impossible to find a suitable launching place beneath the steep and crumbling banks. Lieutenant Albert Smaezny, Commanding 8 Company led his men towards the crossing site, which they reached without any opposition from the enemy. 'But there were no boats and we had to wait quite a while before they arrived' recalled Smaezny. 'At first there were only two and they couldn't take more than two men each. Some time later two rubber dinghies appeared with their British sappers. It was a very slow business, especially as we were losing boats all the time. The night was dark, but the enemy must have realized what was afoot and from time to time illuminated the river and its banks with flares and then their Spandaus went into action. I managed to get across without mishap and as soon as I had crossed I was taken to the HQ of the 4th Parachute Brigade in Oosterbeek to get my orders. In the morning I found that I had only 35 men with me.'

Captain Harry Faulkner-Brown of the 4th Parachute Squadron, Royal Engineers, recalled: 'I was ordered to take fifteen of my sappers down to the river to ferry across some of the Polish Brigade. We got to the river at 2100. It was very dark, which was good for security. The river then was about 100 yards wide with a strong 4-5 knot current. Close inshore a series of groins checked the current but in midstream it was running very fast, so fast that when some men tried to cross in an RAF rubber dinghy they were carried two miles downstream by the current while they rowed from one bank to the other, about 150 yards. Incidentally, that carried them well into the German lines but they were not observed and reported back later that night. The only boats available

94 Quoted in *A Tour of the Arnhem Battlefields* by John Waddy (Pen & Sword 199, 2001).

were six two-man rubber dinghies, normally used for reconnaissance.

'Our first plan was to tie signal wire to either end of the recce boat and pull it across from one side while those on the other bank paid out. As the boats held only two men each it meant that twice as many could cross than would be the case if one man had to be in the boat to row. But we had great difficulty in getting the lines across due to the swift current and the bottom of the river was so stony that in each case the signal wire was severed before we could get a boat back with a load. So we had to row the Poles over individually. About midnight I decided that the only way was for the battle-weary sappers to row the boats using the two tiny oars. This proved difficult, especially for the less expert watermen. One strong officer, Lieutenant David Storrs, rowed across the river and back 23 times, which, coming on all that had been already done that week, was quite a feat of endurance, bringing over each time one fully equipped Polish airborne soldier. [95]

'There was mortar and MG fire during the night as the Germans were near enough on either side to put down crossfire. By day we could not cross as the fire would be observed and be too deadly. The next day we rested and had our first real sleep since landing. But it rained and there was no head cover so we were all pretty miserable. But I found a wrecked German QM truck and in it were some coffee and sugar and we made a brew. It brought us to life again.'

Men even made rafts out of cans and boards and anything else they could lay their hands on, but crossing the fast flowing water on these improvised craft proved a cruelly hazardous undertaking. Many of the men drowned as their rafts overturned, others were swept downstream and into captivity by the strong currents. The rubber dinghies which Myers had mentioned to General Sosabowski were not much more useful than the rafts. By three o'clock in the

95 David Valentine Storrs of the Royal Engineers with tired detachments taken out of the line from all Sapper units in turn, tried for four nights running to ferry the Poles across the River Lek. On the first night he was quite unable to do so and not a man landed on the other side but on three successive nights, under fire and in two-man reconnaissance boats, he bravely got men across. On the second night Storrs himself rowed across the fast running river 26 times and brought 21 Poles into the bridgehead over from the South bank. In daylight on 21 September Storrs assisted the GSO1 (Lieutenant Colonel Charles Mackenzie) and Lieutenant Colonel Eddie Myers in crossing the river on their journey to report on the situation to XXX Corps and on 22/23 September he again successfully crossed the river, met the GSO1 on his return from XXX Corps, at a prearranged rendezvous and safely brought him back into the bridgehead area. 'On two occasions' reads his citation for the immediate award of the Military Cross, 'Lieutenant Storrs, regardless of his own safety, successfully organised parties to put out fires in the Divisional HQ area caused by enemy shelling - in one instance a large petrol dump fire - in another an Motor Transport park. His endurance, his courage and his devotion to duty and leadership displayed by this officer throughout the whole period of the occupation of the bridgehead area, were of the very highest order'.

For actions against the enemy at Oosterbeek, Captain Brown was awarded the Military Cross. His citation recorded that between the 20th and 22nd September this officer with 30 other ranks was attached to Major Wilson's 21st Independent Parachute Company. He held a part of the front which was very exposed to the enemy fire. During the period this officer made several sorties to drive off enemy massing for an assault. He led a small party which destroyed an SP gun and regardless of the enemy fire at close range continuously went from trench to trench giving his men encouragement. His two senior officers were killed and most of his men became casualties but by his personal courage and example he encouraged his few remaining men to drive back nine determined attacks by the enemy and not one yard of ground was surrendered.

morning only one rubber dinghy was still undamaged. Soon afterwards Sosabowski gave the order that any further attempts to get his men across the river should be abandoned for the moment. The Germans put up flares and sprayed the river banks with machine-gun fire and mortar bombs burst in the water before Poles could dig in. By 0300 the next morning only one rubber dinghy remained undamaged. About 55 men and a few cases of ammunition and supplies had been able to cross.

Charles Mackenzie and Ernie Myers made their way towards the river near Oosterbeek Church and moved stealthily to the spot where Myers, after a previous visit to the Poles had concealed an inflatable dinghy near the river, south of Oosterbeek Laag church. It was one of the very few dinghys still left unpunctured. They inflated it in a building at Oosterbeek and dragged over the fields and then carried it down towards a small ditch which led to the river. For some distance they floated the dinghy along the ditch. Suddenly, they found themselves being escorted by a sturdy sergeant-major armed with a Bren. 'We started in the ditch' Mackenzie recalled 'but eventually had to get out because it is full of horrible things. We then walked down the hedge towing the rubber boat behind us. We had another chap, Storrs, with us; and he saw us into the boat.' They turned left, crouching as they followed a hedge leading to the river. The mist had cleared now, but there was a certain amount of haze when they got to the water's edge. The river looked formidably wide and they quickly discussed which of them should row. 'I rowed across,' says Colonel Mackenzie 'and Myers steered. He swore at me for splashing. There were one or two shots fired but they were a long way above our heads. We got over. We parked the boat in a little bay and crawled away from the bank. There was a flap on this side too. We had got through to the Poles on the wireless to meet us. There was a battle going on; and we couldn't make out which were Poles and which were Germans.'

They crossed the wide expanse of open polder beyond, moving across it cautiously towards Driel. Occasionally there was a muffled burst of machine-gun fire in the damp air, but they were not touched. There were no Poles to be seen and they walked across the wet ground feeling alone and isolated in the cold morning light. And then at last they caught sight of two steel helmets. It was impossible to say at this distance whether they belonged to Poles or Germans. Mackenzie and Meyers jumped into a ditch and lay there for two or three minutes watching and waiting. Eventually they persuaded themselves that the two half-hidden figures must be Poles. Mackenzie stepped out of the ditch first clutching a white handkerchief in case of emergency while Myers stayed put to cover him in case the men were Germans. Myers watched Mackenzie go forward and then jumped out of the ditch, overwhelmed with relief, as he saw him wave his arm cheerfully over his head. One of the two figures was a Polish parachutist, the other a British liaison officer. They had each brought two bicycles with them for the two emissaries and so the four men rode off through the river haze to General Sosabowski's Headquarters at Driel, where they found the Polish Brigade under attack by German troops from Elst, supported by guns north of the river. It was clear that the Poles had been losing and were still losing, men to the German guns sited on the commanding promontory north of the river from which the Border Regiment had been pushed the day before. Amid all this hectic activity, Major-General Sosabowski was making inspirational tours of his brigade on a bicycle. By giving the Germans so much trouble in the Driel area, the Poles were indirectly assisting the 43rd Division in its attempts to break through.

Mackenzie stressed how vital it was to get as many men as possible over to join the Division. 'General', Mackenzie said to Sosabowski, 'every man you can get across the river to help 1st Airborne will be invaluable. Even five or ten might make a difference.' But what could he do, Sosabowski protested, without rafts or boats? 'I think we can help', Myers said. 'There are some small three-man rubber dinghies which can be pulled backwards and forwards across the river by hawsers.'

'They made what arrangements they could for the Polish Parachute Brigade to be ferried over' recalled Mackenzie, 'but no one was very hopeful, for there was a great lack of boats or materials from which rafts could be built. While the Polish engineers discussed this with Myers, Mackenzie signalled Horrocks with the news of the Airborne Division's plight. Using the wireless set belonging to the troop of the Household Cavalry which had pushed through Oosterhout ahead of the 43rd Division and had now reached Driel, he transmitted a message which read: 'We are short of ammunition, men, food and medical supplies. DUKWs are essential. Two or three would be sufficient. If supplies do not arrive tonight it may be too late.'

During the day three Household Cavalry armoured cars had reached Driel and late that evening Mackenzie set off to find Browning, Myers and Mackenzie set out in these in an attempt to locate Lieutenant General Browning in Nijmegen. They had not gone far before they encountered an enemy armoured vehicle. The car in which Mackenzie travelled presently drew near to a windmill, around the corner of which poked 'a dirty-looking green nose'. It belonged to a Tiger tank, which went at once into action and at the end of the encounter Mackenzie found himself with the reconnaissance car upside down in a ditch. He crawled away and after some time two Sherman tanks arrived and cleared a passage. The other two cars, with Myers in one of them, pushed on to Nijmegen where Mackenzie later rejoined Myers at Browning's Headquarters between ten and eleven the next morning. The state of their appearance, after several days of battle and crawling across riverbanks, was somewhat shabby and the always impeccable Browning regarded them as 'putty coloured like men who had come through a Somme winter'. Despite the best efforts of these two officers to give Browning a clear understanding of the plight of the 1st Airborne Division, they left his presence with the feeling that they had not been able to convince him of the severity of the situation. Mackenzie had also signalled Lieutenant General Horrocks with information about the Division's critical situation at Oostebeek. Horrocks replied: 'Everything will be done to get the essentials through.'

When Urquhart received Horrocks' message of encouragement which had been relayed to him by the Poles, he asked for a strong mobile column with DUKWs, as well as supplies and two companies of infantry riding on tanks to be sent to Driel. 'However good were Horrocks' intentions' recalled Urquhart 'the progress of xxx Corps was discouragingly slow. Oosterhout was not cleared until about 1700 by an attack supported by more than a hundred guns. It was close country with many orchards. The battle is said to have yielded only 139 German prisoners, one obsolete tank, five flak guns and an 88-mm gun. And the casualties of the battalion of the 43rd Division involved in this action totalled nineteen wounded. Within the perimeter men were being killed and hundreds of soldiers were being wounded a second time as they lay in nine overcrowded buildings used by the medical services. Some of the wounded were killed on their stretchers as the German mortars blasted the area... Thus we remained alone, unaware of the disappointing events on the south side of the river. We were still concerned to keep open this vital bridgehead through which Monty could come through with his drive into Germany. It was costing the 1st Airborne Division dearly.'

Mackenzie's and Myer's return journey was made without incident and Mackenzie reported to General Urquhart that night, having concerted plans for an evacuation now seen to be inevitable. At Driel meanwhile, Myers oversaw preparations to ferry more Poles across the river, this time using the assault boats of the 130th Infantry Brigade. Despite this improvement, the Poles had been given no crews to man the craft and so had to make the best of the situation themselves, resulting in slow crossings and an inadequate number of men across the river by morning. Myers wrote, 'I can find no fault with their attempts; they did as much as they could. They had not been trained in river crossings and the Arnhem plan had not envisaged one and no one had any proper boats. But the less said about their watermanship the better.'

Saturday night was a clear one. The rain had stopped and the sky was full of stars. At about 1900 as usual the mortar fire had quietened and in several sectors it was 'almost uncannily quiet'. To the west and south the horizon was a dull red after attacks by Bomber Command; and closer at hand the flames from the burning gas works poured out of the black smoke and cast a flickering light over the ruined buildings and the waters of the river. After midnight, however, the prodding attacks began again. SS-Obersturmbannführer Harzer, knowing how close the 2nd Army was now to the Neder Rijn, had given orders that the British Division must at all costs be destroyed before the relieving force arrived. The KOSB and the Reconnaissance Squadron were obliged to pull back in face of tanks and flame-throwers rolling forward across the lines to their trenches and blasting their houses into ruins from less than 50 yards range.

Horrocks, still intent on thrusting forward, ordered further crossing operations to take place that night. The entire Polish Brigade was to cross into the perimeter, together with supplies for the Airborne Division. The 43rd Division would then make a major crossing to the west to enlarge the bridgehead. A liaison officer reached the Polish Brigade with orders to start crossing at 2100, using assault boats to be provided by 43rd Division. The boats did not arrive on time and it was not until 0300 the next morning that the operation started, with the fire support of the 5th Dorsets on the river bank and artillery of the 43rd Division. Due to the late arrival of the boats (only twelve, some without paddles and no 43rd Division sappers) only 253 Polish paratroopers managed to cross the river in the few hours of darkness that were left. Neither the Poles (or the Dorsets, who followed on the night of 24/25 September) were able to reach the Airborne Division in numbers large enough to alter the outcome of the battle. The Poles were sent in groups to reinforce vulnerable points of the perimeter, mainly at the MDS crossroads and with the Borders near Hemelseberg, where they fought bravely for the remaining two days of the battle. A British officer said: 'I had to meet them, organise them into squads and send them off with guides to the sections of the perimeter to which they were to go. It was very unpleasant for we were under fire all the time. They fought like demons. The Poles didn't have to be told to get snipers (and by then there were plenty of snipers who had infiltrated into our position). They just went after them and got them.'

Fighting went on all around the perimeter. The wounded were looked after with great devotion by surgeons who would remain at their posts to the last. At 1300 on 23 September a German officer who had driven up to the British lines in a half-track flying a large white flag approached Brigadier Hackett and under a large Red Cross flag 'threatened that unless British troops withdrew from a house being used as a casualty clearing station on the main road running through the perimeter, he would be forced to blow the MDS to pieces. 'We are about to deliver an attack on this side of the perimeter' he explained 'and I intend to put down a mortar and artillery concentration on your forward positions. We know that you have wounded there and we do not wish to put down a barrage that will hit them. I am asking you to move your forward positions 600 yards further back.' The withdrawal would have entailed the abandonment of the whole Divisional Headquarters area and neither Hackett nor Urquhart to whom the decision was referred for confirmation could agree. Half an hour later, however, the German officer agreed not to blow the MDS to pieces provided that the British did not fire from the immediate vicinity of the aid post. When the expected bombardment came, it was delivered further south and the casualty clearing station was left outside the barrage area. [96] On the next day these threats were renewed, although the Germans were well aware that their own wounded to the number of 150 or more were being cared for by the same doctors. Eventually many of the wounded, both German and English, were taken by the enemy back into Arnhem.

At the Schoonoord Hotel and at the Tafelberg and at the Vreewyk, another hotel now used as a hospital, there was hardly any water. And in the forward RAPs the conditions were even worse. At the Tafelberg, when a shell had burst on

96 On the same day when a tank opened fire at close range on the ter Horst house in Oosterbeek Laag, Bombardier E. C. Bolden, the courageous medical orderly and the Rev. S. Thorne, the chaplain, went up to it carrying a Red Cross flag. Furiously shaking the flag and giving 'the most comprehensive display of East London invective' that Padre Watkins had ever heard, Bolden demanded that the tank commander immediately withdraw, as the house was in use as a Regimental Aid Post. The German commander drove his tank away. On another occasion a self-propelled gun fired two shells through a dressing station window. A British surgeon came out angrily waving a Red Cross flag and asked the German officer in command, 'what the hell he thought he was up to'. The German said, 'Oh, sorry' and he also drove away.

the roof smashing the pipes and a cascade of rust-coloured water had poured down on to the wounded men an orderly mopped up the valuable liquid with a blanket and squeezed it into a bucket. All the rain water he had been able to collect during the day had long since gone and not a drop, wherever it came from, could be wasted. There were not enough blankets, either, not enough morphia, not enough bandages. Operations were performed under conditions of appalling difficulty or not performed at all. But in every makeshift hospital, dressing station and RAP the doctors and their orderlies although reaching the limits of their endurance, still continued doggedly and with great skill and courage to do all that they could for the wounded men in their charge. At the RAP near Oosterbeek Laag church, Mevrouw ter Horst asked Dr Martin if there were many dead. 'Thousands of them', Dr Martin said. His hands hang between his knees [she says], an elbow leans against the table; he is very tired. Slowly he looks up with an expression of melancholy in his dark eyes. I say calmly, 'This house won't be smashed.' He nods, 'I prayed for that.' And then suddenly: 'And if we are hit again, I hope it will kill them all right off.' He pointed to a figure under the stairs with hair matted to a bandaged head. 'He just banged his head against the radiator and he was gone... We can't do anything.'

Fire, thirst and hunger were among the tribulations grimly endured. As time wore on, more and more of the houses, so stoutly defended, were set ablaze and became untenable. Hit by a phosphorus bomb, a house usually began to burn in earnest some five minutes later and this short interval gave to those holding it just time to move to another. After the first forty-eight hours, food became very short and towards the end was entirely lacking. The Germans cut off the town water supply and to the pangs of hunger those of thirst were added. 'We went four days without food,' says Sergeant Quinn, 'but we could still get water from a well. 'In this he and those with him were luckier than most. There were vegetables in the gardens-potatoes, cabbages and some tomatoes - but without water it was difficult to cook them. There were apples to be had from the trees and some men of the 156th Parachute Battalion' found a bakery and had bread and bottled cherries.' The 21st Independent Parachute Company was more fortunate than many of their fellows. 'We lived' its commander reports, 'on two meals a day, mostly of tinned vegetables. Once a kid ran across the lawn of my headquarters and we killed and ate it.'

The cellars of certain houses were found to contain small stocks of food and occasionally of wine,' Champagne, Graves, a light claret and Bols gin;' 'There just weren't any army rations after the first day,' reports an officer, 'but there were some tame rabbits, one of which I fed. He used to scratch at the wire of his hutch as I went by and I'd give him a leaf of lettuce or cabbage. One day a parachutist on the scrounge walked off with my rabbit, dead... I made him hand it over and left it between my batman's trench and mine, where it got blown to pieces by a shell. Chickens didn't seem to mind the mortaring at all. They lost a few feathers but went on pecking and scratching about quite calmly. 'Such food as fell from the air went to the Regimental Aid Posts.

On occasion there would be a lull and the tired men were able to relax for a few precious moments. 'In the evening I would go to my trench,' said one of them, 'and smoke a pipe. I used to look at an apple tree which grew nearby and had red apples on it and then I watched the stars come up.' Near that spot 350 years before, another poet, the gentle Philip Sidney, had watched those same stars as he lay dying of a mortal wound.

'Market-Garden' Timeline

Friday 22 September (D+5)

The weather is very bad and, after waiting until midday, Airborne Army cancels all its missions. Fog has been widespread over England and the Low Countries throughout the morning and is replaced in the afternoon by stratus with ceilings about 1,000 feet and in places as low as 300 feet. In the course of the afternoon rain spreading over England from the west lowers the ceiling to between 500 and 1,000 feet and reduces visibility to between 1,000 and 2,000 yards. There are no resupply flights from England though 38 Group stated in its report that they could have been flown. The advancing disturbance could have made the return to base very 'hazardous and this risk may have been the decisive consideration. The 8th Air Force did dispatch two groups of P-47s to patrol the Arnhem area. They fly 77 uneventful sorties and return safely.

Shortly after dawn renewed attempt by XXX Corps to reach 1st British Airborne begins with orders from Horrocks to take all risks. **0830** A few armoured cars of the Household Cavalry find a route through to the Poles at Driel. Late afternoon A single infantry battalion (5th Battalion of the Duke of Cornwall's Light Infantry with some tanks) reaches the Poles. **0900** General Student's attack on Hell's Highway begins and breaks through to cut the largely undefended section of road between Uden and Grave. 101st Airborne, now under XXX Corps, obtains 119 rocket-firing Typhoon sorties from RAF 83 Group along Hell's Highway during the day.

Early evening The 5th Duke of Cornwall's Light Infantry and some tanks of the 4/7th Dragoon Guards join up with the Poles at Driel. At Oosterbeek two of Urquhart's staff officers, including his G-1, Lieutenant Colonel Charles MacKenzie, cross the river in a rowing boat and tell Sosabowski that even a few platoons or a couple of companies could make all the difference in the airborne perimeter. **After nightfall** The Poles begin planning to cross the Lower Rhine, but no boats arrive from XXX Corps before dawn. Sosabowski, acting on Horrocks' orders, manages to get a couple of platoons (about 60 men) across the river towards Heveadorp under intense German fire with four rubber boats, all that are available. About 35 Poles survive to join the Border Regiment. A plan for 5th Battalion DCLI to follow them later in the night is called off as no further boats or DUKW amphibious craft have arrived.

Saturday 23 September (D+6)

After morning fog, the first good weather since the start of 'Market-Garden'. **1300** The delayed last wave of airborne reinforcements takes off in the largest 'Market-Garden' airlift since its first day. Escorted by fourteen fighter groups of 8th Fighter Command, 654 troop carriers and 490 gliders fly the northern route almost without incident to land at **1500.** The US fighters engage over 150 enemy fighters and claim 27 destroyed. 82nd Airborne receives 3,385 troops in 428 gliders, mainly the delayed 325th Glider Infantry Regiment, which should have arrived four days' earlier. 101st Airborne receives 907th Glider Field Artillery Battalion and the last of 327th Glider Infantry. The seaborne tails of both divisions also arrive from England through the Normandy beaches, completing their deployment. 1st Battalion of 1st Polish Parachute Brigade, which had turned back on 21 September, is dropped at Oude Keent, a disused airfield just outside Grave which 1st Airborne Corps planned to use for resupply. (For some reason HQ Airborne Army in England does not despatch the special units to improve and operate this airfield until 28 September and a valuable opportunity is lost). The battalion then marches northwards to join its brigade, which has been placed under 130th Brigade of 43rd Division by Horrocks. The Airborne Division gets its first close-support from ground attack and fighter-bomber aircraft of 2nd TAF, which pound the German positions and rake enemy convoys heading into Arnhem but, like the artillery support, it is too late. At Driel, 41 C-47s of the 315th Group loaded with 560 troops and 28 tons of supplies and equipment are dropped to Sosabowski. They arrive over LZ 'O' at 1643 without loss, damage, or casualties after a milk run which stands in singular contrast to the experience of the glider serials which had flown to that zone just ahead of it. Whether this was because it flew the left hand lane 1½ miles west of the gliders or for some other reason is nowhere explained. A green light, flashed too early, made ten troops jump about five miles short of the zone and two others were brought back. The remaining troops and all but twelve out of 219 parapacks dropped on or close to the zone. Most were well concentrated near the pathfinders northwest of Overasselt. About 18 pilots, impressed by the concentration of gliders, troops and vehicles near the riverbank opposite Grave, dropped their loads there. The troops were quickly assembled, but spent the night in the Groesbeek area as reserves for the 82nd Division.

By the evening 130th Brigade with more river crossing equipment has linked up with the Poles at Driel. Sosabowksi sends 200 men of his 1st Battalion across the Lower Rhine in rubber assault boats borrowed from the Royal Engineers to join 1st British Airborne.

Index